C000042587

HIS WORD FOR TODAY

VIMA DASAN S.J.

HIS WORD
FOR
TODAY

Daily Homilies for Weekdays
(Years 1 and 2)

ST PAULS

ST PAULS PUBLISHING
187 Battersea Bridge Road, London SW11 3AS, UK
www.stpauls.ie

Copyright © ST PAULS 2001

ISBN 085439 617 9

Set by TuKan DTP, Fareham, Hampshire, UK
Printed by The Guernsey Press Co. Ltd., Guernsey, C.I.

ST PAULS is an activity of the priests and brothers
of the Society of St Paul who proclaim the Gospel
through the media of social communication

CONTENTS

YEAR 2

PREFACE

Divine Scripture is the feast of wisdom for it treasures the Word of God. Take it out of our homes and the last glimmer of hope for a safe and stable tomorrow will vanish with its going. It is not surprising, then, that the Second Vatican Council in its constitution on the Sacred Liturgy (51) declared, "the treasures of the Bible are to be opened up more lavishly so that the richer fare may be provided for the faithful at the table of God's Word. In this way, a more representative portion of the Holy Scriptures will be read to the people over a set cycle of years."

Through the liturgical cycles of years, we enter into the life of the Church. In everyday life there are higher points and low points, peak days and ordinary days. So too, in the life of the Church, there are special seasons such as Advent, Christmas, Lent and Easter. But most of the year, like most of our life, is very ordinary. However, the Sundays and weekdays in Ordinary Time are not that 'ordinary', for in every celebration of the Mass in ordinary time, the participants are offered twofold extra-ordinary banquet: the Eucharist and the Word of God. This book, *His Word For Today* contains brief homilies on the two Scriptural readings of each weekday in the two-year cycle of Ordinary Time.

There is an abundance of homilies in print, which contain excellent and useful treatments of scriptural or theological analysis of the readings of the day. But homilies in this book do not claim to have such an extended treatment of the scriptural texts. In my preparation of these homilies, I had uppermost in mind the immediate and personal needs of the people as they endeavour to live their faith in everyday life. Of course, my preparation always began with a careful reading of the two scriptural texts for the day, which led me to come up with a theme common to both readings, at least in most cases, and then the theme was reflected in the context of people's daily lives. Therefore, I would like to call these homilies 'incarnational'. But in doing so, I hope that I have not sacrificed the exegetical and theological integrity of the scriptural texts.

There are different groups of people who come for daily Mass: those who come daily, others who attend regularly, and others who participate occasionally. These homilies are for them all. By listening to them, I hope they will come to understand what the Word of God says in the readings and what it says to them personally. In other words, the listeners will not only understand the Scripture a little more, but also understand themselves a little better in the light of the Word. Hence, these homilies are meant to be Scripturally informative, spiritually uplifting and practically challenging.

There is still another group of people: those who would like to come for daily Mass but can't; and hence, they spend daily some time at home, prayerfully reflecting on the liturgical readings of the day, thus finding a sense of being more in tune with the rhythms and movements of the liturgical year.

These homilies are for them also. They will find in them inspiring reflections on life's basic truths, challenging questions to ponder, thought-provoking stories, and even occasional jokes to get them laugh at themselves. It is hoped that such a variety of entries would create in the readers a deeper sense of what is important, a clearer sense of our spiritual life and a more profound sense of the essence of life's journey.

These homilies are for busy priests, in particular. Every priest knows that he should make time to study, to reflect and pray as a preparation for his homilies; but a busy priest deserves an aid, a 'starter' for his own preparation. And each of the homilies in this book intends to be nothing more than a starter, not a substitute for one's own preparation.

That is why I have made these homilies very brief ones, between two to three minutes in length. Brevity of the homily has been made possible through various ways. One is that I took seriously the advice from Dale Carnegie: "Find a good beginning and a good ending, and put them pretty close together." Brevity was made possible also because of a single message that I have tried to put through each homily. Early in my priestly training a homiletic professor told me: "Don't go to the pulpit just to say something. Go with something to say." Any priest who uses this book will go to the pulpit with something to say.

I would like to end this Preface with an observation from Vatican II: "The Church has always venerated the divine Scriptures just as she venerates the body of the Lord, since from the table of both – the Word of God and the body of Christ – she unceasingly receives and offers to the faithful the bread of life, especially in the sacred liturgy. For, inspired by God and committed once and for all to writing, they impart the Word of God himself without change, and make the voice of the Holy Spirit resound in the words of the prophets and apostles. Therefore, like the Christian religion itself, all the preaching of the Church must be nourished and ruled by sacred Scripture."

Vima Dasan, s.j.

Year 1

ABSOLUTE TRUTH

Readings: Heb 1:1-6; Mk 1:14-20

Philosophical ideas have legs. They walk off the academics' desk down the stairs of their ivory tower into the streets and into our heads. For example, a philosopher floats the idea that there is no absolute truth because we all see differently in the end. This idea reaches the market place. The result is a kind of despair. People give up the search for truth, for they believe it is not possible to find absolute truth, if there is one. But Jesus said, "I am the truth." How could he say that? Because, "In many and various ways God spoke of old to our fathers; but in these last days he has spoken to us by a Son... the very stamp of God's nature" (Heb 1:1-2). Therefore, in Jesus, "time is fulfilled and the Kingdom of God is at hand" (Mk 1:15). That means, Jesus reveals God in the most authentic way, because his way is based on the one absolutely sure and unquestionable source, the very essence of God. Christ's testimony, therefore, has the value of absolute truth. Our inability to find truth does not actually mean that truth does not exist at all; it only means that we can't find it. Hence, we may be frustrated and feel lost. But that should lead us to conclude that we need help, and the help is in Christ.

THE CENTREPIECE

Readings: Heb 2:5-12; Mk 1:21-28

Human beings are designed to be the apex and fulfilment of creation. Yet, we must confess that at times we seem to ride through life on a beast within. As we see apes mischievous, wolves savage, or the vultures ravenous for its prey, so we find human beings base, unjust and selfish. See how bureaucratic, economic and political forces wildly out of control, dehumanising and overpowering individuals! But God's original design for humankind is still in place. It has begun to come true in the risen Christ. God sent him to this world, "crowned with glory and honour, putting everything in subjection under his feet" (Heb 2:7-8). And Christ demonstrated his lordship over evil when he exorcised a man possessed by an "unclean spirit" (Mk 1:26). In his ministry and by his death and resurrection, Jesus provides for all those who come to him the release from moral and spiritual debilities. Therefore, in Jesus our personal failure can be the start of a new direction for us, and our experience of sin can enable us to appreciate the gift of forgiveness and spiritual rebirth. This is why, twenty centuries have come and gone, and today Christ is the centrepiece of the human race and the leader of the column of progress.

WEDNESDAY – WEEK 1 / YEAR 1

STRONGER AT THE BROKEN PLACES

Readings: Heb 2:14-18;   Mk 1:29-39

Whether we like it or not, pain is part of the whole fabric of life. To escape suffering completely, we would have to live in some sort of sterilised and cushioned module with no risk of infection or accident. However, there is nothing that the body suffers that the soul does not profit by. The world may break everyone, but afterwards many are stronger at the broken places. For example, if there were no suffering, trouble or difficulty in life, there would be no courage, patience and forgiveness or compassion. Why is it that as soon as he was told about Peter's mother-in-law's sickness, "Jesus came and took her by the hand and lifted her up?" (Mk 1:31). The answer is: "Because he himself has suffered" (Heb 2:18). Hence our suffering not only refines us, but makes us strong enough to bear and share the sufferings of others. That is why great people do not loose their self-possession when they are afflicted. This does not make suffering easier to bear. While afflicted, we would still need to go to someone. That person could well be Jesus Christ, who cannot only sympathise with us, but can help us through our suffering, since he had fully shared in our human suffering in all its forms.

THE CONTAGIOUS LOVE

Readings: Heb 3:7-14;   Mk 1:40-45

Some are called untouchable outcasts, yet all are created in the image of God. Some are called street kids, yet none is born on a road-way. Some are identified as refugees, or asylum seekers, yet the whole world is God's parish. Some are not given jobs because of colour or tongue, yet our God is the Father of all. Some countries are called the first world, others the third, yet God creates all human beings to share in his glory. Even in the Church, some are left sitting on the fringes of fellowship as marginals of the Church, with lives battered and broken but aching for love. As it were to symbolise the purpose of his mission, Jesus cures, in today's Gospel, a leper (Mk 1:42) who had been excluded from society as an outcast and reintroduces him to society. After Christ came, even leprosy ceases to be contagious; What actually became contagious is love. Anyone who comes into the love of God in Christ, is caught by that love which calls all in the words of an African poem: "Eat and drink together; talk and laugh together, enjoy life together; but never call it friendship until you have wept together." Do we hear the voice of this love in our hearts? "Today, when you hear his voice, do not harden your hearts" (Heb 3:14).

BE RESTED

Readings: Heb 4:1-5, 11;   Mk 2:1-12

A frantic mother called her pastor one day. She had a bad case of 'nerves'. He thought he heard a child's voice over the phone, so he asked, "Is your child upset or worried as you are?" "Why, of course not", she replied. "But why not?" he asked. "I suppose she puts her faith in me and let me do the worrying", she answered. "Then make a transference; try to think yourself as a child of God, and just as your child puts her faith in you, you put your faith in God and you will have good night's rest." Those who put their faith in God will have true rest. Those Israelites who did not share the faith of those who did listen to God, were excluded from the temporal rest of Canaan, while those who did, entered into the place of rest (Heb 4:3). Likewise, the paralytic in the Gospel was forgiven of his sins and cured of his disease, because he believed Jesus when he said, "I say to you, rise, take up your pallet, and go home" (Mk 11). We too, if we believe in the promise of God made in Christ, can have rest. The rest he gives is not lying on a beach all day; it is not a never-ending vacation. His rest is our trust in God's power to act.

SATURDAY – WEEK 1 / YEAR 1

THE SAFE WAY

Readings: Heb 4:12-16;   Mk 2:13-17

When we pray, we pray quickly because we are talking to God. But when we read the Bible, we read slowly because God is talking to us. The Word of God is "living and active" (Heb 4:12), precisely because it is God talking to us. As he talks to us, he guides us on the right path. But the path may run at times on a zig-zag line. For example, the Word will call us, now, to love ourselves, and then, to love others as well; now, to ask God for our daily bread, and then, not to worry about our material needs; now, to dominate the earth and all living beings in it, but then, not to impoverish environment for selfish purposes, and so on. Yes; the Word of God leads us on a path that is ever ascending, but always twisting. That is why, many a time, we give up following God's Word. If we have done that, let us come back to God seeking his forgiveness, for his has to be the Safe Way. Never lose your confidence in the forgiving mercy of the Lord. Remember that he came "not to call the righteous but sinners" (Mk 2:17). If the concept of God revealed by Christ has any validity or any use, it can only be that he understands our human weakness and embraces us again as we come back to him to place us back on the right path to our fulfilment.

INTERNET

Readings: Heb 5:1-10; Mk 2:18-22

Talking to a group of deaf children, the interpreter frequently will point gracefully to the palms of her hands, and pointing to the palms is the sign for Jesus Christ. How fitting is this sign for Jesus! Jesus is the only real and effective contact person between God and humanity because he is God in divine nature and man in his human nature; Hence he is the one "designated by God as high priest after the order of Melchizedek" (Heb 5:10). Before Jesus came on earth, people had to fast and do penance in order to reach out to God, but now, we all can come in contact with God in and through Jesus. Therefore Jesus said to the people that God becoming man in him is a time for rejoicing and dancing, as they do when the bridegroom arrives. "Can the wedding guests fast while the bridegroom is with them?" (Mk 2:19). In other words, why should one keep his arm in a cast after it is healed? No. But, Jesus, the high priest, the sole connecting link between God and humanity has shared his priesthood with all those baptised in him. Do we exercise our priestly function by being connecting links between God and our fellow human beings? The Internet connects us to thousands of things on the earth. Though far apart, through it, we can embrace and speak in love to thousands. Are we prepared to serve as God's Internets bringing people in contact with God?

PRO-PEOPLE

Readings: Heb 6:10-20; Mk 2:23-28

As I was walking around a cemetery, I noticed a marble tablet with the following inscription:In Memoriam: Rev A. Judson, born 9 August 1788, died 12 April 1850, converted Burmans and the Burman Bible-his monument, his record is on High." It is true. God keeps a record of all the good deeds we have done in this life and he rewards them either here on earth or in heaven. "God is not so unjust as to overlook your work" (Heb 6:10). We must never think of God as harsh, inhuman, anti-people. He is pro-people. He cares for us. He loves to reward us for the good deeds done in his name and in carrying out his holy will. In order to point out to us how much God is interested in human joy and fulfilment, Jesus said: "The Sabbath was made for man, not man for the Sabbath" (Mk 2:27). Suppose you have a big property, but you are so kind hearted that you gave your possessions away to all the needy who approached you for help. And in the end, you are dying, leaving behind no property on earth. Do you think that you are dying in poverty? No. God is going to reward you for all the charity you had done to others. After your death, you will have considerable property to go to. God is pro-people whose reward is far beyond our expectations.

WEDNESDAY – WEEK 2 / YEAR 1

THE SHOCK OF THE NEW

Readings: Heb 2:14-18;   Mk 1:29-39

When the English Labour Party changed its name from 'Labour' to 'New Labour', the Conservatives raised the slogan: *New Labour, New Danger!* Likewise, when Jesus, pledging himself to a new deal with humanity, bypassed the old traditions for the sake of the new world order, Pharisees thought that Jesus was a danger. In fact, everything about Jesus was new starting from birth for he was born not of a human father. His priesthood was new for, like Melchizedek, Jesus derived his priesthood directly from God his Father (Heb 7:16). It is no surprise, then, that he cured a man of his withered hand on a Sabbath (Mk 3:5), when the established tradition prohibited even such a deed of compassion on a Sabbath. With Jesus, a new world order was coming into view, and he was establishing the ground rules for it, with its pillars such as justice, love, mercy and peace. In the New World as Jesus saw it, every human law and structure must be oriented towards the total welfare of every human being on the globe. History has proved that behind every stage of human progress, there has been a new way of thinking. I don't mean that human civilization progresses because in every war we kill people in a new way. On the contrary, true human progress depends on the world order that Jesus has established.

THURSDAY – WEEK 2 / YEAR 1

CHURCH AT ITS BEST!

Readings: Heb 7:25-8:6; Mk 3:7-12

The Mass is the Sacrament of sacraments. At Mass, Jesus Christ continues to act "the ideal High Priest" (Heb 7:26) as he did on Calvary. The death and the resurrection of Jesus are not only historical events, but a source of continuing power for the moment, and the power of Jesus' death and resurrection have been captured sacramentally and made available to us through the Mass. Through our celebration of the Eucharist, Jesus continues to build us as his people forgiven and healed, moulding us into one people. So, as the people of our Lord's time, "afflicted in any way, were crowding forward to touch him" (Mk 3:11), we, even today, crowd around the Eucharist to touch and to be touched by the same Jesus, so that we continue to grow into a loving and caring community. Mass is the Church at its best! But, as we come in big crowds around the Eucharist, do we know each other as brothers and sisters in Jesus Christ? If we are anonymous to one another as we approach Christ, if we are indifferent to each other's needs, I am afraid, Christ himself may remain anonymous to us. As Christ calls us to participate in the sacrifice of the Mass, he calls us to "get up!"– Up, out of our self-centred living! Up, out of our indifference! Up, out of our fears and paralysis, when the Spirit stirs our conscience to reach out to those who are hurting.

FRIDAY – WEEK 2 / YEAR 1

WHY? WHY? WHY?

Readings: Heb 8:6-13;   Mk 3:13-19

These days, divorce has become so cheap, that all a boy needs for a divorce is a wife! Divorce has become so cheaply justifiable that some women no longer say that they are getting a divorce, but being recycled! It was not this bad with the people of Israel, but still, they too divorced God who had made a covenant of love with them. But God being who he is, six centuries later, established a new covenant (Heb 8:6) in Christ. God made a promise that even though human beings might prove unfaithful to him, he would not; Rather he will keep on loving us, shaping us into a people of justice and peace, hope and joy. It is in order to go and proclaim this Good News that Jesus "appointed twelve" (Mk 3:14). But then, why is it that peace is still not triumphant, justice does not yet rule on earth, and sin is still present with its painful consequences? Where are the effects of the new covenant, mediated by Jesus Christ? Perhaps we have to look for the answer in ourselves. Are we, the baptised, continuing the mission of Christ, entrusted to his twelve apostles, to live our lives as the people of the new covenant, doing everything we can to bridge and heal the gap between people, and enable them to return to God their Father?

SATURDAY – WEEK 2 / YEAR 1

IS SACRIFICE CRAZY?

Readings: Heb 9:2-3, 11-14;   Mk 3:20-21

Words, like eyeglasses, can blur everything, if you are not careful. One such word is 'sacrifice'. A man says, "I have given up salt; I had to make the sacrifice of it for the sake of my health." Is it true sacrifice? No. True sacrifice is not that you give up something so that you can get something better for yourself. True sacrifice is the surrendering of oneself for the sake of others. Jesus made such a sacrifice. The priests of the Old Testament could not sacrifice their lives in the service of the people. But Jesus did. (Heb 9:12). Such a sacrifice seemed crazy even to his relatives who complained that "he is beside himself" (Mk 3:21). Our own world today is not much different. Its civilised slogan is "Drown not yourself to save a drowning man!' Therefore, don't be surprised if people think that you are a freak when you make a worthwhile sacrifice for the happiness of another. Instead, remember the great saints who were willing to sacrifice their very lives in the service of others, because they were convinced that under certain circumstances, it is not worthwhile to live; The universe is so vast and so ageless that the life of one person can only be justified by the measure of his or her sacrifice for others.

MONDAY – WEEK 3 / YEAR 1

SLANDER

Readings: Heb 9:24-28;   Mk 3:22-30

Justin Martyr once said: "By examining the tongue of a patient, physicians find out the disease of the body and philosophies of the mind!" A slanderous tongue reveals not only the diseased body but also a diseased mind. There are different ways of assassinating a person: by pistol, sword, poison, or by calumny. They are the same in their results except, that the last is more cruel. The Scribes in today's Gospel were indulging in the most atrocious form of calumny against Jesus when they said "By the prince of demons he casts out demons" (Mk 3:22). The truth about Jesus is that he is the personification of the total goodness of God and he destroyed the sin of humanity by the magnanimous "sacrifice of himself" (Heb 9:26). And yet, the Scribes said that Jesus got his energy and directives from the devil. All sins are forgivable but not this one, for it is "against the Holy Spirit" (Mk 3:29), because it designates the highest good to the most heinous evil that calls God himself a devil. Everyone in the crowd has the power to throw dirt: nine out of ten have the inclination to do so. But we must resist this inclination. Remember that slander like coal will either dirty your hand or burn it.

BRIDGE-BUILDERS

Readings: Heb 10:1-10;   Mk 3:31-35

The word 'community' has become a warm word. In recent years, we hear of community development, community studies, community policing, community care, community health and so forth. Anywhere in the world, you can meet literally thousands of people who are involved, one way or another, with restoration of local communities. There are bridge-builders often working in areas where different cultural and religious traditions encounter one another only in conflict. It is a very heartening sight to see. After all, why should human beings be divided on the basis of language, culture, or colour? As long as we believe in God as our common Father, and are ready to do his will, we are already bound together as brothers and sisters by a bond deeper and stronger than that which ties natural family members. Jesus who came to do his Father's will (Heb 10:7) also affirmed: "Whoever does the will of God is my brother, and sister, and mother" (Mk 3:35).Yes; the spiritual nature of our link to God our Father places us within a network of a new, lasting, vital relationship to each other. Let us promote this network in every way we can, till the new universal community envisaged by Christ is born.

THERE IT STANDS!

Readings: Heb 10:11-18;   Mk 4:1-20

Century follows century, there it stands! Empires rise and fall, there it stands! Dynasty succeeds dynasty, there it stands! The Word of God is indestructible. God has been sowing his sacred Word in human hearts all through history. That was his promise: "I will put my laws on their hearts and write them on their minds" (Heb 10:17). That is why, every human being is now able to discover God's directives, for their lives, within themselves. Jesus, too, like "a sower (who) went out to sow" (Mk 4:3,) spread the words of eternal life, which are captured for us in the Gospels. His word informs us about the Saviour of the world; it reforms us, for in it, we find the ideal and the standard, by which we ought to live. It transforms us, because in it, we are brought face to face with God's grace. Information, reformation, transformation; the Gospel has them all. But the Lord's Word must fall in the good soil to bear fruit. The shallow mind, the hard heart, the easily diverted and the morally weak, are not suitable soils. A contagious enthusiasm to receive the Word, and a conducive soil to cultivate it, would do more to rid the present world of its distress and despair, than all the plans and strivings of humanity.

THURSDAY – WEEK 3 / YEAR 1

COMMUNITY PEOPLE

Readings: Heb 10:19-25;   Mk 4:21-25

In the human body, the head does not receive blood to store it up; while it pumps blood in at one valve, it sends it out at another. The same is true of all the fluids in a healthy body; they are in a constant state of expenditure. If any cell in the body should begin to store up its secretion, its store should soon become the cause of inveterate disease. Thus the whole of the human system lives by giving. Do we want to enjoy fulfilment in being followers of Christ? The only way is to enter "through the curtain, that is, his flesh" (Heb 10:20). In other words, a self-fulfilling life in Christ begins with self-giving to his body, the community of believers. All that we are, and all that we have received from God are meant to be shared. That is, we are expected to put the lamp not under the bed, but on a stand (Mk 4:21). Our times are revealing more and more clearly than ever, just how interconnected we all are on this ever shrinking planet, and therefore, how necessary it is to become community people who weave patterns of peace between warring nations, and patterns of love between hating sides; who weave a pattern of hope among the hopeless, and a pattern of joy among the sorrowful.

TRIAL'S BEST MUSIC

Readings: Heb 10:32-39; Mk 4:26-34

Handel, the great musician, lost his health; his right side was paralysed; his money was gone and his creditors threatened to imprison him. Handel was so disheartened that he almost despaired for a brief time. But his faith prevented, and he composed his greatest work, *The Hallelujah Chorus* which is part of his great *Messiah*. Each of us can recall a similar experience in the past, when our faith brought us safe through a most despairing situation, filling us with new vigour for a more fulfilling life. However, we must not conclude that with one test of our faith in the past, our journey of faith will be hereafter one long smooth sailing. No. Our faith will again and again be tested. At those testing times, we must recall the times when our steadfast faith in the past, in the midst of sufferings, gave us "a better possession and an abiding one" (Heb 10:34). Another reason why we should not give up faith when it is tested is this: As a seed which a farmer has thrown on the land is "sprouting and growing night and day, how, he knows not" (Mk 4:27), the seed of God's Kingdom already planted in our hearts, is steadily growing by our repeated acts of faith, and we are sure to reap an abundant harvest. Let us hope; Hope is trial's best music.

SINKING?

Readings: Heb 11:1-2, 8-19; Mk 4:35-41

Notice how a spider builds her web. She casts her film to the wind feeling sure that somewhere it will adhere and form the beginning of her web. She emits the slender filament to the breeze, believing that there is a place provided for it to fix itself. It was in this fashion, Abraham "went out, not knowing where he was to go" (Heb 11:8), trusting only in God's promise. We, too, like Abraham the father of our faith, must cast forth all our endeavours, confident that God will find a place for them. As we journey through this sea of life, we are sure to face storms of tribulation. At those moments, we are called to believe in the presence of God with us, unlike the incredulous disciples who, caught in a storm, cried out, "Teacher, do you not care if we perish?" (Mk 4:38). God does care for us, especially when we are in difficulty. Without this faith, we would be like the man who has fallen in a river but does not know how to swim. He becomes frightened, so he sinks; so he struggles to keep afloat, so he sinks even deeper. If he dropped his fear and allowed himself to sink, his body would come up to the surface on its own. Can we drop our fears when we are thrown into life's storms, believing that God continues to remain our life's support?

MONDAY – WEEK 4 / YEAR 1

ANY SECRET CHRISTIAN?

Readings: Heb 11:32-40; Mk 5:1-20

A woman who was showing a massive piece of family silver apologised as she took it from the cupboard. "Dreadfully tarnished," she said, "I can't keep it bright unless I use it." That is just as true of faith as it is of silver. You can't keep faith bright unless you use it and share it. In fact, sharing of faith-stories builds up and enlarges faith community. Therefore, the author of Hebrews shared the heroic faith stories of pre-Christian age such as those of "Gideon, Samson, Jephthah, David, Samuel and the prophets" (Heb 11:32), with early Christians whose faith was cooling down. During our Lord's ministry, after driving out a legion of evil spirits from a man, Jesus told him, "Go home to your friends, and tell them how much the Lord has done for you" (Mk 5:19). It is impossible to know the value of faith without desiring to see others, too, brought in. "As soon as I was converted," said a convert from Islam, "I wanted to be the means of conversion for all those whom I had ever known. There were a number of young men that I had played cards with, and transgressed with. The first thing I did was, I went to their houses to see and share my faith story with them." Is there any secret Christian? If so, how did you come to know it?

TUESDAY – WEEK 4 / YEAR 1

BLIND UPWARD!

Readings: Heb 12:1-4;   Mk 5:21-43

Every human being lives by faith, the non-believer as well as the saint. People believe a lot of things they don't actually see. For example, if a friend phones and says he just bought a new car, we believe him even though we don't see the car. Used in spiritual matters, faith means accepting and believing things that are beyond this world. Is there really a God? Do we still live after we die? Does how we live, choose and decide in this life, affect a final and lasting life? We say, "Yes" to such questions, simply on the strength of Jesus' words, though we don't clearly see yet. Jesus is the "pioneer and perfecter of our faith" (Heb 12:2). Faith in Jesus fills us with hope, aids us to walk courageously through tough paths of life on earth. Jesus proved that he has power over a prolonged illness, by curing a woman who had suffered a haemorrhage for twelve years (Mk 5:29), and over death itself, by raising Jairus' daughter from death (Mk 5:42). There can be no hope without faith in Christ, for hope is rooted in him alone. In a sense, faith is blind, except upward! It is blind to difficulties and deaf to impossibilities. It listens only to Christ. Faith in him will lead us where we can not walk; Reason has never been a mountain climber, but faith is.

WEDNESDAY – WEEK 4 / YEAR 1

THERMOSTAT UNDER CONTROL

Readings: Heb 12:4-7, 11-15;   Mk 6:1-6

Do we have any idea how much more fruitful we could be, if only we had a little help? That help comes from God when he places us in the fire, in the melting pot of distress, rejection and pressure. Like a loving father who trains his child by putting him through discipline, God corrects and trains us to maturity through pain and suffering. Therefore,

"My son, do not lose courage when you are punished by God" (Heb 12:5) Here is the good news: You might be in the fire today, but God is controlling the thermostat. He knows how hot it needs to be to bring out the best in you. Can you think of anyone you would rather trust with the thermostat than the God of love and wisdom? We need his correction. God did not exempt even his own Son from this portion of suffering. The rejection Jesus experienced in today's Gospel (Mk 6:6) is only one example of his suffering which reached its climax on Calvary. Yet God raised him. Every test has degrees. Only God knows the temperature required to burn away our imperfections and to set us free to do his will. When we belong to God, the fire burns off only the chains that shackle us, freeing us to fulfil God's purpose. He has invested too much in each of us to let us sink.

THURSDAY – WEEK 4 / YEAR 1

THE NEXT GREEN

Readings: Heb 12:18-19, 21-24;   Mk 6:7-13

Recently, one of my parishioners wrote to me and asked: "If I'm suffering because of my own mistakes, do I still have the right to expect God to bless and use me?' I replied: "Yes. God's grace is not based on your character; it is based on his." God will forgive us of all our wrong doings if we return to him humble and repentant, and that is why Jesus sent out his disciples in pairs to preach repentance (Mk 6:12). When God established his new covenant of love with us, in the blood of Jesus shed on the cross, it was a moment of weakness and humiliation for Christ, in contrast to the moment of the old covenant when God appeared to Moses in all his majesty and power (Heb 12:21). The apparent weakness and humiliation of Jesus was a sign that God offers his love and forgiveness in Christ, to those who acknowledge their weakness and frailty and seek his forgiveness. I am not a golfer, but I can tell you this: the most important shot in the game is the next one. The sooner you can forget your last 'slice' and get your mind on the next green, the sooner you will turn your defeat into victory. So too, the sooner we put away from our mind our past failures and return to God repentant, the better for us.

THE BEST CHEER

Readings: Heb 13:1-8; Mk 6:14-29

As the saying goes, "Welcome is your best cheer." So John the Baptist spent the whole of his life in the work of welcoming Christ into this world. He preached to the world how it should welcome the Saviour. But as a reward for this welcoming work, he received martyrdom. King Herod's servant "went and beheaded him in the prison" (Mk 6:17). Those of us who have fallen in love with Jesus Christ our Saviour, wish to welcome him into our lives, whatever the cost may be. But, is Jesus anywhere about us? He is indeed, in the guise of refugees, and strangers. Whenever we show hospitality to strangers we receive Jesus himself. "If you give a cup of cold water to the least of my brothers, you give it to me", Jesus once said. So, "Do not neglect to show hospitality to strangers, for thereby some have entertained angels unawares." (Heb 13:2). Shall we therefore be extra hospitable to migrants and refugees? The language they speak sounds different, but the feelings it expresses are the same. They need a family because they have left theirs to work for other families. The colour of this people is different, but the colour of their blood is the same. They cry for justice and peace in different ways, but our God is the same.

TOUCHED BY LOVE

Readings: Heb 13:15-17, 20-21; Mk 6:30-34

One of the deepest longings in the human heart is the desire to be loved for oneself alone. When you are touched by love, it reaches down into your deepest fibre. Hence, Jesus "the great shepherd of people" (Heb 13:20), spent the greater part of his public life in doing good works for the needy in society, so that they could experience the joy of being loved. When he saw crowds like "sheep without a shepherd, he had compassion on them" (Mk 6:34), and did whatever he could in order to make them feel good. During peek hours, stand at a city railway station or a public square or a main thoroughfare. You will see a sea of faceless people rushing here and there. But you know something? Among them, there should be hundreds who are living frustrated lives, chiefly because they have not experienced true and genuine human love. May we look at such people, first, in our own families, communities, and work places, who long to be loved, and offer them our love in some concerned way? It is difficult to love yourself, if you are not first loved. Like someone who has been lost for years in a forgotten place, the person you love rejoices in being found. Your love somehow transfigures the sad gravity of life in them.

MONDAY – WEEK 5 / YEAR 1

LIKE A TRAMPLED FLOWER!

Readings: Gen 1:1-19; Mk 6:53-56

A little boy, being asked what forgiveness is, gave this beautiful answer: "It is the odour that flowers breathe when they are trampled upon." God acted like this flower towards the first human beings when they rebelled against him and brought upon humanity sufferings and death. God not only forgave the rebellion, but also began working on remedying the painful consequences of it. And how did he do that? He sent his Son Jesus to restore us back to his friendship, to heal our wounds and to recreate us. Hence wherever Jesus went, people "ran about the whole neighbourhood to bring sick people." (Mk 6:55). The healing ministry of Christ shows that suffering, which is an evil was not a curse laid upon humanity by God, since whatever he had created, "God saw that it was good" (Gen 1:10). On the contrary, it was the result of human rebellion against God, and yet God forgave us and began breathing, like a trampled flower, the sweet odour of restoration. Can we also be magnanimous like God, in forgiving others who have hurt us? Can we still love them as God's children and help them to become better and richer human persons? To forgive the hurts and still love the enemy is Godlike. Revenging one, makes you but even with him; but forgiving, sets you above him.

TUESDAY – WEEK 5 / YEAR 1

LIKE HEART BEAT

Readings: Gen 1:20-2:4; Mk 7:1-13

Our gratitude to God needs to be as regular as our heart beat. God created our world and saw that it was good. But when he created the human being in his own 'image' after his 'likeness' (Gen 1:26), he must have found the being to be very good. We resemble God by our intelligence, free will and love. How grateful are we to God for all this? Gratitude seems to be an idiotic word, for it is readily found on people's lips, but seldom exists in the human heart. We hope that the words of the Scripture, "this people honours me with their lips, but their heart is far from me" (Mk 7:6) may not be true of any of us. If our heart is grateful to God for the intelligence he has given us, then we must make it our life's business to use it to search for full truth about ourselves, about God and about this world, though there are times when there is nothing harder to see than the naked truth. If our heart is grateful to God for the freedom, then we ought not to join those people who are clamouring for freedom to do what ought not to be done. If our heart is grateful for the capacity to love, then our love for others has to be what Blake describes: "Love seeks not itself to please, nor for itself has any care; but for another gives its ease, and builds a heaven in Hell's despair."

WEDNESDAY – WEEK 5 / YEAR 1

THE DEFILING FACTOR

Readings: Gen 2:4-9, 15-17; Mk 7:14-23

It is a common saying: "Cleanliness is next to godliness!" Does it mean that when I eat with washed hands and wear clean clothes, I am godly? Not really. When cleanliness of the external is made an essential, but godliness of the inner person is neglected, how can cleanliness be next to godliness? As Jesus says, "There is nothing outside a man which by going into him can defile him; but the things which come out of a man are what defile him." (Mk 7:16). In other words, man does not live by soap alone. Among vices that come out of a man, 'avarice' tops the list, these days. When all other vices are old, avarice is still young. Just look at the ecological devastation that is being caused by so many greedy people in the world. After creating human beings, "the Lord God took the man and put him in the garden of Eden to till it and keep it" (Gen 2:15). God gave us a world of nature for the use of all humanity. But it is appalling to see how the avarice of human beings has spoiled the 'garden', polluted the air, fouled the rivers, turned the grasslands into deserts, forests into wastelands. It is this pervasive human greed that is making our civilisation unclean and this world uninhabitable. As you know, big mouthfuls often choke!

THURSDAY – WEEK 5 / YEAR 1

FEMALE DIGNITY

Readings: Gen 2:18-25; Mk 7:24-30

"Equality consists in the same treatment of similar persons", said Aristotle. Man and woman are similar; and yet, even today, in some cultures, equality for woman is a mortuary word. The words of Adam: "This at last is bone of my bones and flesh of my flesh" (Gen 2:23), signify that man and woman share the same human nature, the same rights and privileges, the same divine destiny. And yet, one wonders how women, in some cultures, became just pawns and slaves to men. Men who flatter women do not know them, men who abuse them know them still less. The fact is that, next to God, we are indebted to women, first for life itself, and then for making it worth having. The future of society is in the hands of mothers; if the world was lost through a woman, as the Bible says, she is needed to save it. That is why Jesus' respect for women was unbounded. He could never refuse any woman any favour as we see him in today's Gospel. He yields to the appeal of a non-Jewish mother to cure her daughter, saying, "You may go your way, the demon has left your daughter" (Mk 7:29). It is heartening to see in some cultures of today, that women are steadily becoming persons first, and wives second, and that is as it should be.

FRIDAY – WEEK 5 / YEAR 1

DEAF AND DUMB?

Readings: Gen 3:1-8; Mk 7:31-37

It is God alone who can give ultimate fulfilment, and if we try to achieve it by ourselves, we are doomed to fail. This is the attempt made by our first parents. They ate the fruit forbidden by God hoping to become "like God, knowing good and evil" (Gen 3:5). They became deaf to God's instruction and fell deep into the valley of guilt. Once the guilt of sin grabbed their conscience, they began to flee when none was pursuing them, like a thief who fears every bush as an officer. When God called, they were unable to face him. They became dumb. Are we somewhat in a similar predicament? Perhaps we remain deaf and dumb in prayer, because our conscience is weighed down by some guilt. Prayer is a dialogue in which we hear God and we speak to him. But our guilt may prevent us from doing it. If so, we need not get discouraged. Jesus can remove these spiritual impediments as he did to the man "who was deaf and had an impediment in his speech" (Mk 7:32). But for the Lord to do the same for us, we need to confess our sins, the cause of our guilt feeling. There smites nothing so sharp as guilt-fear, nor tastes so sour as shame that results from it. But the Lord can forgive and heal the guilt.

GOD IS A PROVIDER

Readings: Gen 3:9-24; Mk 8:1-10

Many mammoth oaks are said to have nearly vanished from most famous forests on earth by the monstrous coils of ivy, which entwine themselves about the trees' trunks, like some unsightly serpents entwined about the bodies of their prey. The sin of our first parents was like ivy, which nearly destroyed the oak of their bliss in the Garden. Their sin disrupted the created order: woman has childbirth pain; man has to labour hard to earn his living, husband and wife relationship becomes infected with dominance and submission, and death becomes the end of one's ambition. However, in what the merciful God said to the serpent, he made a promise to send a Saviour to defeat sin and death for ever (Gen 3:15). The miracle of loaves and fish (Mk 8) symbolises the Eucharist which the Lord instituted to continue to provide for us a way of overcoming the degenerative effects of our repeated sins. This must give us the hope that God will never abandon us however rebellious we turn against him. When we are much discouraged by the roughness of the way to holiness, when the cross we carry seems heavier every day, and when some cloud overshadows and hides our Father's face from view, remember that God is a Provider.

WE HAVE HAD ENOUGH!

Readings: Gen 4:1-15, 25; Mk 8:11-13

In olden times when there was a war, it was a human-to-human confrontation. The victor in battle would directly see the blood and suffering of the defeated enemy. This was true of Cain. He killed his own unarmed brother Abel and relished looking at his blood (Gen 4:8). Nowadays it is much more terrifying, because a man in an office can push a button and kill millions of people and never see the human tragedy he has created. The mechanisation of human conflict poses an increasing threat to peace. But, peace in the world has to begin with peace within each of us. When we have inner peace, we can be at peace with those around us. We must control the anger and hatred in ourselves. If Cain had controlled his anger and jealousy against his brother he would not have killed him. We have had enough of hatred, which aims a gun at another and pulls the trigger. We have had enough of anger, which explodes to shatter joy. We have had enough of jealousy, which denigrates the grace it envies. May we have a new awareness of the battlefield within ourselves and new ways of channelling aggressive instincts! May we have new attempts to befriend those who are different from us, and new readiness to forgive and reconcile.

TUESDAY – WEEK 6 / YEAR 1

WEED UP THE GARDEN

Readings: Gen 6:5-8, 7:1-5, 10; Mk 8:14-21

There are at least two things about which we should never worry. First, the things we can not help. If we can not help them, worrying is certainly the most foolish and useless. Secondly, the things we can help; if we can help them, let us set about it and not weaken our powers by worry. After all, there is the Providence of God. See how he saved the future of human race by saving Noah, even when God's justice compelled him to punish humanity with a devastating flood (Gen 6:8). God always provides; therefore we must weed our garden, and pluck up the smallest roots of worry; if we let them get a start, they will crowd out all the beautiful things that ought to grow in our heart. But let us remember that the ultimate goal of God's providence is the return of humankind back to its final home. This means, that for the sake of a spiritual good, God may allow us to suffer at times from want of even some essential material needs. At those moments, we must not get very anxious as the disciples of Christ who became very worried over a short supply of bread, even after having witnessed a miracle of the multiplication of loaves by Christ (Mk 8:19). At times of want, we need to remember that whoever falls from God's right hand is caught into his left.

WEDNESDAY – WEEK 6 / YEAR 1

THERE IS HOPE

Readings: Gen 8:6-13, 20-22; Mk 8:22-26

Does God love us? If so, why does he not put an end to human misery? That is the question we often ask. But God has not left us hopeless. After the destructive flood receded, he promised: "I will never again curse the ground because of man," but added: "the imagination of man's heart is evil from his youth" (Gen 8:21). In this, we see not only the promise of immense hope, but also the root cause of human misery which resides in the human heart. God created us to live in peace together, but we have failed, because we have loved ourselves too much, and neglected the needy; we prefer to manufacture weapons of war rather than instruments of peace. God gave us a beautiful world to take care of, but we have polluted it; in our pride, we want to be like God by creating people by cloning! By the wrong we do with all the science and technology, we sit crying among the broken dreams and shattered lives, but there is still hope. Our faith assures us that God will keep providing us some means of salvation from our misery. As the blind man in the Gospel, who by the repeated healing action of Christ, finally "saw everything clearly" (Mk 8:25), the human race will one day be completely freed from the degenerative powers of evil.

LOOK UP TO THE RAINBOW

Readings: Gen 9:1-13; Mk 8:27-33

Not to get what you have set your heart on, is almost as bad as getting nothing at all. That is frustration. You put time and effort into work which turns out to be useless; you are all ready to start a project but you can't find some indispensable tool or a piece of paper. You do a good job for which someone else is rewarded. We seek happiness but find misery and death. All of us, now and then, find everything just too much. So we are frustrated. But our faith assures us that our God of mercy and love is guiding us even through frustrating existence, to a fulfilling glory. After God had saved Noah from the flood, he made the rainbow (Gen 9:13). The rainbow may be taken as a symbol not of an immediate destruction of all evil, but of God's promise to guide us through life's pain and suffering. Hence, Jesus, the embodiment of God's promise of mercy and love, undertook the work of redemption, not in an ideal world but in a world still disfigured by sin. As we know, he too had to suffer many things before rising again (Mk 8:31). When life's stress drags us down, when our strength is all but sapped, when the way ahead is shattered, let us think of the rainbow and believe that God takes what is left of life, and renews it all by his love.

DAZZLING!

Readings: Gen 11:1-9; Mk 8:34-9:1

The power of science and technology is dazzling: to create and clone life in the laboratory, to send words and pictures thousands of miles away by the touch of a button. We live in a world of spaceship, satellite, of computer and test-tube. Advances in genetic engineering have given us the power to intervene in the structure of DNA, the stuff of life itself. In a way, we are Godlike in our achievements, with power to create and destroy. That is why, it has become necessary to temper the scientific progress by the moral imperative, and to add divine wisdom to human knowledge. To exclude God from human calculation, and to rely solely on human power, without seeking to do the will of our Creator, is to build a tower of Babel (Gen 11:9), a symbol of self-destructive human arrogance. Jesus asks us to renounce every inclination to become an affront against God. He asks us to be ready to lose one's life itself (Mk 8:35), in order to gain the true and full life God has offered in Christ. We face a future, which contains much promise, but threats as well. Hence, religion is of vital importance today, for it testifies to the spiritual values of truth, justice, love and peace, which alone can form a sound basis for lasting human fulfilment.

SATURDAY – WEEK 6 / YEAR 1

THE BELIEVING THEORY

Readings: Heb 11:1-7; Mk 9:2-13

A schoolboy said of his headmaster: "A fellow can't tell my headmaster a lie, because he always believes what you say." The headmaster's belief in the honour of his boys, laid an obligation of honour on the boys. Suspicion begets suspicion. That is why God believes in us. He believed in us and sent his Son to die for us. Christ gave us teachings and challenges of staggering height because he believed that we would rise to his expectations. Can we apply the same 'believing theory' to our belief in God? Believe in God's promises and they will turn into facts. It is very well to believe in God when you have other props, but believe in him when every prop is knocked away, and a new door will open to you. It is in this sense, "Faith is the assurance of things hoped for, the conviction of things not seen" (Heb 11:1). The same is true of our faith in Jesus Christ. God said on Mount Tabor: "This is my beloved Son, listen to him" (Mk 9:7). To listen to Jesus, we must believe in him and if we do, his promises will come true in our lives.

For example, believe that "blessed are the poor in spirit", and you will experience the Kingdom of God within you. Believe that "blessed are the merciful", and you will obtain mercy.

MONDAY – WEEK 7 / YEAR 1

FREEDOM IN FETTERS?

Readings: Eccl 1:1-10; Mk 9:14-29

Many people possessed by powers that empty them of their true selves, don't seem to belong to themselves. Their freedom is in fetters. They are at the mercy of forces more powerful than they are. Of course, since the beginning of human history our freedom is held captive by so many constraints. Our will is frustrated by so much of despair, and our hearts are so blemished that it is difficult for us to find love in them. What can deliver us from this tragic condition? Human skills or scientific knowledge can't do this. We need wisdom. But, "all wisdom comes from the Lord and is with him forever" (Sir 1:1).This wisdom of God, which is power, and can deliver humanity from its dark and evil forces, is available in Jesus Christ, who is within the reach of every human being. As Jesus drove out the evil spirit from the boy possessed by it with a command, "come out of him" (Mk 9:25), Jesus can even now breathe God's own power into anyone who comes to him, and turn him or her into a new creature. Do we believe in the power of Jesus to do this for us? A strange thing has happened to people of today: in becoming literate, they have lost the ability to recognise the power of God where it is really found.

LIKE LITTLE CHILDREN

Readings: Sir 2:1-13; Mk 9:30-37

The world is increasingly suffering from the pernicious influences of the anti-Kingdom values of glory and honour, status and power, authority and independence. Jesus, as it were to warn us of this danger, "took a child, put him in the midst of them" (Mk 9:36) and put his arm around him, signifying that a child is the prince of God's Kingdom. The child is quite happy to be small, but the mustard seed too is small but one day it can grow into a big tree. The child is quite content to walk behind its father trusting in his leadership which is safe. We are called to be childlike in our relationship with God. Sirach asks us to "cleave to him" and "trust in him" (Sir 2:3,6) like a child. When the adults always claim to be able to manage their affairs on their own, how happy are those who, like little children, keep on knocking on the door of heaven until it opens. When the adults are reasoning and arguing about who will occupy the first place, how happy are those who, like little children, are content in being lower in command. When the adults build their shady little kingdoms on power and greed, violence and exploitation, how happy are those who, like little children, abandon themselves totally to God's mercy.

FLOWERS DON'T COMPLAIN

Readings: Sir 4:12-22; Mk 9:35-40

Some gardeners are going down to a pond and carry in their big pots refreshing liquid to the flowers. A child comes into the garden and wishes to help and yonder is a little watering pot for him. The little water pot, though it does not hold so much, carries the same water.

And it does not make any difference to the flowers whether the water came out of a big pot or a little pot, so long as it is the same water. So too, it does not matter who works for the Kingdom of God; it does not matter to which denomination of faith one belongs, provided what the person does helps towards building up God's Kingdom of truth, love and peace. Such a person loves wisdom which is God's will and "who ever holds wisdom fast will obtain glory" (Sir 4:13). This is what Jesus meant when he said, "He that is not against us is for us" (Mk 9:40). We are to accept anyone as doing good and accomplishing God's purpose, when they don't actively oppose his will. The wisdom of God is not enclosed within the registers of our dusty Catholic sacristies. St Augustine wrote: "Non-Catholics are found inside Catholic Church and Catholics can also be found outside Catholic Church. Many of those who seem to be outside are inside, and those who seem to be inside are outside."

THURSDAY – WEEK 7 / YEAR 1

SCANDAL HAS WINGS

Readings: Sir 5:1-10; Mk 9:41-50

Our chief want in life is somebody who shall, by his or her good example, inspire us to do what is good. But bad example, which is called scandal, is often what we see, especially when peers get together. Love and scandal are said to be the best sweeteners of tea! For example, take drug-abuse. Friends and acquaintances provide drugs to new comers into the group and teach the new friend how to use them. In the course of time, the person begins to excuse drug- abuse. Jesus says, "If your hand causes you to sin, cut it off" (Mk 9:44). He is not asking us to literally cut off the hand used in a scandal. He asks us to sacrifice the immoral pleasures, which some parts of our body may offer, for the sake of greater spiritual benefits. But our evil actions originate from evil inclinations. Therefore, we are asked not to walk "according to the desires of our heart" (Sir 5:2). We are asked to 'circumcise' our heart of its evil inclinations before they loom into scandalous deeds.

Remember that our influence on others is negative or positive, never neutral. Especially, the impact of scandal on others is fast and ferocious. A lie has no leg, but a scandal has wings.

FRIDAY – WEEK 7 / YEAR 1

MARRIAGE DEMANDS DIVORCE!

Readings: Sir 6:5-17; Mk 10:1-12

A young man knocked on the door of a house. A voice from within said, "Who is it?" The young man said, "It is me. I've come to ask permission to marry your daughter." The voice from within said, "You are not ready; come back in a year." A year later, the young man returned and knocked again. The voice from within said, "Who is it?" "It is us. We've come to ask your permission to marry." The voice from within said, "You are now ready. Please come in." Marriage is thinking and acting as one, for in marriage "they are no longer two, but one" (Mk 10:8). God made them male and female, not just to procreate babies, but also to be faithful friends to each other in good and bad times. "A faithful friend is an elixir of life" (Sir 6:16). Their friendship doubles their joy and divides their grief. When we meet with difficulties we think of our relatives, but when we are on the brink of danger, we rely on our friends. People must marry for faithful friendship. To marry someone for money or beauty is like buying a house for its paint and plaster. The cause of many broken marriages is selfishness in one form or another. Hence, a successful marriage demands divorce, a divorce from one's self-centredness.

SATURDAY – WEEK 7 / YEAR 1

DIAMONDS IN FLESH

Readings: Sir 17:1-13; Mk 10:13-16

A diamond in the rough is a diamond; before it ever sparkles, it is made of diamond stuff. Of course, someone must find it or it will never be found. And then, someone must grind it, or it will never be ground. But when it is found, when it is ground and when it is burnished bright, it sparkles everlastingly. A child is like a diamond, for "God made them in his own image" (Sir 17:3). That is why, Jesus "took them in his arms and blessed them, laying his hands upon them" (Mk 10:16). Adults, especially teachers and parents, have the sweet obligation of burnishing the diamond-like children by training them in a way that the image of God in them shoots forth its light. It is tragic that modern media has to talk so much about child-abuse. Among many forms of child-abuse, one is psychological. Children are psychologically abused when they are rejected, criticised excessively, punished unrealistically, humiliated persistently, shown love sporadically and threatened with abandonment. An old sexton in a cemetery took special pains with the little graves. I asked him why. He said, "Sir, about those larger graves, I don't know who are the Lord's and who are not; but, you know, it is different with children."

MONDAY – WEEK 8 / YEAR 1

GOLD CHAINS

Readings: Sir 17:20-29; Mk 10:17-27

Riches are chains of gold, but still chains. They chain our spirits down to earthly things so strongly that we can't move towards God, the only true good. Most of the luxuries are not only not indispensable, but positive hindrances to the elevation of human spirit. Therefore Jesus told the rich young man, "Go, sell what you have, and give to the poor" (Mk 10:21). Riches are sometimes called 'mammon' in the Scriptures. Mammon refers to not only material possession but stands for any idol in our life, any created thing, which becomes the focus of our praise, reverence and service. For example, when I become dedicated to a particular ritual, particular creed, particular ideology as more important than my worship of God and service of neighbour, that particular thing has become 'mammon' to me. If we realise that we have become enslaved by any such mammon, God is pleading with us to repent and choose him again as our supreme good. He will forgive us and take us back in his arms. "How great is the mercy of God, and his forgiveness for those who turn to him" (Sir 17:29). When we fully embrace God, we are fully satisfied, for the love of any other, has been changed into the love of God.

TUESDAY – WEEK 8 / YEAR 1

SINGING AFTER WEEPING

Readings: Sir 35:1-15; Mk 10:28-31

How did the Apostles make a sacrifice of their lives for the sake of the Gospel of Christ? Matthew was slain by a sword. Mark expired in Alexandria after being cruelly dragged through the streets of that city. Luke was hanged. John was put in cauldron of boiling oil. Peter was crucified. James the elder was beheaded. James the younger was thrown from the lofty pinnacle of the temple. Bartholomew was flayed alive. Andrew was bound to a cross. Thomas was run through his body with a lance. Jude was shot to death. Matthias was stoned and beheaded. Barnabas was stoned to death. Paul was tortured and beheaded. All of them gave their lives believing in the reward Christ had promised: "in the age to come eternal life" (Mk 10:30). Yes, after the cross, a crown of life; after weeping, a song; after the night of sorrow, a bright and glorious dawn. Jesus also promised: "a hundredfold now in this time" (v.30). This promise confirms Sirach: "The Lord is the one who repays, and he will repay you sevenfold" (Sir 35:11). The number seven refers to plenitude. Whenever we have suffered something in the service of the Gospel, have we not experienced the truth of the Lord's promise?

LIKE A FRUIT TREE

Readings: Sir 36:1-2, 5-6, 13-19; Mk 10:32-45

As the light of the moon is swallowed up by the brightness of the sun, so the shining achievements of men and women are swallowed up by the glory of God, for it is with God-given human faculties that human beings are able to achieve so much. But, what about our own glory? We pray to God: "Fill Zion with the celebration of thy wondrous deeds and thy temple with thy glory" (Sir 36:14). How do human beings share in God's glory? Jesus answers: "Whoever would be great among you must be your servant" (Mk 10:43). The Lord has planted each of us like a fruit tree in his vineyard of this world and we must bring forth good fruits by serving our fellow human beings; and if we do not, we shall lose even our leaves, and stand like a winter's tree, bare and withered. If we do not serve others, we will become like an arrow, which falls short of its mark or a candle which smokes but yields no light. A life spent on only self-service is a wasted life, a life without the flower and glory of existence. In fact, it is no life at all; it is only an animated death. On the other hand, how glorious would be our life, both in this life and the next, if we reach out to others in humble and loving service after the example of Jesus, the Servant of servants!

KEEP THEM OPEN

Readings: Sir 42:5-26; Mk 10:46-52

In his book *Letters from the Desert* Carlo Corretto describes the lovely nights he found in the deserts of Arabia into which he flew, to be in close touch with God: "How dear they were to me, those stars," he writes; "through spending my nights in the open, I had come to know them by their names. I could now distinguish their colour, their size, their position, and their beauty." Yes; the love and wisdom of God are revealed in the marvels of his creation. "The work of the Lord is full of his glory" (Sir 42:16). God's creation is an unlimited broadcasting system through which God speaks to us if only we tune in. A spiritual master told me: "when you look at a tree and see a tree, you have really not seen the tree; when you look at a tree and see a miracle, then, at last, you have seen a tree." To be able to see the love and wisdom, the might and majesty of God in every created thing, we need to have eyes of faith kept open. If they are shut, we are spiritually blind. As babies, when we are baptised, we receive our eyes of faith, but as we grow old, faith becomes dimmed. The only person, who can open them, if we allow him to do so, is Jesus Christ. Hence, if we are losing our eyes of faith, let us pray to the Lord in the words of Bartimaeus: "Master, let me receive my sight" (Mk 10:51).

WILL IT ENDURE?

Readings: Sir 44:1, 9-13; Mk 11:11-26

A fellow, trying to tell his sweetheart how much he loved her, exclaimed, "Why, I would die for you!" Promptly the sensible girl replied, "It is off! I don't want to marry a corpse!" The Lord Jesus

does not, often, ask us to die for him; he asks us to live for him. When
we live only for him and in the manner he expects us to live, we not
only enrich our own life, but our life enriches the lives of other people,
so enduringly that our Christian influence lives on even after we have
passed from this life. There have been in the Church such illustrious
Christians, "whose righteous deeds have not been forgotten", and their
prosperity remains "with their descendants" (Sir 44:10-11). But such a
total dedication to Christian life requires strong faith. Faith is root for
the tree of life. Without deep faith, our Christian life is like "a fig tree
withered away to its roots" (Mk 11:20), and hence can't bear any fruit.
Children inscribe their names in capitals in the snow and in the
morning's thaw the writings disappear. May we ask:Have I written my
life in the snow? Will my Christian life endure the lapse of years? Has
there been anything immortal in it, which will survive the speedy
wreck of all sublunary things?

SATURDAY – WEEK 8 / YEAR 1

AN ENDLESS EXPLORATION

Readings: Sir 51:12-20; Mk 11:27-33

Why was Solzhenitsyn driven out of Russia by the communist regime?
Not because the regime felt he might unseat them; it was a desperate
attempt to plug up the dreadful wellspring of truth, a truth that might
cause dangerous transformation in the social consciousness of Russians.
So too, the Scribes and Pharisees who felt in their heart that Christ
must be the expected Messiah, were not willing to accept the truth,
fearing that it will destabilise the religious establishment of which
they were leaders. Hence they became insincere in their answers to
Christ's questions when they said, "We do not know" (Mk 11:33).
Thank God, we have honestly accepted the truth about Christ. But, our
knowledge of Christ is only an entrance into the wisdom God. Our
exploration of Christ, who is the Wisdom of God made incarnate,
must go on throughout our life. We should be able to say, "I sought
wisdom openly in my prayer and I will search for her to the last"

(Sir 51:13-14). Jesus, in his three years of public ministry, has revealed more than all the moralising of all moralists, and all the philosophising of all the philosophers since the world began. How can one, then, fathom Christ within one's life span?

MONDAY – WEEK 9 / YEAR 1

BEING MERCIFUL

Readings: Tobit 1:3; 2:1-8; Mk 12:1-12

Although the attributes of God are all equal, mercy shines with even more brilliancy than justice. There is largeness in God's mercy like the largeness of the sea. In his mercy, God does not snuff out the smouldering wick or break the bruised reeds. Through a story about the owner of a vineyard, Jesus describes God's enduring mercy towards his people. He sent his prophets but they killed them, and finally God sent his own "beloved Son" (Mk 12:6) whom also they killed. Tobias is pictured as a man of great charity and mercy. First he wanted to share his meal with a poor man, and then he went out of his way to bury a murdered stranger (Tob 2:7). Jesus called us to feed the hungry, but many are satisfied just discussing about world hunger in seminars; he asked us to visit the prisoners, but many creep off quietly to a chapel to pray for their release; he asked us to clothe the naked, but many are just debating the morality of naked appearance; he asked us to visit the sick, but we often blame the government for lack of proper health-care system. What is true mercy? It is not the impersonal concern that prompts the mailing of a check, rather it is the personal concern which demands the giving of one's soul.

THE BEST POLICY

Readings: Tob 2:9-14; Mk 12:13-17

Honesty is a good thing for it is truth in action; In fact, an absolutely honest person is the noblest work of God and Christ was such a one. Hence the Pharisees rightly began their conversation with Jesus saying, "Teacher, we know that you are true" (Mk 12:14). However, if you are absolutely honest, you get often martyred. Yet, Tobit was not afraid of being totally honest. Despite his misfortune of being blinded, he ordered his wife to return the young goat to its owner, for he thought that she had stolen it, when in fact, her employer had given it to her as a bonus (Tob 2:13). The saying, "Honesty is the best policy" is very true. If we are dishonest, people will hate us, and at the same time, our dishonesty causes suffering to others. Large-scale dishonesty leads to large-scale sufferings. Farmers work the land, but their produce brings them little profit; the women work with thread and cloth, but their labours bring them little return; the children work in factories, but to little benefit. Often, these people work to pay back the debt they owe their oppressors. Are not such sufferings of the poor and the weak, often due to the dishonesty of some rich and powerful people towards their fellow human beings whose labours they exploit?

GOD OF LIFE

Readings: Tob 3:1-11, 16-17; Mk 12:18-27

Like fields, mountains and animals, we know that we belong here *on* earth. However, unlike them, the quality and passion of our longing, make us restlessly aware that we can not belong *to* the earth. We are involved passionately in the world, yet there is nothing here that can claim us completely. When we forget how partial and temporary our belonging must remain, we put ourselves in danger of disappointment, for we compromise something eternal within us. We are created for eternal life. In today's Gospel Jesus is not concerned with answering a silly question about marriage. His concern is about our entering into our everlasting life, a life in which we will be "like angels in heaven" (Mk 12:25). We pray to the Lord for so many material things, but do we pray for eternal life? When we pray for material needs the Lord often answers our prayers in his own way, as he did to Tobit and Sarah. Their afflictions were so overwhelming that they asked God to let them die (Tob 3:6). But God answered their prayers by giving them not death but new life, with joys and gifts far exceeding all their expectations. This is because our God is not a God of death but of life. Pray to God for eternal life, while doing his will, and you will get it.

THURSDAY – WEEK 9 / YEAR 1

AN ENDURING MARRIAGE

Readings: Tob 6:10-11; 7:1, 9-14; 8:4-9; Mk 12:28-34

What is it that will sustain a marriage between man and woman to the end? The answer is simple: love. But, mere human love is not enough. If human love is put on a pedestal as an idol, they will soon discover that the stem of human affection can not bear its weight. This is not to demean human love; it is only to insist that it is only human, a spark that falls from the great hearth of love which is God. Therefore, the spouses must first love God with all their heart, soul, mind and strength (Mk 12:30). If they do, each one will be able to love each other as oneself. Love of God is the root, love of neighbour is the fruit, of the tree of life. Neither can exist without the other, but the one is the cause and the other is effect. It was made evident in the case of Tobit and Sarah. Their love for each other as husband and wife sprang from their love for God. They loved God as his Children, and so Tobit said to his wife: "Sister, get up and let us pray that the Lord may have mercy upon us" (Tob 8:4). In response, God saved the life of Tobit from death. Yes, indeed; the marriage-relationship is not the antithesis of the God-relationship; rather, the one is the type of the other.

FRIDAY – WEEK 9 / YEAR 1

THE MASTER KEY

Readings: Tob 11:5-17; Mk 12:35-37

There are many locks in my house and all with different keys, but I have one master key that opens them all. So too, God has many treasures and secrets all shut up from human beings; we can try our best to open them but we can't. We need a master key that opens them all and that key is Jesus Christ. That is why we address Jesus as our Lord. He himself acknowledged this title when he said to the Scribes "David himself calls him Lord" (Mk 12:37). Because he is the Lord, Jesus Christ is our Head. Everyone knows that it would be far better to loose our feet than our heads. Adam had feet to stand on, but we have lost them by his disobedience. Yet we have found a Head in the Lord Jesus Christ. Because he is our Lord, he has sovereign power over everything that may happen to us in our lives. If we remain faithful to him in times of suffering, he has the power to turn tragedy into moments of insight. Just as pressures can transmute coal into diamond, so the Lord can turn our pains into a vehicle for greater blessings. As the Lord of creation he can do this for us either directly or through any elements of creation as he did to Tobias; his blindness was cured by applying fish gall on his eyes (Tob:11:11). Jesus is our Master Key.

SATURDAY – WEEK 9 / YEAR 1

THE HONEYCOMB FLOWS

Readings: Tob 12:1, 5-15, 20; Mk 12:38-44

There are three kinds of givers: the flint, the sponge, and the honeycomb. To get anything out of the flint, you have to hammer it and then you can get only chips and sparks. To get water out of a sponge, you must squeeze it and the more you squeeze it the more you will get. But the honeycomb just flows. It is called generous giving. Generous giving, in one sense, is giving to others more than their due. Tobias did that when he instructed his son to give his travelling companion more than the figure agreed on (Tob 12:1). In another sense, generous giving is giving to a worthy cause until it hurts the giver. The poor widow in the Gospel did that, by putting in the treasury two small coins that was "her whole living" (Mk 12:44). Why should we be generous in giving? Firstly, when we give to the needy, we give to God. Secondly, giving brings honour to the giver. Did you ever see a tombstone with a dollar sign on it? I haven't. I have known so many people who lived as though their only ambition is to accumulate. But I have never known one who wanted the final judgement to be based on what he or she had accumulated. One wants people to read in his or her obituary, not a balance sheet of one's wealth but an account of one's service to humanity.

MONDAY – WEEK 10 / YEAR 1

THE DIVINE FRIENDSHIP

Readings: 2 Cor 1:1-7; Mt 5:1-12

If God really loves us, why does he not put an end to war, poverty, hunger, sickness, and all the misery we see everywhere? If God cares about me personally, why am I in such a bad shape? Such questions are often raised less by those who have tasted suffering, than by those who had merely heard and read about it. The victims of poverty, oppression and war, are often more deeply convinced of God's love than others are. For them, the suffering and dying of Jesus is the most convincing sign that God really loves them and does not leave them in the lurch. They really believe in the beatitude: "Blessed are those who mourn, for they shall be comforted" (Mt 5:4). They really experience God as "the Father of mercies and God of all comfort" (2 Cor 1:3). A real friend is not someone who can solve all your problems, or who has an answer to your every question. A real friend is someone who does not walk off when there are no solutions or answers, but sticks by you and remains faithful to you. This is the friendship Jesus offers to those who suffer but still believe in him. For these people, Jesus is the faithful friend who treads with them in the lonely road of suffering, comforting them all the way.

TUESDAY – WEEK 10 / YEAR 1

"YES" TO HIM

Readings: 2 Cor 1:18-22; Mt 5:13-16

While wonderful in its continued conquests, technology has often impoverished people in their essential human life, by depriving them of their inner spiritual dimension, and stifling their sense of true and higher values. The primacy of the spiritual is being questioned. We can see this in modern trends of opinions, fashions and media. They often excuse everything, and the result is an unbounded permissiveness. It is in this world, Jesus asks us to be "light of the world" (Mt 5:14), dispelling the gloom consequent upon the increasing moral decay; and to be "the salt of the earth" (v.13), keeping alive the core of spiritual values, thereby stemming the decline of ethical standards. But, apart from Jesus Christ, we can never serve this decaying world as its light and its salt. Why? Because "all the promises of God find their Yes in him" (2 Cor.1:20). This means that the Yes we said to Jesus at our baptism must be daily repeated. He is the Light; may we say Yes again, and see him as our way and follow him. He is the Truth; may we say Yes again, and believe in him. He is the Life; may we say Yes again, and keep searching for him deeper and deeper.

WEDNESDAY – WEEK 10 / YEAR 1

OUR GOOD WORKS

Readings: 2 Cor 3:4-11; Mt 5:17-19

Can we ever make a black man white by pelting him with snowballs? Never. But we are trying to do a similar thing, when we try to be saved by mere observance of God's law. Law has a purpose:our heart is like a pool and the law stirs the mud at the bottom of the pool, reveals how foul the waters are and compels us to acknowledge the evil within. But it is not the observance of the law that can remove the evil; only God's grace can do the cleansing. To many Pharisees, mere doing of the law was the essence of religion. Jesus corrected this view about laws by saying, "I have come not to abolish them but to fulfil them" (Mt 5:17). What in effect he was asking us is that we observe God's law from the motive of love, thereby fulfilling the purpose of the law. Of course, when we obey God's law, we are doing good works; but we must remember that we are saved not by our good works but by the free grace of God. As St Paul says, "Not that we are sufficient of ourselves to claim anything as coming from us; our sufficiency is from God" (2 Cor 3:5). Personally speaking, I have got hurt more by good works than by bad ones! My bad works always drove me to the Saviour for mercy; my good works often bloated my ego.

THURSDAY – WEEK 10 / YEAR 1

A CRAZY IDEA

Readings: 2 Cor 3:15–4:1, 3-6; Mt 5:20-26

A blanket is no longer a blanket if it does not keep you warm. So too, a religion you and I profess, is no religion if it does not lead to one's inner transformation. A great and foolish king complained that the rough ground hurt his feet; so he ordered the whole country to be carpeted with cowhide. The court jester laughed and said, "What an absolutely crazy idea, your Majesty! Why all the needless expense? Just cut out two small pads to protect your feet!" Do we want to make our world warless and bloodless? Let us first get our interior selves transformed. War begins with anger in our heart. So Jesus says that if we feel we have something against another, "Leave your gift there before the altar and go; first be reconciled with your brother" (Mt 5:24). This is why, when God wants to bless us, he first blesses us with gifts which transform our inner self to the likeness of his Son Jesus Christ. As St Paul says, God "has shone in our hearts to give the light of the knowledge of the glory of God in the face of Christ" (2 Cor 4:6). A Christian is not a person who is trying to do something, but one who has received something interior, a person to whom something has happened within.

FRIDAY – WEEK 10 / YEAR 1

"PLUCK IT OUT"

Readings: 2 Cor 4:7-15; Mt 5:27-32

Absolute purity in human sexuality, whether married or unmarried, could be a battle with our darker impulses more arduous than medieval crusades! And yet Jesus asks us to keep fighting, and goes further saying: "If your right eye causes you to sin, pluck it out" (Mt 5:29). Are we to take it literally? No. If we paint a fox preaching in a vicar's backyard, nobody imagines that a real fox is meant, but that craft and hypocrisy of the vicar in the pulpit are described. So too, when Jesus says "pluck the eye out" what he means is: do not allow your eye to rest too long on an object of temptation for it will lead to sin of impurity and even to adultery. Why purity in sexuality? For one thing, when we succumb to lustful appetite, we suffer disquiet of heart, remorse of conscience and lose the very peace we sought after. If there is one overriding motive for preserving purity of mind, heart and body from sexual sins, it is that one day we are meant to rise from the dead, body and soul glorified. "He who raised the Lord Jesus will raise us also" (2 Cor 4:14). We have been promised that the indestructible glory and power of God that we carry in our perishable bodies will one day raise us to imperishable bliss.

SATURDAY – WEEK 10 / YEAR 1

WORDS ARE PEGS

Readings: 2 Cor 5:14-21; Mt 5:33-37

The Emperor Constantine is said to have refused to be baptised until he was on his deathbed. He did not want his sins remitted until he had got them all committed! This story may sound funny but there is a message: Baptism washes away all our sins and reconciles us with God. Since at baptism we are baptised into the death and the resurrection of the Lord Jesus, we are born anew." If anyone is in Christ, he is a new creation" (2 Cor 5:17). But then, our new life in Christ must become visible in our daily dealings with our fellow human beings. Our reconciliation with God must lead us to get reconciled with those whom we have hurt. One area that may need reconciliation is the sadness or loss we may have caused to others by our false promises. "You shall not swear falsely, but perform what you have sworn" (Mt 5:33), is a law set down by the Lord himself. Apart from false oaths, do we indulge in religious language for manipulative and evasive purposes? Have we indulged in casuistry that retains the vocabulary of faith but sucks out its substance? Are we given to religious double talk that sounds solemn and elevating but says nothing? All words are pegs to hang ideas on, not to hang people on a cross!

MONDAY – WEEK 11 / YEAR 1

UNPROVOKED ASSAULT?

Readings: 2 Cor 6:1-10; Mt 5:38-42

Violence seems to be the rhetoric of our times. There are people who will tell you: "Be peaceful, be courteous, obey the law, respect everyone; but if someone puts his hand on you, send him to the cemetery." But Jesus says, "If anyone strikes you on the right cheek, turn to him the other also" (Mt 5:39). This saying can not be taken literally. What Jesus is asking us to do is not to harbour a spirit of resentment and not return violence with violence. Instead, if someone injures you, show yourself the master of the situation by doing something to his or her advantage. If one gets some pleasure out of hitting you and you let the person hit again, you are performing an act of grace. For this we have a model in St Paul who says: "As servants of God we commend ourselves in every way through great endurance" (2 Cor 6:4). Our sense of justice naturally prompts retaliation to unprovoked assault. But as servants of God, we are advised to leave justice to God. Though the mills of God's justice grind slowly, yet they grind exceedingly small; though with patience God stands waiting, he grinds all with exactness. After all, what use for peace in the world, if we retaliate with violence?

LOVING OUR ENEMIES

Readings: 2 Cor 8:1-9; Mt 5:43-48

In order to unlock nature's potential, scientists once made this experiment: They transmitted 200 TV programs simultaneously on a cable the size of a human hair! But, should everyone of our experiments deal with 'things'? Is there anyway to help human beings to unlock some of their human potentials? Jesus' response is surprising: "Love your enemies" (Mt 5:44), he says. How will it work? Firstly: pray for your enemies. Persistent prayer for the enemy whom we naturally dislike brings about remarkable change in our feeling and attitude towards the enemy. Secondly:lend the enemy a helping hand when that is what he or she needs. Such kind acts will produce a sense of shame leading to a change of heart in the enemy. But, is it possible to love our enemies in this way? It is possible if we keep in mind what Jesus has done for us: "Though he was rich, yet for your sake he became poor, so that by his poverty you might become rich" (2 Cor 8:9), and died for us on the cross. All other matters in the Gospel are important and none of them is to be cast into the shade. But the death of the Son of God, so that we sinners may live, is the central sun of all these minor luminaries, a death that must inspire us to love our enemies.

A DOLLAR AND A CENT

Readings: 2 Cor 9:6-11; Mt 6:1-6, 16-18

A big silver dollar and a little brown cent were one day rolling along a sidewalk. The dollar said to the cent: "You poor little cent, you cheap little mite; I am bigger and more than two times as bright; I am worth more than you, and written on me in bold letters is: In God we trust." "Yes, I know," said the cent, "I am a cheap little mite; I am not big or bright; yet you don't go to church so often as I." Even some well-to-do people who come to church are so miserly that they often put in the collection box only a few cents and that too, because there are no smaller coins available! St Paul encourages us to give generously and gives a reason too: "He who sows bountifully will also reap bountifully" (2 Cor 9:6) from God. In fact, God himself will be our reward for what we give. That is why, while giving, Jesus asks us not to parade our alms giving, but expect that "Your Father who sees in secret will reward you" (Mt 6:4). We are becoming more and more aware of the needs of people throughout the world. While giving we must see ourselves as part of all humanity. May our superfluities give way to our neighbours' conveniences, our conveniences to our neighbours' necessities and our necessities to their extremities.

THURSDAY – WEEK 11 / YEAR 1

WHAT IS NEW?

Readings: 2 Cor 11:1-11; Mt 6:7-15

Today, there is a craze for what is new and fashionable. A modern slogan, especially among the youth, is: "Let us have some new clichés." As Homer put it, "It is always the latest song that an audience applauds the most." In fact, many deceive the public by calling what they say as new, when in fact, they are only saying something as if it had never been said before. This craze for novelty seems to have crept into early Christianity. St Paul warned Christians against accepting a new gospel but different from the one they had accepted from him (2 Cor 11:4). The world may have many religions, but it has only one Gospel. The whole Gospel is contained in Christ and Christ is God's everything for our total need. How can there be a different Christ other than what the Gospel portrays? Dazzled by novel methods of prayer, many of us have also lost our appreciation for the *Our Father*, the prayer that Jesus himself taught us (Mt 6:9). No matter how holy we become, we can never outgrow this complete prayer. And no matter how ignorant we think we are of the theology of religion, we can still say the 'Our Father' daily, deriving great spiritual nourishment.

FRIDAY – WEEK 11 / YEAR 1

"WHAT I GAVE, I HAVE"

Readings: 2 Cor 11:18, 21-30; Mt 6:19-23

It is good to have money and things that money can buy; but it is good too, to check once in a while to make sure you haven't lost the things that money can not buy. Money can't buy truth; in fact, when money speaks, truth is often silent. Money can't buy love, happiness or what it did last year. There is certain prudence in saving money, but how much real security can we find in saving money? "Do not lay up for yourselves treasures on earth" (Mt 6:19), says Jesus, for permanent treasure comes not from saving but from giving away generously to the needy. We are asked to be generous not only with money but in any thing we give for love of God and neighbour. Paul was so generous in the work of proclaiming Christ that, for the sake of the Gospel, he accepted very severe hardships such as lashes, shipwrecks, starvation and similar sufferings. How generous are we in giving of ourselves to God and others? God himself will be our reward for what we give now. As an old gravestone said of the dead man: "What I spent I had; what I saved, I lost. What I gave, I have." Our generosity in giving reacts upon the quality of our own happiness in this life and in the next.

SATURDAY – WEEK 11 / YEAR 1

LETTING GO

Readings: 2 Cor 12:1-10; Mt 6:24-34

Very often, the greater the dependence on God, the more power there is over the things of the earth. St Francis of Assisi had a power over birds and animals, which is not given to many mortals. The more one is the instrument in the hand of God, the more readily God works through that instrument. If a pencil rebelled against the direction of the hand, less writing would be done. "Seek first God's Kingdom and all these things shall be yours as well" (Mt 6:33), said Jesus. Paul emphasised the same message in his own way: "When I am weak, then I am strong" (2 Cor 12:10). True spiritual strength lies not in holding on to things but in letting go of them. Only by letting go and letting God in, can we open ourselves to a greater power. A child brings to me his broken toy, and with tears, asks me to mend it. But when I start mending it in my own way, he won't let me do it. He hangs around and tries to help me in his own way. Suddenly he snatches it back and cries, "How can you be so slow?" "My child," I say, "what could I do? You never did let go!" That is what God says when we do not give him our total loyalty and let him run the rest of our life. How can a lamp that won't allow it to be plugged into a socket become a light?

MONDAY – WEEK 12 / YEAR 1

THE BLINDING LOG

Readings: Gen 12:1-9; Mt 7:1-5

We judge ourselves by our best intentions and others by their worst faults! There is a Last Judgement when God will judge each and every one of us. And yet, many of us are in a hurry to judge others here and now, very often unjustly. Why is it? It is our love of self. The love of self, to which we are prone, is gratified when we can identify the failings of others and justify a high opinion of ourselves. The expectation of our competitive and materialistic society leads us into the trap of assessing people according to their looks, wealth, social status, intelligence or morality, and encourages us to form a quick judgement that highlights their weaknesses and makes us feel superior to them. Jesus gently ridicules our love of self which is like a 'log' (Mt 7:3), blinding us to our own faults. It is time that we, like Abraham (Gen 12:4), leave this homeland of our self-love, and journey into the 'promised land' which is not a piece of real estate, but a new way of life, a life of selfless love, of understanding and compassion to others. If we leave our selfish way of judging our fellow human beings who are our brothers and sisters in God, like Abraham, we too will enjoy a marvellous thing in our 'promised land':a close intimacy with God.

THE DEAD SEA TEACHES

Readings: Gen 13:2, 5-18; Mt 7:6, 12-14

In former times, people were closer to their neighbours. People were poorer too and more dependent on each other. They firmly believed in the saying: "A good neighbour is better than a bag of money." But in the fragmentation of contemporary life, people live in great isolation and distance from each other. A neighbour can be dead for weeks and we do not notice. Each individual, each home is an isolated monad with no bridge to the neighbour. What is worse is that practically everything in our modern society is based on the idea that you do indeed have to look out for yourself, and it is weak and foolish not to be assertive on your own rights and to let someone take advantage of you. Jesus urges us to turn this selfish orientation around: "Whatever you wish that men would do to you, do so to them" (Mt 7:12). The story of Abraham illustrates that God takes care of those who are generous and unselfish with others. For example, Abraham allowed Lot to take the better portion of his land (Gen 13:11), and he received from God the entire land of Canaan. All the time receiving from others is no good. What makes the Dead Sea dead? It is all the time receiving and never giving out.

OUR HEROES

Readings: Gen 15:1-12, 17-18; Mt 7:15-20

All heroes are honoured in their generations and are the glory of their times. But how do we pick our heroes? Jesus says: "You will know them by their fruits" (Mt 7:16). Our criteria ought to be not their achievements of success in this world, nor their popularity or social prestige, but the fruits of the Spirit such as faith, hope and charity seen in their lives. We can see how God's choice of Abraham to be the father of his people is justified by Abraham's thinking and his whole manner of life. His finest fruit is his faith and trust in the Lord's promise. Though a hundred years old, he believed in the word of God: "Your own son will be your heir" (Gen 15:4). Because Abraham believed he has become the father of all believers. Who are our heroes now? Whom do we want to emulate in life? Whoever excels in the fruits of the Spirit must top the list of our heroes. As you know, teenagers mostly gossip about their heroes. 'Hero-worship' can be healthy, provided your hero's life style stimulates you to deeds of heroism for God and humanity. Those who stir up the young and the old, (at least in the evening of their lives) to unselfish campaign for justice and peace, and lift up the masses above the commonplace meanness of earthbound mediocre life, are true heroes.

THURSDAY – WEEK 12 / YEAR 1

IS GOD A STOPGAP?

Readings: Gen 16:1-12, 15-16; Mt 7:21-29

We are living in God, in God's action, as a fish in water. Every moment, therefore, is the message of God's will. Every external event, and even thoughts and feelings within us, is God's own touch. Everything we come into contact, the whole of our daily circumstances whether pleasures or pains are God's working. Hence, in order to experience God's promises in our lives, we must submit willingly even to God-sent pains. This is something Hagar, the slave girl of Sarai failed to do. She ran away, pregnant with the child of Abraham, in order to escape from Sarai's ill treatment. But the angel of the Lord intercepted her and said, "Return to your mistress and submit to her" (Gen 16:9). Jesus too, calls us to do God's will whatever it might be and warns us against mere lipservice to God. Building the house of religion on any other found-ation, is like building "a house upon the sand" (Mt 7:26). God can not be used as a stopgap. His will must be found at the centre of life; Not only in health and vigour but also in sickness and weakness, not only in pleasures and joys, but also in pains and sorrows, not only in life but also in death, we have to embrace his will.

THE DIVINE ENERGY

Readings: Gen 17:1, 1-9, 15-22; Mt 8:1-4

God is not only our goal; he is also the way by which we get there. He is the life we need on our journey. His life is supernatural power; it is divine energy. Other forms of energy may carry us to the farthest stars. But only divine energy can get us to rise above ourselves. What we can not do with our natural power, can be done by God with his supernatural power, if it is for our eternal good. It was out of the realm of human possibility for Abraham and Sarah, to become parents at their very advanced age; but God using his supernatural power gave them a child, Isaac (Gen 17:19). Likewise, Jesus cured a man's leprosy, an incurable disease in his time (Mt 8:3), using his divine power. Leprosy is compared to sin in the Scriptures, for, as leprosy eats away human flesh, so sin eats into human soul, especially our sins against fraternal charity, such as anger and bitterness. But if we approach Christ repentant and ask for forgiveness, he will revive our drooping spirit by means of his divine energy, which is a spiritual force. Spiritual forces are so much more powerful and mysterious than those of matter. If God could fill you with his spiritual energy, as he does to his saints, you will feel like one of those birds, seen blown around, surfing above a high wind.

AT ANY TIME, IN ANY PLACE

Readings: Gen 18:1-15; Mt 8:5-17

The Word of God brings peace and contentment as no human word can. Sometimes, it brings straight away healing from physical illness. A centurion's servant (Mt 8:13) and Peter's mother-in-law (v.15) were healed by the Word of Jesus. Sometimes, God's Word may not bring immediate healing, but it will bring meaning to the pain. After all, our happiness hinges not on good luck, but on peace of heart and peace of heart comes if we find meaning in a thing. God speaks to us in and through even the most troublesome predicaments. God can speak at any time, in any place, through any source. The Word of God came to Abraham from a completely unexpected source: three travellers (Gen 18:2), to give him hope and assurance. God speaks when your friend comes to you in pain, when a neighbour tries to hide her tears, when your enemy reaches out a hand or when a stranger cries out for help. Some one told me that she heard the Lord while taking her dog for a walk! For myself, it was while taking a shower that the Lord put into my mind the idea of writing this piece. God is not limited by any condition that we lay down. So, we need to widen our horizon and expect him to speak to us at any time, in any place.

MONDAY – WEEK 13 / YEAR 1

VIGOROUS FAITH

Readings: Gen 18:16-33; Mt 8:18-22

A vigorous believer is like one walking through a strange country on a dark night. Thomas Merton rightly said:'Christian faith is a principal of questioning and struggle before it becomes a principal of certitude and peace." Abraham's faith was vigorous because it was not afraid of asking questions such as: "Will you indeed destroy the righteous with the wicked?" (Gen 18:23); but after asking all his questions, he finally accepted what the Lord had to say. But the faith of the man in the Gospel, who wanted to follow Jesus, was not vigorous. It is true that he too like Abraham proposed his own view of discipleship; but when the Lord said, "Follow me, and leave the dead to bury their own dead" (Mt 8:22), he did not accept. Is our own faith vigorous? If it is, we would question the doubtful implications of our faith, but in the end we would yield firmly to Jesus and to what he has to say. Developing an understanding of the reasonableness of our faith gives you an inner confidence, as you deal with the problems of a complex world. As one artesian well piercing to the spring, is of more value than a hundred tubes thrust into the surface, one spiritual truth vigorously believed is far more worth, than the whole of the creed received from custom or compliance.

TUESDAY – WEEK 13 / YEAR 1

KEEP MOVING

Readings: Gen 19:15-29; Mt 8:23-27

We are a pilgrim people. We are to keep moving from our past into a new future. Our God is a God of new creation. As a bird in an egg can never fly, so we can never become a new creature unless we crack the shell of our past, a past darkened by clouds of selfishness, of injustice, of anger, of violence and harmful addictions. God is calling us to travel into new opportunities for humanity and ourselves. He is ready to heal us of the hurts we may have experienced in the past, and ready to bind up old wounds, so that our reconciliation with God and one another, may burst forth into endless possibilities for peace and harmony. We are not to look back as Lot's wife did (Gen 19:26), as we move away from our past. If we keep moving into the future holding hands with Jesus, we will enter into a land of closer unity of respect and understanding, love and peace. In our journey, we may be afraid at the sight of human beings, still waging war against each other, in boiling blood and with a fiery greed for victory. But we need not give up our journey. Christ may appear to be sleeping as he once did in the boat (Mt 8:24), but in fact he is not. Keep moving even in the dark; Treasures lie hidden in darkness, and only those who walk in the night ever see the stars.

WEDNESDAY – WEEK 13 / YEAR 1

BITTER NATIONALISM

Readings: Gen 21:5, 8-20; Mt 8:28-34

Divine providence reveals a solicitude that seeks to assure the essential destiny of all human beings without exception. It emphasises the personal intervention of God who wants to act as the compassionate shepherd of all without any exception. He takes care of everyone. His vigilance does not overlook anyone. See how the son of Abraham born to the slave girl is exiled by a jealous Sarah; yet the Lord hears the cry of the poor child. He takes care of Ismael and promises to make a great nation of him (Gen 21:13). This same all-embracing compassion and protection of God is illustrated by Jesus when he cured two demoniacs (Mt 8:32); Though these men were not Jews, Jesus came to their rescue. To God, there are no foreigners, as far as his love goes. We are called to imitate God's universal love. For example, while being loyal to our country, we need to avoid racial prejudice and bitter nationalism. Bitter nationalists have broad hatred and narrow love towards people of other ethnic origins. Fanatical nationalism is like a silly cock crowing on its own dunghill, and it is a form of idolatry that all Christians ought to shun.

THURSDAY – WEEK 13 / YEAR 1

HEROISM IN THE GREATEST

Readings: Gen 22:1-9; Mt 9:1-8

One day, a Korean missionary was travelling with a friend through the country. The friend was amused to see in a field a young man pulling a plough and an old man holding the handles. "They must be very poor", remarked the friend. "Yes", was the reply. "When the church was being built, they wanted to give something for the house of God; so they sold their only ox and gave the money; that is why, this spring, they have to plough like that." "What a sacrifice!" exclaimed the friend. "They did not call it a sacrifice," said the missionary, "they were glad to have an ox they could sell." When God wanted Abraham to offer his only son Isaac as a burnt offering (Gen 22:9), he was ready to do it. Great sacrifice would not be a problem to one who knows how generous God has been in sacrificing his only Son Jesus Christ on the cross, as atonement for the sins of all humanity. so that he can even today say to any sinner: "Your sins are forgiven" (Mt 9:5). Often, the sacrifices that are required of us in daily life are trifles; but perhaps, are we waiting for occasions to make heroic sacrifices? Let us not forget that heroism in the least is the pledge of heroism in the greatest. Unless we can leap up under the trifling sacrifices, we go down under the great ones.

FRIDAY – WEEK 13 / YEAR 1

TO LOVE A LEAF

Readings: Gen 23:1-4,19;   24:1-8, 62-67;   Mt 9:9-13

God was love itself long before he created human beings and hence his love for us has to be all-inclusive. But he needed a spring board from which to launch his all embracing love. The spring board was the Old Israel of which Abraham was the father (Gen 24:7), whose descendants were linked together by the same gene. But God sent his own Son from the line of David, with a mission to form the New Israel to which both Jews and Gentiles, the virtuous and sinners would belong by faith. The Pharisees who could not accept this universal love of God, protested when they saw Jesus befriending the Gentiles and eating with sinners (Mt 11). Do we love all people discriminating none? The tragedy of the world is that so many people are unloved. Roses always look beautiful and smell sweet, and hence they are a prize to be possessed. Sweet briar, however, has fragrant leaves and they are never so fragrant as when it rains. The small people of the world are like these leaves; they have something fragrant about them, particularly when the rain of pain falls in their lives, but do we love the small as we love the big? Anyone can love a rose, but it takes a great deal to love a leaf. It is ordinary to love the marvellous, but it is marvellous to love the ordinary.

SATURDAY – WEEK 13 /YEAR 1

ROOT AND FRUIT

Readings: Gen 27:1-5, 15-29;   Mt 9:14-17

Once upon a time, there was a monk who decided to live only on crusts, and as a result, he upset the whole monastery by making all the monks hunt for crusts to satisfy his desire for mortification. He thought he could become holy and pleasing to God even though he disrupted the lives of his fellow monks. Rebeka did a similar thing; She instigated her younger son Jacob (Gen 27:15), to deceive his blind father to obtain his blessings, which Isaac had intended for his elder son Esau. Probably, Rebeka felt that the future of the family would be better served with mild mannered and peace loving Jacob, than with Esau who was of wild manner and carefree, and hence, God would be pleased with her action. But in doing so, she completely forgot that she was doing a great injustice to Esau. Jesus revealed that what pleases God is above all our love for our neighbour. He called his message of love "the new wine," and said that "neither is the new wine put into old wineskins" (Mt 9:17). What he meant was that in order to safely receive this new wine of love we must first rid ourselves of our thinking that we can please God even though we do harm to our neighbours. May we never forget that love for God is the root and love for neighbour is its fruit.

MONDAY – WEEK 14 / YEAR 1

OUR INNER TOWER

Readings: Gen 28:10-22; Mt 9:18-26

Human life runs between two extremes: adversity and perplexity. Therefore, wise people seek God for their protection. They know that those who have God for their protection have an inner tower that is never depressed by adversity nor inflated by prosperity. But how do we have God with us? Does he come to us? Yes, indeed. He walks into our soul with silent steps. God comes to us more than we go to him. Never will his coming be what you expect and yet never will it disappoint. God came to Jacob in a dream, standing there over him (Gen 28:12). The ladder he saw in the same dream reaching from the earth to the heavens indicated the constant coming of God into human lives. God's power reached and healed a woman who touched the cloak of Jesus (Mt 9:22). It found its way through the touch of Christ's hand to raise a little girl from the sleep of death (v.25). Into every believer, God comes through the sacramental signs. By the mere fact that we turn on the faucet, water comes out. So too, the divine life of God is poured into our soul by the mere fact that we receive the sacrament in faith. John Henry Newman prayed: "My Lord and my Saviour, support me in the strong arms of thy sacraments."

THE HARVEST IS PLENTIFUL

Readings: Gen 32:23-33; Mt 9:32-38

Once I heard a group of street children in Calcutta singing the rhyme: "While other children are enjoying their homes and gardens, the garbage heap is my garden, the dirty street is my home. When they sing, 'Jesus loves the little children', am I included or not?" Street children are only one section of the poor in the world, who need saviours and shepherds. What Jesus saw many centuries ago is still true today: "The harvest is plentiful, but the labourers are few" (Mt 9:37). The Church needs anyone who can serve people in need. God calls every one of us to do something for the poor and the needy. We don't deny that accepting God's call to serve the poor, can be a constant struggle similar to that of Jacob who "wrestled with God until daybreak" (Gen 32:25). It will be a struggle because we are persistently drawn away by our own selfishness, by the allure of money, pleasure and comfort. May we be faithful to God and to his poor, by letting go of whatever pulls us away from service. If our love for the poor dries up, may we remember that there are two kinds of dryness: one that trots, and this is dryness of love without God; the other is dryness that ripens, and that is when one grows through the first heat of sacrifice.

WHAT IS MISSING?

Readings: Gen 41:55-57; 42:5-7, 17-24 Mt 10:1-7

Even when everything you want is on your table and everyone you love is there in your life, you still feel something missing; you are not able to name what is missing. If you could, you might be able to go somewhere to get it. You feel that something that is vital to you lies out of your reach in the unknown. The hunger to fill this vacuum drives some people to accumulate possessions, but they are still disappointed, because this hunger is for the Divine. It is to satisfy this hunger that God sent his Son Jesus Christ. God once used Joseph to rescue his starving brothers and father from famine (Gen 42:19). In that Joseph was the foretype of Jesus who came to satisfy the hunger for God. When we see Jesus feeding the hungry and "curing all kinds of diseases" (Mt 10:1), we are reminded that these are his signs calling us to see in him the answer to our eternal hunger. God is not beyond Christ, but is in him. Therefore, let us not try to satisfy our hunger for the Divine away from Christ; If we do, this hunger will only drive us out of truth and shelter of love, setting us on a haunted journey, on a never-ending path in quest of something that is missing.

THURSDAY – WEEK 14 / YEAR 1

SHARING A SMILE

Readings: Gen 44:18-21, 23-29; 45:1-5; Mt 10:7-15

I once wrote to a wealthy and influential businessman requesting a subscription to a worthy charity. I promptly received a curt refusal, which ended by saying: "As far as I can see, this Christian business is just one continuous give." After a brief interval I answered, "I wish to thank you for the best definition of the Christian life that I have yet heard." Jesus has asked us not only to give to the needy but give without charge. "You received without pay, give without pay" (Mt 10:8). Sold by his brothers into slavery, Joseph had risen, by the sheer gift of God, to a position in Egypt practically equal to the Pharaoh himself. Knowing that this favour was from God and not just for his own benefit, he forgave his brothers' treachery and supplied them with food in times of famine (Gen 45:4). It is not only our material possessions but all that we have are God's gifts. He is asking us to share them with others freely. Just think of this one gift: smile! It is a gift that enriches the receiver without diminishing the giver; a gift that can be given in a flash, but can have an impact that lasts for ever; a gift that is of no earthly value until it is given away; a gift which, no one is so poor that he or she cannot share.

FRIDAY – WEEK 14 / YEAR 1

GOD JOURNEYS WITH US

Readings: Gen 46:1-7, 28-30; Mt 10:16-23

God can draw good out of evil because, while the power of doing evil is ours, the effects of our evil deeds are outside our control, and therefore are in the hands of God. Jacob brought his whole family with all his descendants and settled in Egypt under the protection of his son Joseph (Gen 46:6). But later, when the new Pharaoh came to power, they had to lose their social status and been put to work as slaves. However, God made use of this trial of Israel as a purifying experience in preparation for the extraordinary experience of Exodus. The early Christians, as foretold by Christ (Mt 10:22), were hunted by the state, rejected by the religious establishment and ridiculed by their own families. But through such persecutions, God brought them only closer to the Lord. Our God is a God who journeys with his people. Why is it that the absurdities of life lead some minds to despair, while the same lead others to hope and greater peace? It is because the latter realise that the struggle is worth their best; that God is not in his heavenly head quarters calling the shots, but himself keeps coming down into the muck and mud of all the meaninglessness of our life; and that he is forming and shaping our lives through our trials and tribulations.

SATURDAY – WEEK 14 / YEAR 1

WHO IS IN CONTROL?

Readings: Gen 49:29-33; 50:15-26; Mt 10:24-38

I asked a friend of mine, "Do you believe in chance?" He laughed and said, "The harder you work, the luckier you get!" Clearly, he did not believe in chance. But there are a lot of people who believe in it. "Every man," said one, "even the most blessed, needs a little more than an average chance to survive this world." But personally, I don't believe in chance. Can chance explain events in our life? No. If it did, it has made a football of human life, a plaything of irrational influences. Events are not governed solely by accidental causes, but by a benevolent intention of God which organises the entire frame work of human life for the sake of our superior destiny. It was not by chance that the brothers of Joseph who approached him seeking help, but fearing that he would take revenge on them, found him to be very forgiving and friendly, saying: "I will provide for you and your little ones" (Gen 50:21). It was God's benevolent plan working for them. God's benevolent plan neglects no details of our life. "Even the hairs of your head are all numbered" (Mt 10:30). This is so, because by virtue of his immense love, God attaches value to everything that concerns us. The so-called 'chance' is caught up in the solicitude of God's providence.

MONDAY – WEEK 15 / YEAR 1

MY MOTHERLAND!

Readings: Ex 1:8-14, 22; Mt 10:34-11:1

We call our native country either Fatherland or Motherland, because, as its citizens, we are expected to love our country, as we love our parents. But Jesus asks us to love him more than we love our father and mother. "He who loves father or mother more than me is not worthy of me" (Mt 10:37). In a sense, he calls us to love him more than we do love our country. It means that if we have learnt to see Jesus in the poor and the needy, we will love them more than we love the welfare of our country, when they come into our country seeking help. The Egyptians did not do that. The Israelites, who had come to settle in Egypt in order to escape famine, were viewed as foreign intruders and were accused of taking the Egyptians' jobs and occupying some of their country's best lands. Even the part played by Joseph in saving Egypt from famine was forgotten, and the Israelites were made into slaves (Ex 1:11). But is the situation different in our world today? There seems to be no country in the world without its asylum seekers; but how are they treated? Referring to asylum seekers in England, the late Cardinal Hume said: "It seems to me that the reception given to those applying for asylum is an illuminating indicator of the state of a society's moral health."

DIVINE PROVIDENCE

Readings: Ex 2:1-15; Mt 11:20-24

God provides every human being with all that is required for acquiring our supernatural destiny. It is with this final goal of humanity in view, that God's providence extends to all aspects of human life, both spiritual and material. Since God's dominion over the earth is complete, his gracious will must extend to all material conditions of life with its own spiritual purpose. The fascinating story of how Moses, while an infant, was rescued from death (Ex 2:9), illustrates God's providential care of his chosen one. Despite the machinations of an evil ruler in Egypt, God was powerful enough to bring his plan for Moses to completion. Some scientists object to the idea of divine providence, because they see it as the Creator's interference into the functioning of the laws of nature, which he himself has established; and hence they call him a dictatorial ruler. To them, divine providence tends towards magic and superstition. Yes, indeed. Providence of God will not be credible to those who limit themselves to an exclusive scientific conception of the universe. Even Hitler had to admit divine providence: "I go the way that providence dictates, with the assurance of a sleepwalker," he said. But one wonders whether he really meant it.

THOSE LITTLE THINGS

Readings: Ex 3:1-6, 9-12; Mt 11:25-27

All good things have small beginnings. The mighty oak starts with a tiny acorn. From a tiny seed, most wonderful plants and flowers spring forth. From a tiny seed of love many lives have been changed. Do you feel you are small in talents, in good looks, in health, in possession, in education, in social status and so on? Do not get disheartened. Little things grow into big things. Be grateful for many little things in your life, for Jesus promises the Kingdom of God to the little ones. He thanked his Father for revealing the riches of his Kingdom to mere 'babes' (Mt 11:25). Moses had become a shepherd working for his father-in-law. His life was simple and unassuming and he could not be counted among the learned and the clever of this world; but it is to Moses that God revealed himself (Ex 3:4). We all like to become like babes, as Christ would want us to become. But how? First, we must believe in God's wonderful promises; Visualise God going before you, preparing the way to make the seemingly impossible become possible. Secondly, accept the teachings of Christ as true and live by them, so that God's promises may come true in your personal life.

THURSDAY – WEEK 15 / YEAR 1

"I AM WHO I AM"

Readings: Ex 3:13-20; Mt 11:28-30

There are times in life when there is nothing more difficult than the absence of God's presence. But in fact, God is never absent from our life. In the midst of physical and emotional pain, we cry out to God and wonder if God hears or cares. The truth is that he cares. God revealed himself to Moses as a personal God when he gave his name as: "I am who I am" (Ex 3:14). God is not an inanimate object or a vague, nebulous force in the universe. In giving his name to Moses, he revealed his desire to enter into an intimate relationship with every human being. This intimacy of God is even more evident in the person of Christ, the God made flesh, who invites us to come to him for refreshment and rest (Mt 11:28). May we, then, turn all our anxieties over to God, express all our fears to him and react to life's trials first by trusting God. When we feel God is absent, it is appropriate to question, cry, complain and even argue with God. But as we wrestle with God, let us always affirm that in spite of our feelings of pain and abandonment, God is God who cares and who is with us in our troubled journey. As John Donne wrote: "God's hand is in every translation; and his hand shall bind up all our scattered leaves again."

FRIDAY – WEEK 15 / YEAR 1

HAVE WE PASSED?

Readings: Ex 11:10-12:14; Mt 12:1-8

There are, in effect, only two forces in the world. One is the force of expansion towards God and towards others, and that force is called love. The other is the force of withdrawal into oneself, and that is called selfishness. By defending his disciples against the criticism of the Pharisees, when they picked some ears of grain to satisfy their hunger on a Sabbath (Mt 12:2), Jesus revealed that the Sabbath was meant to be a means towards an expansion of love for God and neighbour. The very core of the liberation accomplished by Christ's Passover from death to resurrection consists in our being delivered from the sins of selfishness, the most radical of all evils. The event of Passover, the greatest one in the history of Israel, when God freed his people from the slavery of Egypt (Ex 12:11), was only a forerunner of the Christian Passover Christ achieved for us by his death and resurrection. But how far have we passed from self-love to love of others? Christ's Passover has made available the grace needed to make this passing; but how earnest are we in making use of the grace? Some are so addicted to self-love that they are like the condemned man who is proud of the vastness of his prison wall. I hope none of us would fall into this category.

SATURDAY – WEEK 15 / YEAR 1

IS HE AN ABSENTEE GOD?

Readings: Ex 12:37-42; Mt 12:14-21

Is our God an absentee God, sitting idle, ever since the first Sabbath, at the outside of his universe? Should we believe in a God who exists in all his perfection, creating imperfect human beings in order to make them run the risk of hell? These and similar questions are raised by some atheists as reasons for not believing in God. Nietzsche said something more cruel about God: "God is a thought that makes crooked all that is straight." I believe that the main difficulty people encounter in relating to God is their wrong image of him. They imagine that he is a God who is demanding love, fidelity, obedience; that he is a punisher, that he makes us suffer and leaves us alone in suffering; he is a God of judgement and condemnation. But the God whom the Scriptures reveal is just the opposite. It portrays him as a loving and caring Father, keeping night watch "to bring the Israelites from the land of Egypt" (Ex 12:42), and a God who is tender and merciful who "will not break the bruised reed or quench a smouldering wick" (Mt 12:20). Some of us tend to do away with things that are slightly damaged. We say, "Well, he has a problem with drinking; we would better not take the risk of getting involved with him." But God does get involved with him too.

MONDAY – WEEK 16 / YEAR 1

DO WE NEED A SIGN?

Readings: Ex 14:5-18; Mt 12:38-42

God never wrought a miracle or sign solely to convince us that he exists, because his ordinary works are convincing enough. Yet, some people are constantly looking for wonders and signs to believe in God, in his love, wisdom and power. The Israelites experienced the deliverance from Egypt, which was sign enough to believe in God guiding them. But after freedom, they asked for another sign (Ex 14:11). They needed a new sign at every turn. Similarly, after all that Jesus had said and done, the Scribes and Pharisees were not satisfied. They wanted some new signs to believe in him (Mt 12:38). But the only sign Jesus gave was himself, a Christ crucified on the cross and raised to life. What about us? After all that we know about Jesus, his life, his teaching, his works, death and resurrection, do we still need a sign to believe in him? It is reason that creates motives for believing. Faith is to religion very much like credit to business. Just as one must have a reason for giving credit, so too, one must have a reason for believing. The conclusion of reasons for accepting the testimony of Jesus Christ are not mathematically certain. Yes, but they are morally certain. They are very much like the certitude that you have that you were born of your own parents!

GET IN TUNE

Readings: Ex 14:21-15:1; Mt 12:46-50

There are peculiar storms in the Indian ocean-typhoons and monsoons. They are peculiar in that they do not move very rapidly. They do not move from east to west, or north to south; instead, they play around a circle. Hence, when the navigators run into a monsoon, they locate its centre and go round it. By and by, they narrow the circle; when they get into the centre, they are in dead calm. This storm is like God's will. Try to get out of it, and you will find it a destructive force. Get into it, you are in a calm and you find it good. This is what happened to the Israelites when they obeyed God's marching orders through the Red Sea (Ex 14:21). Calling us to obey God's will, Jesus says, "Whoever does the will of my Father in heaven, is my brother, and sister, and mother" (Mt 12:50). Those who live by God's will, will have a life full of excitement and expectancy. They can expect even miracles, because by doing God's will, they belong to the special family of Jesus Christ. Anything can happen to them at any time, because they are in tune with a higher power, and are working from a higher level of God's own wisdom. Daily, early morning, get your heart in tune with God's will. A sensitive musical instrument has to be tuned before it can be played.

OUR GOD OF ABUNDANCE

Readings: Ex 16:1-5, 9-15; Mt 13:1-9

God is a God of abundance, not a God of scarcity. He has made with us, not a contract but a covenant, that he will feed our body and soul generously. See how he fed the hungry Israelites in the desert by raining down bread from the heavens (Ex 16:4). Jesus reveals to us God's abundance, when he compares his divine word to seed which a farmer goes out to sow (Mt 13:3) in abundance. The words he spoke are the divine seeds which give us spiritual nourishment yielding happiness and peace in abundance, depending on the kind of soil our hearts are. Whether it is material food or spiritual food, God does not give us just enough, but more than enough. God is a generous giver. But we can only see and enjoy God's generosity, when we too are generous in our love for him. As long as we say, "I will love you, God, but first show me your generosity", we will remain distant from God, and unable to experience what God truly wants to give us, which is life in abundance. If our love for God is generous and true, we will allow Christ's words to take flesh in us. As he said, his word is life and spirit in abundance; but to experience its power, we must allow it to live and move and have its being within us.

THURSDAY – WEEK 16 / YEAR 1

SEE HIM, HEAR HIM

Readings: Ex 19:1-2, 9-11, 16-20; Mt 13:10-17

God's goodness surrounds us at every moment. We walk through it almost with difficulty as through thick grass and flowers. God manifested himself and spoke to the Israelites in the awesome movements of nature, through peals of thunder, lightning flashes, dense cloud and loud trumpet blasts (Ex 19:16-19); Even today we can see his beauty in a sunset, his power in a mighty wind, his loving care in life-giving rain. See the majesty of God in the stars, his wisdom in the intricacy of human body, his intelligence in the reach of the human mind and his splendour in the complex elegance of the natural world. As God spoke to the Israelites through Moses, today God speaks to us through the leaders of his Church. He also speaks to us through our fellow human beings. When someone, for example, tells me, "I have been thinking of you, today" or "I missed you" or "I wish you were here" or "I really love you", it is God himself speaking to me. Such words of affirmation and love are like bread. We need them each day over and over again. They keep us alive inside. Are our inner eyes and ears open to recognise God and hear him speak whenever he chooses to? "Blessed are your eyes, for they see, and your ears, for they hear" (Mt 13:16).

OUR SPIRITUAL SPACE-SUITS

Readings: Ex 20:1-17; Mt 13:18-23

Greed is a bottomless pit that exhausts the person in an endless effort to satisfy the need, without ever reaching satisfaction. Greed not only enslaves one to endless unhappiness, it also enslaves millions to unnecessary poverty. There is so much poverty in the world because, though there is enough in the world for everyone's need, there is not enough for everyone's greed. Hence, among the Ten Commandments God gave his people, he commanded us not to covet others' property (Ex 20:17). The Ten Commandments are God's words which are like seeds (Mt 13:19). They can bear much fruit in our life, if we put them into practice. The Ten Commandments do not infringe upon our freedom. On the contrary, they set us free. For example, it is not greed to enjoy a good concert. But if you sit down to eat a good dinner and enjoy the concert at the same time, you loose the freedom to enjoy either of them fully. That is why the Ten Commandments prohibit greed. They are like the space-suit. The space travellers have to be confined within a space suit for survival. It protects them against hostile environment and is tethered by a lifeline to the ship. Thus, rather than inhibiting the freedom of the spacemen, the spacesuit offers a lifeline to safety.

TRY AGAIN

Readings: Ex 24:3-8; Mt 13:24-30

Poet Yeats wrote: "Things fall apart; the centre can not hold; mere anarchy is loosed upon the world; the blood-dimmed tide is loosed and everywhere the ceremony of innocence is drowned." How rightly he pictured the presence of evil in the world! However, not just evil, but also good, in fact, more good can be found in the world, as in a field where weeds grow with the wheat (Mt 13:25). But, why does God allow evil people to thrive with the good ones? Because, every sinner is potentially a holy person. By not eliminating evil from human lives, God gives every bad one time to be converted and to find his or her destiny in the end. The Israelites promised to abide by the laws God gave them through Moses (Ex 24:3). But at every turn of their spiritual journey, they violated them. Yet, God continued to care for them, for he knew they were in the right direction, in spite of their repeated unfaithfulness. In our own individual selves, we will find virtue and vice intertwined. We must not become impatient with ourselves. When a small child learning to walk falls down, it is not discouraged but picks itself up and tries again and again until it has mastered the art of walking. So too, if you fall, pick yourself up and try again.

MONDAY – WEEK 17 / YEAR 1

THE MUSTARD SEED

Readings: Ex 32:15-24, 30-34; Mt 13:31-35

The mustard seed is very small and insignificant. Pliny the Elder, a contemporary of Jesus, wrote a great book called *Natural History,* in which he describes all the plants that were known in the Mediterranean world. He says only two things about the mustard plant: It is medicinal; so it did have some value. But he asked people not to plant it, because it tends to take over the entire garden; it is a weed that can not be stopped. When Jesus compared the Kingdom of God to a mustard seed (Mt 13:31), he was building on two images of the mustard seed to describe the Kingdom: like the mustard seed, his Kingdom is therapeutic, but it is a weed. As therapeutic, it is life giving, it is healing, it is medicinal. As weed, however, it is like virus, that is, his Kingdom promotes 'stupid' things such as non-violence and simple life. But he has planted it and it is going to take over. We don't know when it is going to take over, but Jesus has planted his eternal truth in the world and it is going to take over. It is going to grow with great difficulties, because there is going to be opposition, but it will prevail; it will eventually take over the whole world.

TUESDAY – WEEK 17 / YEAR 1

NO "IFS" IN HIS HEART

Readings: Ex 33:7-11-34:5-9, 28; Mt 13:36-43

There are no *ifs* in God's heart. God's love for us does not depend on what we do or say, on our looks or intelligence, on our success or popularity. God's love for us existed before we were born, and will exist after we have died. It is this unconditional love that we see in his dealings with Israelites. No matter how often and how greatly they had sinned, God would yield to Moses' prayers for their forgiveness, because he is "a God merciful and gracious, slow to anger, and abounding in steadfast love and faithfulness" (Ex 34:6). It is God's unconditional love that allows his Church, to be not only a haven for the virtuous, but also a refuge for sinners. He patiently allows weeds of evil to grow along with grains of goodness in his field (Mt 13:38). Does this mean that God does not care whether we are good or bad? No; because God's love would not be real if he did not care. To love without condition does not mean to love without concern. God's unconditional love means that he continues to love us even when we do evil things. God continues to wait for us, as a loving parent waits for the return of a lost child. It is important for us to hold on to the truth that God never gives up, even when he is saddened by what we do.

WEDNESDAY – WEEK 17 / YEAR 1

BLUES FLY AWAY!

Readings: Ex 34:29-35; Mt 13:44-46

It is no honour to Christianity, if a Christian should sit under a juniper tree, hang his or her harp upon a willow and walk about the world in the shadow of death and despair. If I am a true Christian, I have discovered the risen Christ in some way, a discovery which should fill me with great joy, for in discovering Christ I have met God. When

Moses met God, the grace and love of God glowed within Moses and overflowed into joy and peace on the outside, with such splendour that he had to veil his face (Ex 34:30), lest people who saw him were blinded! Jesus compares the joy we would find in meeting him to the joy a man finds in discovering suddenly a hidden treasure in a field or a pearl after a search (Mt 13:44-45). This must be so because when we meet Christ, we come into contact with the Kingdom of God. Joy is what makes life worth living, but for many, joy seems hard to find. They complain that their lives are sorrowful and depressing. They wonder whether some people are just lucky, while others have run out of luck. Strange as it may sound, we can choose joy, if we choose to find God in Christ. Strive to meet the risen Christ, and you will be so filled with joy that you will be able to drive the blues away from other peoples as well.

THURSDAY – WEEK 17 / YEAR 1

BEING DRAWN TOGETHER

Readings: Ex 40:16-21, 34-38; Mt 13:47-53

How much we wish to put an end to untold human sufferings! How much we hope, that one day, races will be free from injustices to one another, that nations will use the earth's resources in a way that all may have enough to eat, that war and the possibility of war will be banished altogether, that family life everywhere will be secure and stable, that people will be brought everywhere into fellowship! Will that day come at all? Yes; God is in our midst working with us for the coming of that day. The same God who first made his presence among his people on Mount Sinai, then moved his presence to the Tabernacle Tent which Moses built for him (Ex 40:19), is also present with us now, but in a more powerful way. He is present through the pervasive power of the Spirit of his risen Son, Jesus Christ. The Holy Spirit is the 'dragnet' (Mt 13:47), whom God has cast beneath the sea of human life. You and I struggle for peace and justice; and around us, are some of our own kinds and others of a hundred different breeds struggling. But there is one thing common to us all, namely, we are all being drawn by the dragnet ever closer together, and we are convinced that, in the end, all will be sorted out and brought into harmony.

FRIDAY – WEEK 17 / YEAR 1

CELEBRATIONS

Readings: Lev 23:1, 4-11, 15-16, 27, 34-37; Mt 13:54-58

Birthdays are so important. On our birthdays, we celebrate being alive. On these days, people can say to us: "Thank you for being." Birthday presents are signs of our being a part of our family. As we celebrate birthdays, the people of Israel celebrated throughout their liturgical year the wonders God had worked on their regard to be alive as his chosen people. As the book of Leviticus describes, whenever they came together for a feast of the Lord, they celebrated the fact of being alive as one people by the love and mercy of God. We too celebrate throughout the Church liturgical year the great feasts of our Lord Jesus Christ, remembering his life, death and resurrection. Such memorial feasts are necessary, otherwise we may forget the Lord in whom we are alive and by whom we are brought together as one people. Still a greater danger is that our forgetfulness of him may soon become our rejection of him as our Saviour, a rejection Jesus suffered at the hands of the people of his own home town (Mt 13:58). Birthdays are our big days, since we become the centres of attention. So too, the feast-days of our Lord will be big days both for him and for us, if the Lord becomes the centre of our attention

---

SATURDAY – WEEK 17 / YEAR 1

DO WE PROTEST?

Readings: Lev 25:1, 8-17; Mt 14:1-12

Each of us has some degree of power over other people's lives. Do we use this power to enhance other people's welfare or our own? Worse still, some people try to exert absolute dominion over other people's lives, as if they are little gods. People like king Herod who married his own brother's wife and who killed a man like John the Baptist to please a dancing girl (Mt 14:4,10), are people trying to usurp God's own dominion over human lives. In the Jubilee year which the Israelites celebrated every fiftieth year (Lev 25:11), farms were left fallow, the land that had been sold was restored to the original owner and the slaves were left free. These observances were meant to affirm that no one other than God could exercise absolute control on the lives of others. When we see, today, many landowners trying to control the lives of the coolies who work in their fields, by sending them away nearly empty handed and with unfilled bellies, do we protest? When we see some industrialised nations trying to control the lives of the farmers in agricultural countries, by leaving them to steer the heavy plough through soft oozing mud, guiding the pair of sturdy oxen till the field is tilled, in an age of technology, computer and space travel, do we protest?

MONDAY – WEEK 18 / YEAR 1

THE SECONDARY CAUSES

Readings: Num 11:4-15; Mt 14:13-21

According to reliable statistics, in 1984 six million people were starving in Ethiopia alone. Hence, the 1984 Christmas issue of *News Week* ran this advertisement: "Right-now giant cargo planes are delivering enough food to feed tens of thousands of hungry people a day. Here is how you can help! Your gift of $15 is all it takes to feed a hungry child for a month! Please give whatever you can now." God our Creator is our Father too. Hence he has to see that humanity does not suffer from starvation. But normally, God works through secondary causes of natural phenomena, human initiative, intelligence and concern. For example, God fed the Israelites in the desert with manna. Manna is said to be a sweet resinous substance exhumed from a desert tree; hence, it was a desert food, but given in abundance (Num 11:8). When Jesus fed the hungry people in the desert, he did not feed them from nothing. He worked a miracle using "five loaves and two fish" (Mt 14:17) that were already available. How willing are we to put ourselves and what we possess, at the disposal of God to help the starving people in the world? Should we expect God to deliver more food from heaven to feed the starving or to move the human hearts to share what they have?

HIS ORDINARY CHANNEL

Readings: Num 12:1-13; Mt 14:22-36

The Church is the ordinary channel of God's Word to us. At times, God may send an extraordinary prophet to impel us on a neglected direction. But the Lord gave us as an ordinary guide to reveal without fanfare God's love for us, and to continue the work of salvation for all humankind. Miriam, passing Moses in whom God had invested his authority to lead the Israelites, wanted God to appear in clouds and thunder, lightning and vision; and for that, she was turned into a leper (Num 12:10). The spiritual leadership of the Church may be weak with faults, as Moses was. The Church is holy, yes; but tainted in all its members; and hence it is constantly tempted by lust for power, greed, rivalry and competition, torn apart by arguments, prejudice and authority-conflicts. That is why, the boat with disciples, together with Peter, tossed by the waves of the sea (Mt 14:24), has traditionally represented the Church. It is difficult to believe that God has chosen this human and frail Church to be the ordinary channel of his Word. Yet, we have to believe. We have to believe in the Church with the same faith we believe in God. Believing in Jesus and believing in his Church are two sides of one faith.

WEDNESDAY – WEEK 18 / YEAR 1

KEEP MOVING FORWARD

Readings: Num 13:1-2, 25-14:1, 26-29, 34-35; Mt 15:21-28

A child moves gladly from kindergarten to secondary school, unafraid of the future. Likewise, in our life-long Christian journey, which takes us from love of self to love of God and neighbour, we must accept the change that this journey demands and keep moving forward like a child. We must not be afraid of the future every time we move into a new phase of greater love for God and others. This is something the Israelites failed to do when they were asked by God to move into the promised land, for they were afraid of the "men of great stature" in the new land (Num 13:32). They did not trust in the power of God ready to protect them. In contrast is the Canaanite woman in the Gospel whose trust in the divine power of Jesus was so strong that she refused to give up her pleas until Christ healed her daughter (Mt 15:28). Our journey is like a windmill. A strong wind blows and the sails are turning at great speed. Then the wind drops and the sails stop turning, for they are completely dependent upon the wind for their movement. We too, in our journey from love of self towards love of God and others, depend on God's power. If we put our security in ourselves, we can not move an inch forward, for we will be afraid of the unknown.

THURSDAY – WEEK 18 / YEAR 1

OUR BROKENNESS

Readings: Num 20:1-13; Mt 16:13-23

Jesus was broken on the cross. He lived through his suffering and death, not wanting to avoid them, but embracing them, as his mission. But Peter could not accept a Christ crowned with thorns and dying on a cross. Hence he remonstrated: "God forbid, Lord! This shall never happen to you" (Mt 16:22). He felt comfortable with a gold-crowned Christ, in the tradition of a conquering emperor. What kind of Christ do we want to embrace? A Christ of an elite bourgeois Christianity, or the Christ of a ruling class, a Christ robed in silk, seated on an ivory throne? No way. The true Christ is a broken one. We too are broken. We live with broken bodies, broken hearts, broken minds or broken spirits. We suffer from broken relationships. Jesus invites us to embrace our brokenness as he embraced the cross. He asks us not to reject our brokenness as a curse from God that reminds us only of our sinfulness, but to accept it and put it under God's blessing for our purification and sanctification. In this way, our brokenness can become a gateway to a new life with the risen Christ.

WHAT MAKES FOR JOY?

Readings: Deut 4:32-40; Mt 16:24-28

The key to a joyful life is to keep asking: "What will it profit a man, if he gains the whole world and forfeits his life?" (Mt 16:26). Nothing matters but the ability to rise above the material pull to do God's will. If you are forced to live in one room, you consider yourself a captive. Suppose you live in a building with a thousand rooms; are you freer? No. Multiple choices of means of material pleasures and comforts is never a substitute to joy, nor a guarantee for eternal joy for which every human heart yearns. A writer who has a choice of a thousand pencils is not freer to write a novel than he who has one. To be constantly on the move to new pleasures, never makes for joy. What gives us true joy and guarantees eternal fulfilment is obedience to God's will. So Moses asked his people to keep the Lord's statutes and commandments so that it might go well with them (Deut 4:40). We must never rush ahead unguided by God's will. Nothing is out of step in God's will for us. So, work with it and not against it. If we try to work against it, we will simply exhaust ourselves and will get nowhere, and it will be like swimming against the tide; we will either remain stationary though swimming, or we will be swept back with the force of the tide.

THE OIL OF LOVE

Readings: Deut 6:4-13; Mt 17:14-20

What is love? It is not the desire to have, to own, or to possess, but the desire to be had, to be owned, or to be possessed. This is the kind of love we are expected to have for God. It is his first and the greatest commandment: "You shall love the Lord your God with all your heart, and with all your soul and with all your might" (Deut 6:5). If I love

God in this way, my whole outlook will become optimistic, for I have placed all my security in God. I will always expect the best, always find the best, and always create the best. Optimism leads to power, pessimism to weakness and defeat. Love God with all your heart and see the power of love shining in and through you, creating around you a world of beauty, peace and harmony. When our outlook on life is optimistic, we can lift all those around us, giving them hope, faith and belief in life, for love for God necessarily overflows into love for others. It becomes oil in our hand. I was once shown a big heavy door, which was very hard to open because the hinges were stiff. Then someone placed few drops of oil on the hinges of the door, which was then being gently eased until it could open with the slightest touch. Likewise, when our heart is full of love for God, we ease people's burden with the oil of love.

MONDAY – WEEK 19 / YEAR 1

AT WHITE-HEAT TEMPERATURE

Readings: Deut 10:12-22; Mt 17:22-27

If you have worked long enough for a ship building company, you would know that welding is impossible unless the materials to be joined are at the white heat temperature. Likewise, there is something that needs to be at the white heat temperature for us Christians to be joined together as one family of God. What is it? Is it the parish church? No. Mere brick building can not unite us. Besides, with the coming of Jesus, the temple had ceased to be the centre of God's community. The temple is now replaced by the new community with Jesus as its Lord. The half-shekel temple tax (Mt 17:24), once symbolised allegiance to the temple as the religious centre. But now we are sons and daughters of the Father and our worship is no longer limited to one place. What unites us now as Christians is that Jesus is our brother and his Father is our Father, whom we are called to love and serve with all our heart and all our soul (Deut 10:12). The more dedicated we are to our Father, the closer we become to his Son Jesus and to one another. It is this dedication that has to be at white heat temperature; otherwise, our efforts to try to weld ourselves together into one community will fail, and we will only fall apart.

IN GOD ALONE WE TRUST

Readings: Deut 31:1-8; Mt 18:1-5, 10, 12-14

Trust and obedience are hallmarks of a child. Jesus asks us to "become like children" (Mt 18:3) in our trust and obedience to our heavenly Father, so that we can be counted as "the greatest in the kingdom of heaven" (v.4). Moses trusted in God, and so he urged Joshua to lead the people across the Jordan into the promised land, fearing nothing, and telling him: "The Lord goes before you; he will be with you, he will not fail you" (Deut 31:8). Moses obeyed God as best as he could. Though he was the one who led his people from Egyptian slavery, he obeyed God's command not to cross the Jordan. He obeyed because his trust in God was absolute. He trusted in God alone. Is our trust in God alone? How often do we put our trust in God, plus our job and in our lawyer? How often do we put our trust in God, plus our insurance and savings accounts? How often do we put our trust in God, plus our friends and families? Of course, there is nothing wrong with having a job, insurance, family and bank accounts. In fact, these are all good and necessary. Yet, family and friends may disappoint us; jobs can be eliminated; insurance may not pay; and financial resources can be depleted. Therefore, our ultimate trust must be in God alone.

A QUALITY OF THE HEART

Readings: Deut 34:1-12; Mt 18:15-20

Christian community is primarily a quality of the heart. It is not primarily a matter of particular structures. It is first of all an awareness of Christ's call to inter-dependence, to loving and being loved, to forgiving and being forgiven, to serving and being served, to giving and receiving. When my community is thus a quality of the heart, then I can do what Jesus asks: "If your brother sins against you, go and tell his fault, between you and him alone" (Mt 18:15). However, such a face to face fraternal encounter may not lead immediately to a happy resolution. We may try hard, pray for resolution and peace, may admit our faults and seek forgiveness, may talk about the issues and confront the problem; still, disharmony and distrust might continue to linger. Sometimes, the harder we try to make things right, the worse it might get. Frequently, the difficulty is that we are aware of the symptoms, but the ability and congenial environment to speak heart to heart may be lacking. This only reminds us of our own fragility in a broken world. At such a time, we can only commit these difficult and painful circumstances into the masterful hands of God, awaiting another day and time, for a happy resolution.

THURSDAY – WEEK 19 / YEAR 1

WE ARE WOUNDED

Readings: Jos 3:7-11, 13-17; Mt 18:21-19:1

We are all wounded people. Often, we are wounded by those whom we love and those who love us. That is the tragedy of our lives. Yet, we have to be ready to forgive, not seven times but "seventy times seven" (Mt 18:22), which means we must forgive always, and forgive from our heart. Forgiving is an act of liberation. We set the offender free from the negative bonds that exist between us; we no longer hold the offence against him or her. We also free ourselves from the burden of being the offended one. If we do not forgive, we carry the offender as a heavy load. Why should we forgive? Forgiveness is the cement of a community life. Forgiveness holds us together through good and bad times and it allows us to grow in mutual love. It often appears we are not able to offer forgiveness to others, because we have not been able to receive it when it is offered to us. Receiving forgiveness is difficult because it requires a confession that we have hurt somebody, and the humility to acknowledge our dependence on others. Accepting forgiveness and giving it to others, often may seem impossible, but nothing is impossible for God. God who lives within us will give us the grace to go beyond our offended selves.

MARRIAGE, A BUSINESS DEAL?

Readings: Jos 24:1-13; Mt 19:3-12

Everything God does is out of love. All God's actions throughout the history of Israel recounted by Joshua in the first Reading, manifest his wisdom and love, which, of course, reached its climax in the death and resurrection of his Son Jesus. If we keep God's enduring love in mind, we can better understand his laws, including the difficult ones, such as the law about divorce enunciated by Christ. Permanent union between the spouses is the original will of the Creator (Mt 19:6). Of course, a life-long, self-giving union is not easy. Love can be as powerful as a tempest. But it is also delicate and fragile. It can be wounded and lost. But what Jesus was proclaiming was the vision of love between spouses, which would reflect the enduring covenant relationship between God and his people. If the love such as proclaimed by Christ is the motive for a marriage, then marital life stands a good chance of success. On the contrary, if it is merely a business deal, it will soon break down. A man lived in the wilderness and advertised for a wife: "She must be able to sew, cook, clean, raise children, fish and have a motor boat, which she must bring with her." P.S. "Send pictures of boat and motor." That could be a business deal, not an everlasting covenant.

A DIFFICULT CHOICE

Readings: Jos 24:14-29; Mt 19:13-15

Freedom does mean choice. But the choice itself is our difficulty in life, for the number of choices that a human being can make is so many that, at times, it is a good choice not to choose at all. However, it is impossible for us to be happy either in this world or in the next, unless we choose to trust in God whatever may be our life-situation at any given moment. So Joshua said to his people: "Choose this day whom you will serve" (Jos 24:15). Two families hold funerals for their two teenage girls, tragically killed in a tragic accident. At such times, profound questions about God emerge, such as: If God is in control of our lives, why did he not prevent this from happening? There is no simple answer. But, the questions leave us with a choice about God. Even though we feel deep emotional pain and intellectual confusion, we can still choose either to trust God or give up on him. People who trust God in spite of the tragedies, are those who believe that God who did marvellous things to bring his people into the promised land, still continues to work for our good. An unknown author wrote: "Courage, brother! Do not stumble; though the path be dark as night, there is a star to guide the humble; trust in God and do the right."

MONDAY – WEEK 20 / YEAR 1

NO DUST ON FLYING WINGS

Readings: Judg 2:11-19; Mt 19:16-22

When we applaud an actor on the stage or a returning hero, we are, in a sense, worshipping him, putting a value on his worth. Worship is a sign of value, the price we put on a person. Therefore, to worship God means to acknowledge that he is the source of our ultimate happiness. But there are times in our lives when we push God to the back seat and give his place to lesser gods of our own choosing. For example, the people of Israel repeatedly "forsook the Lord, the God of their fathers" (Judg 2:12); They worshipped, instead, the lesser gods of their pagan neighbours. To the rich young man in the Gospel, his possession was his lesser God. Hence, when the Lord proposed to him to renounce his riches in order to follow him to perfection, he could not, and "went away sorrowful" (Mt 19:22). When the heart is filled with the supreme and transcendent desire after the eternal God, then we realise that there can be nothing outside God that can fully satisfy us, for everything comes from his Hands. Dust never rises very high on the road; the birds that fly high above, have no dust upon their wings. So, if our heart knows how to fly high enough towards God, it escapes the anxieties and the worries, which brood upon the earth.

HUMBLE BUT PROUD?

Readings: Judg 6:11-24; Mt 19:23-30

Humility is like underwear. We have to have it, but we should never show it. And yet, at some banquets, I have heard speakers, when they are given some cup, or degree, or praise, to say: "I am very humble, but proud." One wonders how they could be humble and proud at the same time! Pride is what we think ourselves to be; humility is the truth we know about ourselves. Gideon, a simple farmer, was truly humble. When he was called by God to be a leader of the people, he protested that he had none of the qualities necessary, and added: "I am the least in my family" (Judg 6:15). But humility is not only truth about oneself; it is at the same time confidence in God. Humility is not inaction because of one's weakness, but action in the power of God. It believes in the saying of Christ: "With men this is impossible, but with God all things are possible" (Mt 19:26). Armed with this confidence, the humble Gideon led his people against their enemies to victory. Therefore, a humble person's constant motto is: "I will fear no evil, for thou art with me." Responsibilities are no longer burdensome to a humble soul, for it realises that the Divine works in us. Want of courage is want of humility.

GOD IS DRIVING

Readings: Judg 9:6-15; Mt 20:1-16

Our being born into this world is like getting into a train. All our life, we are driven by God's will for us and its destination is God himself. Whether we like it or not, we can't get out of the train. In moments of utter distress, we may cry to God to stop the train, as a passenger does by pulling the alarm. God may or may not stop. On our part, we must persevere in being driven by God trusting that God knows what is best for us. Whatever we do in life is worth only if it be in accord with God's will. If we insist on following our own will to satisfy our whims and fancies, we will end up like Abimelek who chose himself as king against God's will, with the result that he had nothing to offer his people except harm like a "bramble" (Judg 9:14). Do not be surprised if you see God's will showering more blessings on others than on yourself. In fact that is the kind of God the parable in today's Gospel portrays, a God who gives equal wages to both the first comers and late comers (Mt 20:14). God's ways are indeed strange, but remember that he sees the whole of the picture, where you and I only see a very small portion of it; God sees all the actors in the play of life, when you and I see only the nearest at hand.

THURSDAY – WEEK 20 / YEAR 1

THE EUCHARISTIC GARMENT

Readings: Judg 11:29-39; Mt 22:1-14

"Our Lord does not come from heaven every day to stay in a golden ciborium. He comes to find another heaven, the heaven of our soul in which he loves to dwell", said Theresa of the Child Jesus, referring to our Eucharistic banquet. Jesus in the Gospel compares the Kingdom of God to a wedding banquet. But the Eucharistic banquet is the foretaste of our heavenly banquet. With what disposition of the soul do we come to receive the Lord in Holy Communion? In other words, do we come to the Eucharistic banquet wearing a suitable spiritual 'garment'? (Mt 22:11). For example, we cannot come to break the Lord's bread, without accepting responsibility for the brokenness of the poor in the world. But who actually are the poor? We might think of people who live in slums, people who go to soup kitchens, people who sleep on the streets, people in prisons, in mental hospitals and in nursing homes. But the poor can be also those who feel unloved, rejected, ignored, or abused. It is precisely when we do something to alleviate the distress of the poor, who are either far away or close by, that we are sewing a spiritual garment suitable to wear for the Eucharisic banquet.

MADE FOR LOVE

Readings: Ruth 1:1, 3-6, 14-16; Mt 22:34-40

One day, there came parading in a street of London a lovely little girl with a great Purple Heart flaming on her blouse. Across the Purple Heart were inscribed the words, "Made for love!" Looking at her, anyone would believe it. But God tells us that not just pretty little girls are made for love, but all of us, created in the image of God who is love, are made for love, namely, to love God and our neighbour. "Love the Lord your God with all your heart… and your neighbour as yourself" (Mt 22:37,39). Of course, true love entails sacrifice. Look at Ruth in today's first Reading. After the death of her husband, rather than return to her own country, she decided to stay with Naomi, her mother-in-law, because she believed Naomi needed her (Ruth 1:16). By doing so, she fulfilled the double commandment of love, because she attached herself in devotion both to her mother-in-law and to the God of Israel. But it meant a great sacrifice on her part, for in effect, she had to leave behind her other relatives and their pagan customs. Charity always involves sacrifice. For example, Fr Damian went to the Hawaiian island in Moloka in 1873, served the lepers there, until he too contracted leprosy and died in 1889.

THE UNKNOWN SAVIOURS!

Readings: Ruth 2:1-3, 8-11; 4:13-17; Mt 23:1-12

Why is it that God is still sustaining our violent and homicidal world and continues to give new opportunities? We might think it is because of the peace movements carried out by VIPs, international peace conferences, organised public protests against crimes and the like. But I firmly believe that one of the convincing reasons for God's continued protection of the human race is that some totally unknown people are praying and working in silence; they are unassuming in their acts of love and anonymous in their endeavours for peace. Our Lord's words, "The greatest among you shall be your servant. Whoever humbles himself will be exalted" (Mt 23:11-12) support my belief. A classical example is Ruth. Not once in the entire story of Ruth's affectionate relationship to Naomi or Boaz, is the word 'love' mentioned. This shows that Ruth's love and care for others was unassuming and that is why she became an ancestor of Jesus, in ways more than biological. In God's sight, the things that really matter seldom takes place in public or with pomp. The major part of Jesus' own life was hidden. Our God is a hidden God. Hence, the greatest part of God's work in human history could well remain unknown.

MONDAY – WEEK 21 / YEAR 1

BLIND HORSES!

Readings: 1 Thess 1:2-5, 8-10; Mt 23:13-22

Have you ever seen a blind horse used in a mill? It goes round and round the mill, never getting a step further, but only being whipped continually. The faster he goes the more work he does, and the more he is tired. Religious legalists are like this blind horse. Preoccupied with the observance of the minute details of religious laws, they fail to see that the essence of religion is faith, hope and love. This blindness is Pharisaism, condemned by Christ as hypocrisy (Mt 23:13). Pharisaism scares people away from religion, for it harries them with obligations and obsesses them with guilt. But the new converts in Thessalonica were not given to such hypocrisy. They had imbibed the true essence of religion, and hence they lived by faith, laboured in love and showed constancy of hope in Jesus Christ, for which Paul praised them (1 Thess 1:2). Are we satisfied with mere observance of religious rituals? We need to remember that mere external observances of religion are like the trappings on black horses that drag people to their graves in a funeral procession. Is there any mark of pharisaic hypocrisy in our attitude towards the religion that we have embraced? Of all things that stink in the human nostrils, hypocrisy is the worst.

TUESDAY – WEEK 21 / YEAR 1

WHAT IS WITHIN?

Readings: 1 Thess 2:1-8; Mt 23:23-26

A heart is very much like Africa, a region unexplored. From where come our carnality, greed, pride, sloth and unbelief? Are they not all to be traced to the corruption of our hearts? When the hands of a clock move in an irregular manner and when the bell strikes the wrong hour, you can be sure there is something wrong within. So too, for the wheels of our actions to be right, the mainspring of our motives must be in proper condition. St Paul swears by God "who tests our hearts," that his appeal was never "made with guile" (1 Thess 2:4,3). In contrast, the Pharisees were like white-washed sepulchres who "cleanse the outside of the cup and of the plate but inside they are full of extortion and rapacity" (Mt 23:25). If you should fire at a man and the bullet unexpectedly turned aside, you would be as truly guilty before God as if your victim had died. But human law might not call you a murderer, because it is obliged very much to judge a wrong by the effect. But the Lord looks at the heart and weighs the motive. Besides, the world esteems honest persons. If you can be absolutely relied upon, when you say you will do a thing, you are already of consequence in the world for you carry a passport to universal esteem.

WEDNESDAY – WEEK 21 / YEAR 1

THE MOUNTING EAGLES

Readings: 1 Thess 2:9-13; Mt 23:27-32

See how high the eagle mounts! Does it care for the heavenly blue, or aspire to commune with the stars of heaven? Not a whit. The bird mounts to heaven, but it keeps its eyes ever more on its prey. No celestial impulse is needed; its love of blood suffices to bear it aloft. A hypocrite is like this eagle, in a sense. Hypocrisy is appearance. I appear holy while preaching on holy things, but if my heart has not truly embraced what I preach about, I am a hypocrite in whom there is a conflict between inside and outside. It is to preach without practising, to smile and be a villain. St Paul was not a hypocrite. In his letters, he underscores the authenticity of his ministry. He tells them that his behaviour is in keeping with what he preached (1 Thess 2:10). The Pharisees, on the contrary, were actors who were like "whitewashed tombs" (Mt 23:27), which shine outside, while inside, full of decaying corpses. That is why, they could preach without remorse against things that they themselves were doing. Let us beware of hypocrisy in our dealings with God and our fellow human beings. Do I profess what I don't believe? If I do, I am living more lives than one, and hence liable to die more deaths than one!

THURSDAY – WEEK 21 / YEAR 1

KEEPING WATCH

Readings: 1 Thess 3:7-13; Mt 24:42-51

There are three comings of the Lord: His Second Coming at the end of the world, his coming at the end of one's life, and his coming as we live this day. Any one of these comings can take place at any moment in our life. Therefore, Jesus cautions: "Watch" (Mt 24:42). How do we keep watch? It is by doing God's will always. A musical instrument, when it is out of tune, creates discord. We too, when we are out of tune with God's will, create unnecessary troubles for ourselves. How do we keep watch? It is by starting each day with a willingness to love everyone we may meet. So St Paul prays: "May the Lord make you increase and abound in love to one another and to all men" (1 Thess 3:12). Let our love be like an open book that all persons can read. Love is not blind, for it sees the very best in the loved one, and so it draws forth the very best from others. Again, how do we keep watch? It is by starting each day expecting new blessings from the Lord. There are, of course, the regular blessings: the heartbeat, the sun-rise, tasty food, a loving family, and so on. But who knows, there may be new unusual blessings for the day. When we start the day expecting new blessings, we start it on the right foot and it will be an exciting day.

FRIDAY – WEEK 21 / YEAR 1

SEXUAL BONDAGE

Readings: 1 Thess 4:1-8; Mt 25:1-13

God is a God of surprises. He comes not according to our schedule. Therefore, we need to be always prepared to meet him, whether he comes at the end of the world, or at the end of our life, or at any moment of a living day. We need to be always spiritually resourceful, like the five wise bridesmaids who had taken more than enough oil, to meet the bridegroom at any time he chose to come (Mt 25:4). For a Christian, what is to be resourceful? It is a life of faith translated into action. And there are many obstacles that could drain our faith, driving us to spiritual inactivity. One major obstacle is inordinate sexual indulgence, such as lust and fornication (1 Thess 4:3), against which St Paul is warning all those who wait for the Lord's sudden coming. Those who abuse their body in sexual immorality are in bondage. "Out of a forward will," wrote St Augustine, "lust had sprung; and lust pampered, had become custom; and custom indulged, had become necessary. These were the links of the chain; this is the bondage in which I was bound." Sexual desire is natural and hence morally neutral; but when we idolise it, it turns into lust. It is sad that today we have to live in a sex saturated society!

SATURDAY – WEEK 21 / YEAR 1

LOVE UNFOLDING

Readings: 1 Thess 4:9-11; Mt 25:14-30

Once a chick has emerged from its shell, or a butterfly from its chrysalis, there is no going back; instead there is a continuous unfolding into the new. Similarly, we who were reborn in Christ by the power of God's love at baptism, are called to let that love unfold day by day into increasing acts of service for others. That is why, while acknowledging the brotherly love that was manifest among his converts, St Paul encouraged them to go on making ever greater progress in that love (1 Thess 4:10). The Lord has given each of us, too, different gifts and we are expected to use them in loving service to God and neighbour. If we are not making proper use of the gifts God has given us, at the day of judgement, he will be right if he treats us harshly, as the man in the Gospel treated the servant who had received one talent but did nothing with it (Mt 25:28). How generous are we in the use of our gifts, spiritual, intellectual and material, in the service of our neighbour? The joy of giving is tremendous. For example, if you have a happy and sunny nature, and you give of it wherever you go, it will be returned to you a thousand-fold, for everyone responds to a sunny disposition.

MONDAY – WEEK 22 / YEAR 1

RISE, WE MUST!

Readings: 1 Thess 4:13-18; Lk 4:16-30

Just as a person casts off worn out garments and puts on the new, even so, our embodied souls will cast off our worn out and dead bodies and take on the new at the general Resurrection, when "at the sound of the trumpet of God, the dead in Christ will rise" (1 Thes 4:1). Not just our body, but our whole person, body and soul, will rise glorified under the saving power of the death and resurrection of Jesus. When Jesus announced in the Synagogue that he had come "to proclaim release to the captives" (Lk 4:18)), his message was first down to earth, namely, that he had come to free the poor, and the outcasts, held captives by injustice, greed, pride and hatred. However, his message went still deeper. He proclaimed that he had come to give all those who believe in him the precious spiritual release that includes release of the body held captive in the earthly death. Our human body, with such a glorious destiny, deserves to be treated now with respect. If we have been treating our own body and those of others with disrespect, we have fallen. Of course, the believer falls. But it is one thing to fall down and it is another thing to lie where we have fallen. Rise, we must.

TUESDAY – WEEK 22 / YEAR 1

THERE IS A CENTRE

Readings: 1 Thess 5:1-6, 9-11; Lk 4:31-37

It is by its promise of a sense of power that evil often attracts. But that promise is a lie, for evil has lost its power at the hands of Jesus Christ. When Jesus ordered the evil spirit, "Be silent, and come out of him" (Lk 4:35), and it came out of the possessed man, Jesus revealed that he had come to overpower evil. In deed, he destroyed the seed of evil on Easter Sunday and has already given us, through our baptism, a share in his power over evil. That is why, St Paul calls us "sons of light and sons of the day" (1 Thess 5:5). Therefore, we as believers, have within us the spiritual resources to defeat evil gradually, both in our personal lives and in humanity as a whole. A concrete example would help: When someone hurts us, ignores or rejects us, a deeper inner protest emerges. It can be rage or depression, a desire to take revenge or even an impulse to harm ourselves. It is precisely here, that we have to dig deep into our spiritual resources to defeat evil, and find that centre of power within us, the centre that lives beyond our need to hurt others or ourselves, the centre where we are free to overcome the evil done to us, by forgiveness and love.

WEDNESDAY – WEEK 22 / YEAR 1

SEEDS OF RIPE CORN

Readings: Col 1:1-8; Lk 4:38-44

During World War II, members of a London congregation decorated their church with stalks of ripe corn for a harvest liturgy. That night, the church was destroyed in bombing raid. All that winter, it lay in ruins. When spring came, green sprouts emerged from the church's rubble. All summer long, the sprouts grew. When fall came, the church's congregation reaped a remarkable harvest of corn. The Gospel is like those seeds of ripe corn. Nothing can keep it from bearing fruit. But there are two conditions. For the Gospel to bear fruit, it has to be lived, as well as to be announced. In fact, "the Gospel" (Col 1:5) St Paul refers to, was also called 'living tradition', that is, it was the Good News heard and lived, remembered and celebrated. Jesus himself is seen in today's Gospel, "preaching in the synagogues of Judea" (Lk 4:44) and laying his hands (v.40) on all the sick and curing them. Preaching is a responsibility of every Christian. If a Christian is not called to preach, then he or she is called to send other Christians to do so. Likewise, witnessing to what is preached, is of equal responsibility, if not a greater one. In fact, a good example, is the best sermon. Precepts may lead, but examples draw.

THURSDAY – WEEK 22 / YEAR 1

DECISION-MAKING

Readings: Col 1:9-14; Lk 5:1-11

As we go through life, we are called to make choices, in relation to our personal and professional life: What kind of job we will do, where will we live, whether to stay single or get married and so on. In order to make the best possible decision, we have to have some knowledge of the situation; and of course, our own personal preferences will play a large part in the process. But there is still one more dimension we have to attend to. That dimension is spiritual, which calls us to be "filled with the knowledge of God's will" (Col 1:9) before deciding. If our own personal preferences are different from God's will, we are advised to put them aside in favour of God's will. In this we are called to act as Peter did in the Gospel. Jesus instructed Peter to "put out into the deep" (Lk 5:4), even though Peter had laboured in vain all night. Physically exhausted and demoralised, Peter could have refused to recast the net; but he obeyed the Lord, and was rewarded with super abundant fish. If we insist to choose our own path against God's will, what seemed to be as best, might prove a snare. In my own experiences, what was initially a disappointment to me, turned out to be God's appointment.

FLOWING WITH THE TIDE

Readings: Col 1:15-20; Lk 5:33-39

At times, one has to flow with the tide, not against it. When we feel that change is necessary, we need to be willing to change and not try to resist it. We need to be flexible. We can never let our attitude be "What was good enough for my parents is good for me." Change will never come if this is our attitude, but change must come. "No one puts new wine into old wineskins; if he does, the new wine will burst the skins" (Lk 5:37). This means that the new messages of Jesus about the Kingdom of God require a change in our attitudes and outlooks, for the new has outgrown the old and needs more room. For example, some of us are accustomed to think that if someone does harm to us, it is our right to retaliate. But Jesus' new message was: "Turn the other cheek when someone hits at you." What he meant was that, even when we are hurt, we need to exercise self-control, unselfishness and love for our neighbour, and not take revenge. If this new message is practised by all, there will be no need for so much conflicts in the world. But in order to accept this new message of love from Christ, we need to change our belief in wild justice, which is retaliation. When a plant is pot-bound, it needs to be spotted, to allow its roots to expand.

THERE IS SOMEONE!

Readings: Col 1:21-23; Lk 6:1-5

Life is unpredictable. We can be happy one day and sad the next; healthy one day, and sick the next; rich one day, and poor the next; alive one day, and dead the next. So, who is there to hold on to? Who is there to feel secure with? Who is there in whom to trust at all times? There is someone. He is Jesus Christ. The reason for this is this: Jesus

Christ is the sole mediator between God and humanity. He alone is our direct link with God, our Creator, for he "has now reconciled (us) in his body of flesh by his death" (Col 1:24). Jesus achieved our reconciliation with God on Calvary, and we make that reconciliation ours, by linking ourselves with Jesus. Our being accepted by God as his children or being received lovingly after we have abandoned him, does not depend on our doing some Sunday rituals or by our observance of some precepts of the Church. Jesus said, "The Son of man is lord of the Sabbath" (Lk 6:5). He meant, in effect, that he is the new point of our reunion with the Father, and nothing else can take his place. And yet, there are some ministers of God in the Church, who can preach a sermon without mentioning the name of Jesus from beginning to the end! What do you think of them?

MONDAY – WEEK 23 / YEAR 1

OUR HEALING MISSION

Readings: Col 1:24-2:3; Lk 6:6-11

A local newspaper reported: "A driver rammed a car over the curb and onto a busy sidewalk, then slumped against the steering wheel, apparently unconscious. For nearly an hour, dozens of people walked around the car ignoring the apparent tragedy." Had this incident not actually taken place, we would never believe people could be so detached. Yet, on another level, the same thing happens every day. There are wrecked people whose lives are broken. Do we ignore them? Jesus did not. When he saw a man in the synagogue with a withered hand (Lk 6:10), he called him out and cured him. By doing so, he stated that his mission was to restore what is broken and to heal what is wounded. We his followers have the same mission in today's world to heal people with broken hearts, with wounded bodies, with damaged emotions, and with injured memories. Perhaps, some of us feel we don't have the strength and energy to carry on such a mission. But, St Paul did not think like that. He wrote: "I toil, striving with all the energy which (Christ) mightily inspires within me" (Col 1:29). The risen Christ lives in us also, through his Spirit, as the secret energy with which we too can carry on our healing mission.

TUESDAY – WEEK 23 / YEAR 1

OUR SOVEREIGN

Readings: Col 2:6-15; Lk 6:12-19

It appears that many people today don't anymore believe in ouija boards, palmistry or psychic phenomena. But it is surprising that there are still lots of people who believe in paranormal and preternatural, in supplements, lucky charms, mantras or astrology charts. St Paul says that we don't need them, for Christ supersedes them all with his sovereign power; he "disarmed the principalities and powers, triumphing over them in him" (Col 2:15). That power of Christ is still active in his Church founded on the twelve apostles (Lk 6:13) whom he chose. To them, he transmitted his power and they passed it to their successors in the Church. Though we may believe that the power of Christ is active in the Church, perhaps, many of us believe more in objects other than Christ, such as medals, scapulars, icons, votive candles and the like. These are good objects and are called sacramentals; but in themselves they don't possess any divine power; they are only reminders of the power of Christ and excite us to deeper reliance on the sovereign power of Christ who is the head of the Church. When the whole of Satan's kingdom is subject to the authority of Christ, what else can take its place?

WEDNESDAY – WEEK 23 / YEAR 1

ARE THEY OPPOSITES?

Readings: Col 3:1-11; Lk 6:20-26

Emptiness and fullness, at first, seem to be complete opposites. But in the spiritual life, they are not. In spiritual life, we find the fulfilment of our deepest desires by becoming empty for God. When Jesus declared that the poor, the hungry and the sorrowful are truly blessed people (Lk 6:20-22), he affirmed that those who empty themselves for values higher than the earthly ones, are truly being filled, for they drink from God, the very source of happiness. Jesus is not against happiness, but declares what really constitutes happiness. He is not against money, sufficient food or comfort, but warns us not to pursue them as a source of happiness. Hence, St Paul asks us to "seek the things that are above, where Christ is seated at the right hand of God" (Col 3:1). We know only too well, how Jesus himself lived his life, emptying himself to the death on the cross. However, his moment of complete emptiness and complete fullness became the same. When he had given all away to his Abba Father, he cried out, "It is fulfilled." He, who was lifted upon the cross, was also lifted into the resurrection. So it is with us. When we empty the cups of our life completely, for the sake of God, we will receive from him, the fullness of life.

THURSDAY – WEEK 23 / YEAR 1

NOT LIKE RATTLESNAKES!

Readings: Col 3:12-17; Lk 6:27-38

Some of the most unhappy people in the world are those with emotional photographic memories. They never forget hurts. Every slight ever received is permanently etched in their minds. Some continue to be angry with people who have died years ago. Much unhappiness in life could be eliminated if we extended forgiveness generously and freely. St Paul begs the Colossians to forgive each other, reminding them, "as the Lord has forgiven you, so you also must forgive" (Col 3:13). Jesus goes further and commands, "Love your enemies, do good to those who hate you" (Lk 6:27). For one thing, we do not do any good to ourselves by hating those who have hurt us. A trapped rattlesnake can become so angry that it will bite itself. So too, we end up 'biting' ourselves, not our enemies, when we refuse to forgive them. How do we handle anger and resentment when they begin to take control of us? It may help to recite affirmations such as these: "Beginning now, I release all grudges and hatred. Beginning now, I extend good will towards those who have caused me pain. I allow God's love to flow over me and heal my memories. I allow God's love to flow through me, empowering me to forgive."

BLIND LEADING THE BLIND

Readings: 1 Tim 1:1-2, 12-14; Lk 6:39-42

Before the discovery of radio and television, a telephone operator used to get a daily call requesting the exact time. She was always able to give it authoritatively. This was because she checked her watch daily when the town's factory sounded its whistle at the end of each workday. One day, however, her watch stopped, and she told her mystery caller that she was waiting for the factory whistle. There was a silence. Then the caller said, "This is the factory. We always use your time to decide when to sound our whistle each day." This is a case of a blind man leading a blind man (Lk 6:39). St Paul admits that before he became a believer he was a blind guide of blind people in his persecution of the Christians. He acknowledges: "I had acted ignorantly in unbelief" (1 Tim 1:13). We too, often, are not sure what to do. Some parents cannot even persuade their children of 16 or 18 years old, to go to Sunday Mass. Why? When you tell your spouse that he or she is giving bad example, you are not listened to. Why? Often, the reason seems to be that people, who reject our legitimate corrections, see greater faults in us, faults that we ignore or refuse to acknowledge. The blind can not lead the blind.

OUR SINGLE HOPE

Readings: 1 Tim 1:15-17; Lk 6:43-49

When a beggar asks for money and you give him something out of pity, you are not showing mercy. Pity connotes distance, even looking down upon. Mercy comes from a compassionate heart; it comes from a desire to be an equal. Jesus, God made flesh, did not want to look down on us. He wanted to become like one of us, and feel deeply with us. That is mercy. St Paul saw himself as a living example of God's mercy. He wrote: "I received mercy for this reason, that in me, as the foremost, Jesus Christ might display his perfect patience" (1Tim1:16). We ourselves are the recipients of so much of God's mercy and hence we should show mercy to others. "Blessed are the merciful," said Jesus. But it is not enough to be repeating this beatitude; one must practice it; Otherwise, he or she will be like "a man who built a house on the ground without a foundation" (Lk 6:49). If we don't practice mercy, we will easily become judgmental and intolerant of faults and failures of others with the result, that we ourselves will not receive God's mercy when we need it. Who among us can live happily now and forever without the mercy of God? For those who have everything, as well as for those who have nothing, there is only one single hope: God's mercy.

MONDAY – WEEK 24 / YEAR 1

THE SAVIOUR OF ALL

Readings: 1 Tim 2:1-8; Lk 7:1-10

As human beings, we can not manufacture salvation for ourselves. Eternal salvation must come from the eternal God. And he is Jesus Christ. Christ is the A and the Z of the salvation alphabet. He is the only Saviour for every human being; Therefore, the saving power that flowed from his death and resurrection is present in every person of goodwill, who believes in God and tries to please him. It is this saving power that was present in the Centurion, a non-Jew, which drove him to believe in Jesus, which brought cure to his sick servant (Lk 7:10). Hence, St Paul asks us Christians to bring all the good deeds being done by anyone or any groups, irrespective of their particular creed, to our common prayer. He adds: "I urge that petitions, prayers, inter-cessions and thanksgivings be offered for all men" (1 Tim 2:1). If the power of Jesus Christ is working in every person of goodwill, can we reject anyone, just because they are not Christians, from our common endeavour to build God's Kingdom of truth and love, peace and justice on earth? If we look around us, we will discover that there are many non-Christians, even unbelievers, who stand out by their love and service to humanity, putting some Christians to shame.

AN IMPERATIVE NECESSITY

Readings: 1 Tim 3:1-13; Lk 7:11-17

If we want a stable world, the root of it is a very simple thing. It is a thing so old fashioned that if I mentioned, I might face a derisive smile from many. Yet I can't but mention it. The root is 'love' – Christian love or compassion. If we believe in compassion, then we have a motive for existence, a reason for courage, a basis for hope; Compassion is an imperative necessity for a stable world. We learn compassion from Jesus. See how Jesus, without being asked, went to a sorrowing widow, who had lost her only son, and raised him to life and "gave him to his mother" (Lk 7:15). When we know someone is grieving over the loss of a loved one, we may not have the power to raise the dead. But still, we can show compassion to the bereaved in many other ways. Go to him or her; don't delay. Your visit will tell the person, "I care", "I love you"; but don't say too much. Words get in the way of grief. Sit gently by the person's side knowing that comfort comes from your presence. Allow the person to tell of the loss over and over again. The repetition defuses the intensity of the loss and makes it possible for healing. Open your eyes and be sensitive to whatever the bereaved needs to be done, and do it with the person's permission.

A GUARDED LIE

Readings: 1 Tim 3:14-16; Lk 7:31-35

An excuse is worse than a lie, for an excuse is a lie guarded. I know an individual who is unable to dance, but blames the unevenness of the floor. A person, who is going to commit an inhuman act, can excuse oneself saying, "I'm only human after all." There are people in some parishes who want a pastor who is a saint, but when he comes, they believe he is mad, setting the standard so high. Therefore, if someone more down to earth comes, they gossip about his drinking habits. It is about such people Jesus bemoaned saying, "To what then shall I compare the men of this generation?" (Lk 7:31) It is our belief that the Church of the living God, is "pillar and bulwark of the truth" (1 Tim 3:15), for in the Church, the power, the mercy and the love of God are made manifest to us. But sadly enough, many of those who see the truthfulness of the Church, don't want to embrace it on some excuses. To them, the Church is too otherworldly, if it speaks of eternal values; it is too involved, if it engages in social services and actions of justice. But truth of the matter is that the Church is too inconvenient for them, for their comfortable lifestyle. The person who really wants to do something finds a way, the other one finds an excuse!

THURSDAY – WEEK 24 / YEAR 1

A FAKE HOUSE

Readings: 1 Tim 4:12-16; Lk 7:36-50

In London there is a building called: *The House That Never Was*. It has no door bell or letter box. Nobody visits. Nobody sits on the balcony. More than a million people have walked by, but never noticed anything strange. In fact, it is a fake house cemented on a brick wall. It hides the entrance to an ugly subway tunnel and has been painted to blend with nearby homes. Appearances are deceptive. Do we hide ugliness, loneliness, and insecurity behind a 'sham' front of composure? Do we judge others by their appearances? St Paul tells Timothy: "Let no one despise your youth." Because, though he appeared young, he had been entrusted to set "an example (to his people) in speech and conduct" (1 Tim 4:12)." From the Gospel too, we learn that public ascriptions of status can be deceptive. The woman was known to be a sinner, but she had a heart filled with repentant love. Whereas, the Pharisees who represented a law that called for forgiveness, had not forgiven the woman. (Lk 7:39). Outside show is a poor substitute for inner worth. Fine words and insinuating appearance are seldom associated with true virtue. They are not all saints who use holy water!

MONEY TALKS

Readings: 1 Tim 6:2-12; Lk 8:1-3

Money talks: "Let me have a word with you. I am your servant if rightly used. You will become my slave if you persist in misusing me. I often hear people saying, "the love of money is the root of all evils" (1 Tim 6:10). Yes; it is true if you have a wrong attitude towards me. But, I can be also the root of much good, if you will use me properly. I would like to stay with you for a little while. There may be a real mission that I can perform for you some time. On the other hand, I detest being held tightly. It hurts. When there is something urgent and really useful, let me be on my way. See how some wealthy women financed the mission of Jesus and "provided for them out of their means" (Lk 8:3). I was not intended for you alone. I want to do the greatest possible good. And, please remember that I like to go to churches too. I am always happy when I can work for the Master of all silver and gold, the One who owns all the riches of creation." How do you like this money-talk? I like it. In one of the Catholic churches, I found these words inscribed on the collection baskets: "One dollar spent for a lunch lasts five hours; One dollar spent on a neck tie lasts five weeks; One dollar spent in the service of God lasts for eternity."

THE SEED OF GOD'S WORD

Readings: 1 Tim 6:13-16; Lk 8:4-15

In our local park, a tree had been blown over. During the night a fierce storm had struck and the tree was now lying on the ground. Its roots had broken off just below ground level. Actually the tree had never developed a strong, straight taproot. It had grown for a while, supported by artificial watering and protected from strong winds. Now, its weakness has shown up quite starkly. Our lives are much like this too. God has planted in our hearts and minds his Word, but unless it is tended and cared for, it can quickly succumb to the "worries, riches and pleasures of life" (Lk 8:4-15), without reaching maturity. But if the Word of God is tended and watered by consistent spiritual means, it will bear much fruit. The finger of God scratched the soil and planted a seed, and Mother Teresa left a convent in Albania to minister to the dying in the streets of Calcutta. God is still planting the seeds of his life in our hearts. Is there something that is distracting us away from tending the seeds of God's Word that we have received? The biggest distraction today is the allure of consumer society. "We have to see through the allure of consumerism and materialism," said late Cardinal Hume, "and gear ourselves for the pressures of the pilgrimage."

MONDAY – WEEK 25 / YEAR 1

AM I SHINING?

Readings: Ezek 1:1-6; Lk 8:16-18

A man scoffingly asked, "What advantage has a Christian over any unbeliever like myself? Does not the sun shine on me as on him, this fine day?" "Yes," replied his companion, "but the Christian has two suns shining on him at once – one on his body, the other on his soul." At Baptism, we become the children of the light because Jesus begins to shine on our souls. But we need to let this light shine through us on others. "No one after lighting a lamp covers it with a vessel" (Lk 8:16). We are called to let the goodness of God glow through us. When others see that goodness, they become enlightened. Our smiles, kind words and good deeds are all small reflections of Christ, the one mighty light of the world. If we can help others to see more clearly where they are going, and what they are doing, then we place the light of Christ on a lamp stand. A small child was taken to a Cathedral. She sat watching the sun shining through the windows. She asked her mother, "What are these people on the windows?" "They are saints", was the answer. Then the child said, "Now, I know what saints are. They are people who let the light shine through."

TUESDAY – WEEK 25 / YEAR 1

THE FAMILY OF GOD

Readings: Ezek 6:7-8, 12, 14-20; Lk 8:19-21

I was once standing at the counter of my local train station. I felt a small hand grab my jeans. Looking down, I saw a toddler hanging on to me. She was not mine, but I did not want to scare her by telling her off. Luckily, she let go before she ever noticed she had the wrong legs, and I saw her wander back to her father. We are a lot like that child, often grabbing at the wrong things, thinking that they are what we need, and that is where we belong to. For example, we are a family of God as a parish. But how do we become members of God's family? Some think that it is by belonging to the one parish church, which is a brick building. It is a big mistake. Temple, of course, was once the political, social and religious centre of life for the Jews. That is why, after returning from the Babylonian captivity, they rebuilt the Jerusalem Temple (Ezek 6:16). But after Christ came on the scene, he himself has become our temple and it is by belonging to him that we become members of God's family. And we belong to him as his brothers and sisters when we hear from him the word of God and do it (Lk 8:21). In fact, he has become our eldest brother in the family of God, because he gave us the supreme example of how to hear God's word and do it.

WEDNESDAY – WEEK 25 / YEAR 1

WE ARE SENT OUT

Readings: Ezek 9:5-9; Lk 9:1-6

As fire exists by burning, so the Church exists by mission. We are Christians today due to the missionaries who once came to the homes of our ancestors to preach the Gospel. Were it not for those poor and frequently martyred messengers of the Gospel, armed only with the

Lord's word, the churches in our parishes where we go to worship, would not exist. Those missionaries came in the line of the disciples whom Jesus sent out "to preach the kingdom of God and to heal" (Lk 9:2). It is now our turn to go out and do the same. In our modern time, a good deal of Christian mission, take place through institutions such as colleges, schools, hospitals and welfare centres. But we must regularly evaluate their effect and see whether they are truly a proclamation and witness of God's Kingdom in word and deed, which ought to be the heart of all our missionary works. The cross of Christ firmly roots us in human concerns and needs, and places us alongside the oppressed, the dispossessed, the homeless, the poor and the starving millions of our planet. Therefore, the task of mission for today, is not so much to get the non-Christians into the Church, as to get the Christians out of the Church into the world.

THURSDAY – WEEK 25 / YEAR 1

SCARCITY MENTALITY!

Readings: Hag 1:1-8; Lk 9:7-9

It is more blessed to give than to receive, because we make a living by what we give, but we make a life by what we give; I mean, "life in God". There are a lot of people who give to God and give his people generously. But there are also people who are very stingy. They may give the Lord credit, but are reluctant to give him cash! Prophet Haggai found his people to be so. He found that those who had material means refused to contribute to the building of the temple. He felt that they were more concerned with their own comfort than providing a suitable place for the worship of the Lord. So he told them: "Consider how you have fared" (Hag 1:5). It raises a question for us: How willing are we to give to the church, which is body of Christ who has replaced the temple for us today? Have we got into a mindset that normally tells us: "There is not enough money and food for everyone; so I better make sure that I save enough for myself, for emergency!" This is a scarcity mentality. It involves hoarding whatever we have, fearful that we won't have enough to survive. The tragedy, however, is that what we cling to, ends up rotting in our hands.

BOATS OF PRAYER

Readings: Hag 1:15-2:9; Lk 9:18-22

To see someone in prayer is a touching sight. For a while, they have become unmoved by the grip of society, work and role. The body gathers itself before the Divine, and stillness deepens. The blaring din of distraction ceases and the deeper tranquillity within the heart envelops the body. Jesus often took himself to this kind of prayer, an intense communion with God. Once, "as he was praying alone, the disciples were with him" (Lk 9:18). Jesus must have, in his prayer, asked his Father to enlighten his disciples as to who he was; and his prayer was answered, for at least Peter could declare, "You are the Christ of God" (v.20). Do we ever pray for others as intensely as Jesus prayed for his disciples? It is consoling to remember that there are old and feeble nuns in forgotten convents, who live out their days by creating little boats of prayer, to ferry nourishment to a hungry world. There are also monks in monasteries, whose wonderful chorus of prayer keeps human life civilised and somehow still balanced. In our precarious and darkening world, we would have destroyed everything long ago, were it not for the light and shelter of prayer. Every time you pray for others, you add to the light and harmony of humankind.

THE DESCENDING WAY

Readings: Zeck 2:5-9, 14-15; Lk 9:43-45

Certain seeds won't germinate until they are frozen. That is what gardening experts say. They also say that certain buds must freeze before they bloom. For example, bring a bare branch of forsythia into the house in autumn, and the buds will never open. But bring it in January or February after the buds have been well frozen; they will bloom. So too, a Christian has, in a sense, to freeze in the bitter chill of daily crosses and final death, before he or she can bloom into eternal life. To a Christian, suffering in this life is ultimately life giving, as it was to Jesus. So he reminded his disciples: "The Son of man is to be delivered into the hands of men" (Lk 9:44), referring to his death on the cross. In Jesus, God not only descended to our human condition, when he became a human being, but descended to the total dereliction of one condemned to death. Jesus calls us to take up the same descending way. It is the way of suffering, but is also the way to healing. It is the way of humiliation, but is also the way to resurrection. It is the way of tears, but of tears that turn into tears of joy. It is the way of oppression and persecution and death, but also is the way to full revelation of God's love. Christ has made the dark door of death into a shimmering gate of life.

MONDAY – WEEK 26 / YEAR 1

THE POOR HAVE A TREASURE

Readings: Zach 8:1-8; Lk 9:46-50

Like every human organisation, the Church also is in constant danger of corruption. As soon as power and wealth come into the Church, manipulation, exploitation, misuse of influence, are not far away. How do we prevent corruption in the Church? It is by serving the poor. Whoever is prepared to spend his or her life in serving and helping the people who do not matter much in the eyes of the world, is serving Jesus and his Father. This is what he wanted to convey when he said, "whoever receives this child receives me" (Lk 9:48), for children did not count for anything in Jewish society of his time. Therefore, the true people of God serve the poor. This is the people of God Zacharia saw in his vision, filling the city of God; and God proclaimed: "They shall be my people and I will be their God" (Zach). One of the reasons why we neglect the poor is that we think that they don't offer us anything in return. But the truth is different. The poor have a treasure to offer us, precisely because they can't return our favours. By not paying us for what we have done for them, they call us to inner freedom, selflessness and generosity. Their repayment is spiritual. It is joy, peace and love of God that we so much need, as an antidote for corruption in the Church.

ON THE GROUND OF ETERNITY

Readings: Zach 8:20-23; Lk 9:51-56

Christ is the great central fact of the world's history. All lines of history converge upon him. To him everything looks forward and backward. Do we know why? He is the source of blessing not only for the Jews but also for the Gentiles. He is the Saviour of all. Zachariah foretold that, "many peoples and strong nations shall come to seek the Lord in Jerusalem and to entreat the favour of the Lord" (Zach 8:22). Since Jesus has replaced Jerusalem, it is to him all peoples are encouraged to come now. If we find people who are not coming to the Lord, we, his followers have a duty to bring such people to the Lord in our prayers. The Lord wants to make us a channel of his grace to the whole world, if not through anything else, at least through our prayers. We can not be like the disciples, James and John, who wanted to pray for fire to descend and consume those who did not believe in Christ (Lk 9:54). We must rather pray to the Lord also for the unbelievers of our day, that they be converted to Christ. It is unthinkable what prayer can actually achieve! When you pray, you are on the ground of eternity. Prayer is the activity of the invisible world. It is said that if you pray beside a flower, it grows faster!

TOTAL DEDICATION

Readings: Neh 2:1-8; Lk 9:57-62

A pig and a chicken were once discussing the problem of world hunger. Both wondered what they could do to alleviate human misery. The chicken had a brain wave. They could make a regular contribution of bacon and egg to some relief agency. It might not be much, she argued, but at least it was a personal contribution. "Fine for you," replied the pig, "but for me, that is total dedication." A word like 'dedication' challenges our comfort zones. Jesus tells us in the Gospel that following him demands total dedication; that we must love him more than we love our property, that we follow him without delay and so on (Lk 9:62). Nehemia is an example of a totally dedicated servant of God in spending himself out to rebuild the walls of Jerusalem, the city of God (Neh 2:5). He was not a cloistered monk but a layman. Even today, we can see and admire such total dedication among the laity: in the heroic love of parents for their most vulnerable children, in the professions like nursing, where the financial reward is slight in comparison to the human wear and tear of caring for fragile people, and in the sacrifice of many young people who choose to become full-time volunteers to work with relief agencies in the most devastated areas in the world.

THURSDAY – WEEK 26 / YEAR 1

"AMEN, AMEN"

Readings: Neh 8:1-4, 5-6, 7-12; Lk 10:1-12

Every thing in the railway service depends upon the accuracy of the signals. When these are wrong, lives will be sacrificed. On the road to our Father's house, we need also unerring signals to live this life well or the catastrophes will be far greater. The Word of God in the Bible provides such an unerring signal because God inspired it. Ezra was a man who, by his calling, was devoted to the laws of Moses, contained in the first five books of the Bible. After the return of the people from exile in Babylon, he was overjoyed to rediscover them, and when he explained God's words to his people, they were filled with awe and accepted them with a resounding "Amen, Amen" (Neh 8:6). In our own world, millions are thirsting for the Word of God. Jesus urges, in effect, more and more evangelisers to take God's Word to these people, when he says, "The harvest is plentiful, but the labourers are few" (Lk 10:2). It is impossible to govern the world rightly, unaided by the Word of God. The Bible, or parts of it, has now been translated into about 1027 languages. But that is not enough. The lessons of charity, justice, and equality, which enrich its pages, should be explained to all people, in order that greed, avarice, and iniquity can be blotted out.

FRIDAY – WEEK 26 / YEAR 1

"I CONFESS"

Readings: Bar 1:15-22; Lk 10:13-16

What do we mean when we say "I confess", at the start of the Mass? We mean, "I repent." Without repentance, there is no pardon and without pardon, there is no reconciliation with God. "Repentance", wrote John Milton, "is the golden key that opens the paradise of eternity." That is why, Jesus grieved over the unrepentant people of Chorozin and Bethsaida (Lk 10:13), who could have represented the Jewish nation as a whole. But we on the contrary, do repent and repeatedly repent. When we say, "I repent", I suppose we repent of a particular fault, or wrongdoing or sin. For example, we may repent like Baruch who repented for his people's "not heeding the voice of the Lord" (Bar 1:18). However, if we do really repent for not listening to the voice of God, there must be a tangible sign of it in our actual lives. Knowing the Word of God is not enough; we must apply it. Willing to please God is not enough; we must actually please him. What is the use of hungering to be masters of the world, without hungering to master the evil in our own life? Unless the fruit of repentance can be seen in our lives, there is no evidence of the root of repentance in our heart. You can't purify the water by painting the pump.

SATURDAY – WEEK 26 / YEAR 1

CHILDLIKE FORGIVING

Readings: Bar 4:5-12, 27-29; Lk 10:17-24

To many people, revenge is sweet: to see your enemy perish and pay to justice all he or she owes. "But the weak," said Gandhi, "can never forgive. Forgiveness is the attribute of the strong." Yet, many adults who claim to be strong, can't forgive an offence, leave alone forgetting it. But children are different. They can be fighting with one another one minute and the next minute, they are playing together as the best of friends. In this, they are like God. See how the prophet Baruch proclaims God's readiness to forgive his people: "Take courage, my children, and cry to God" (Bar 4:27). It is this childlike simplicity of the disciples of Jesus, which won from God the power to drive out evil spirits, for which Jesus thanks his Father saying, "I thank thee, Father, thou has revealed these things to mere babes" (Lk 10:21). We too can obtain the same power, in different degrees, a power that sets individuals free to be sons and daughters of God. But, are we childlike in our simplicity? Can we, like little children forgive an offence and forget it? As the saying goes, "To err is human, to forgive is divine." Therefore, if we have not forgiven anyone, we have not yet tasted one of the sublime enjoyments of the Divine.

MONDAY – WEEK 27 / YEAR 1

THE HELPING SECRET

Readings: Jon 1:1-2:1, 11; Lk 10:25-37

"We make our friends," wrote G.K. Chesterton, "we make our enemies, but God makes our next door neighbour." However, our neighbour need not be always the one who lives next door. To the question, "Who is my neighbour?" (Lk 10:29), Jesus replies with a parable, answering, in effect, that our neighbour is any one who is in need of our help. Often we excuse ourselves for not helping others, by saying that the person is in such and such need, because of his or her own mistake. If we are prepared to imitate the Good Samaritan, we will not make such excuses. The secret of helping others is to treat them as we find them, not as they ought to be, not as we want them to be, but as they actually are. After rendering the immediate help, later on, one can lift them up; but at the beginning, there must be acceptance. This is always the way of a physician. The more accurately he can diagnose the actual state of the patient, the better prepared he will be, to use his healing art. If however, we throw a book called *How to make money* at the unfortunate starving one, we are like a medical doctor who starts setting a broken bone, by reading to the patient a treatise on the dangerous effects of broken bones.

TUESDAY – WEEK 27 / YEAR 1

THE GOOD PORTION

Readings: Jon 3:1-10; Lk 10:38-42

The Church ought not blindly to adapt itself to the changing world; rather, it must always witness to the primacy of the spiritual over the material, of contemplation over action, of wisdom over ingenuity, and of character over efficiency. Of course, we need contemplation and action, ingenuity and wisdom, efficiency and character. But it makes a lot of difference when the spiritual comes first. And Jesus confirms this, by praising Mary who chose to sit at his feet and listen to his words, when Martha was busy doing things. The Lord said: "Mary has chosen the good portion" (Lk 10:42). An instant of pure loving communion with God in silent prayer, is more profitable to the Church than all other good works put together, though it may seem nothing were done. Do you know why? From our regular time of meditative communion with God, we emerge refreshed, renewed and rebaptised in the power of the Sprit. In God's presence, we are healed. In his presence we find the courage to live our lives through him, with him, in him and for him. Once we begin to open our heart to God's power, everything in our life becomes charged with meaning. All our doing, all our talking, all our loving, and all our living, find meaning from silent prayer.

WEDNESDAY – WEEK 27 / YEAR 1

LEAVE HIM ALONE!

Readings: Jon 4:1-11; Lk 11:1-4

The *Our Father*, the prayer taught by Jesus (Lk 11:2) addresses first to the concerns of the Father himself: the proclamation of his name, the spreading of his Kingdom, and the fulfilment of his will. And only then, we are asked to pray for our own needs. So often we reverse this order and want God first to satisfy our personal needs, thus turning the providence of God into a tool of our special wants. This is what Jonah tried to do when he wanted God to be an endorser of his own prejudices. He did not want the Ninevites to repent, yet they repented. He was very indignant and fell into a rage (Jon 4:4). He wanted God to destroy them for their sins but God did not, for he is the loving Father of all. Do we get angry with God when bad people enjoy material prosperity? Do we get angry with God when we hear of someone who lived a sinful life all through, but converted at deathbed by true contrition and confession? If we do, we put our own whims and fancies before the concerns of our heavenly Father. Good parents love their children, not because of their achievements, but simply because they are their children. God loves all his creatures because they are his children and let us leave him alone.

THURSDAY – WEEK 27 / YEAR 1

DOES GOD FAVOUR THE BAD?

Readings: Mal 3:13-20; Lk 11:5-13

Life is often ambiguous and complex. We try to live morally, to make responsible choices and to please God in everything. And yet, we don't seem to prosper. Whereas, those who live immorally and don't care about pleasing God, seem to flourish. So we ask, "What is the use of trying to be good, when God seems to favour the bad?" A small Jewish community raised a similar question, after their return from Babylon. They were honest and God-fearing people, but suffered poverty of many kinds, while many other dishonest people were enjoying success. So they came to the desperate conclusion that "it is useless to serve God" (Mal 3:14). But God counselled them to keep praying for deliverance and be patient until he would put down injustice. Jesus promised: "Ask, and it will be given you" (Lk 11:9). When we find ourselves in a situation similar to that of the Jews, we need to be patient praying and hope God would act in our favour in his own time. The following verse was found on the wall of a German concentration camp. It had to have been written by a person with a hope that saw more than a pessimistic present: "I believe in the sun, even though it is not shining; I believe in love, even when I feel it not; I believe in God, even when he is silent."

FRIDAY – WEEK 27 / YEAR 1

THIS IS SPIRITUAL WAR

Readings: Joel 1:13-15; 2:1-2; Lk 11:15-26

St Thomas Aquinas once came to Rome to pay his respects to the Pope. The Pope proudly showed all the wonders of the papal palace, and took him to his treasury and showed him chests of silver and gold received from every part of the world. With a smile on his face, he said, "You see, Thomas, we can't say with Peter, 'Silver and gold have I none.'" Looking the Pope in the eyes, Thomas Aquinas fearlessly replied, "No, but neither can we say, 'In the name of Jesus, rise up and walk!'" What Thomas implied was that when material riches had come in, the spiritual riches had gone. What the Church needs, before everything else, is the spiritual power to wage the spiritual war against evil that has gained cosmic proportion. The prophet Joel already foresaw such a global war between good and evil. Seeing a locust plague as a symbol of a coming clash between good and evil, he exclaimed, "A day of darkness and gloom!" (Joel 2:2). As today's Gospel reports, the cosmic dimension of that battle erupted during the ministry of Jesus when he drove out evil spirits from many people (Lk 11:15). In the footsteps of Jesus, his Church is now engaged in a spiritual war against evil; and she needs spiritual power more than anything else, to win this war.

SATURDAY – WEEK 27 / YEAR 1

THE NON-CONDUCTORS OF EVIL

Readings: Joel 4:12-21; Lk 11:27-28

The wickedness of the world is so great that you have to run your legs off, so you don't get them stolen off. The evil seems to be getting the upper hand day by day. The fear of one evil often leads us into a greater evil. But evil can not be the ultimate victor. The good that is inborn in every human being will keep resisting it. Evil often may triumph, but it can never conquer. That is the promise God gave us: "The Lord will be a shelter for his people, a strong hold for the sons of Israel" (Joel 4:16). One day, this promise will come fully true, when evil will be thoroughly destroyed. In the meantime, we must assist the process of winning over evil, already set in motion by the resurrection of Jesus. How are we to assist? It is by hearing the Word of God and keeping it (Lk 11:28). For example, the Word of God has urged us "to love our enemies and do good to those who persecute us." Suppose each of us keep this Word and practice it! The result would be that personal animosity and antagonism will go. We will become non-conductors of evil. The chain of retaliation will stop with us. Doing so, we would open the possibility of greater understanding and peace among all.

MONDAY – WEEK 28 / YEAR 1

SENSATION SEEKERS

Readings: Rom 1:1-7; Lk 11:29-32

Religion is bread for daily nourishment, if it is fed by faith. Religion is a cake useful only for special occasions, if it is being fed by sensationalism. For many people, in Jesus' time, religion was a magnificent spectacle of extra-ordinary happenings just for excitement. Jesus condemned this attitude by saying, "This generation is an evil generation; it seeks a sign" (Lk 11:29). To believe is our chief duty and the fountain from which all other duties flow. The core of Christian religion is our faith in Jesus Christ, proclaimed as "the Son of God in power according to the Spirit of holiness by his resurrection from the dead" (Rom 1:4). Panic is possible even for Christians if the resurrection of Christ is obscured from our faith. The resurrection of Christ, the "sign of Jonah" as the Lord called it, is the evidence of the validity of all his claims. Is my religion a superficial pursuit of sensational experience or one of faith in the risen Christ? A Christian worker was trying to lead a young man to accept the grace of God by faith in Christ. The young man suddenly turned upon him and said, "I will never believe until I have an experience." The Christian worker flashed back, "You will never have an experience, until you believe."

TUESDAY – WEEK 28 / YEAR 1

ANY EXCUSE?

Readings: Rom 1:16-25; Lk 2:1-11

One evening, I stood watching some pure white flowers on a vine encircling the veranda. I had been told that the buds that hung with closed petals all day, every evening near sunset, unfolded and sent out a peculiar fragrance. A feeling of silent awe possessed me, as I saw bud after bud slowly fold back its leaves, until the vine was filled with perfect blossoms. What else but the invisible touch of the hand of the Creator can work out such marvels in nature? "Ever since the creation of the world," says St Paul, "his invisible nature, namely, his eternal power and deity, has been clearly perceived in the things that have been made" (Rom 1:20). Through the perpetuity of rain and snow that make the earth fertile, we know God's concern for our basic necessities. Majestic fountains and verdant valleys reveal God's beauty and charm. A little bee that builds ten thousands cells for honey, reveals his wisdom. He fills the starlit nights since he is the Father of lights. The stormy billows shout that God is mightier than the seas. Something in each flower's face tells about God's love and grace. Yes, the heavens and skies declare God's glory and the earth takes up the chorus. Can there be still any excuse for anyone not to believe in God?

WEDNESDAY – WEEK 28 / YEAR 1

THE DEMONS WITHIN

Readings: Rom 2:1-11; Lk 11:42-46

No person is born without some faults. He is the best who has the fewest! Yet, we are so quick to blame others for their faults. Imagine the pot telling the kettle: "Get away, black face!" It is a pity that we keep on deceiving ourselves in regard to our own faults, until at last, we start looking at them as virtues! Some people find fault in others as if it were a buried treasure. St Paul warns that "in passing judgement upon (another), you condemn yourself, because you, the judge, are doing the very same things" (Rom 1:1). We criticise others for not doing their duties, and at times, for doing more than their duty, while we excuse ourselves for not doing any of our duties. In this, we are like the Pharisees who loaded men with heavy burdens, when they themselves did not touch the burdens, even with one of their fingers (Lk 11:46). It would be much better if, instead of putting others in their place, we put ourselves in their place. All of this calls us to examine ourselves and to discover the demons within us: the demon of pride, the demon of selfishness, the demon of prejudice, the demon of greed and so on. Let us first discover these demons, and begin to battle with them.

THURSDAY – WEEK 28 / YEAR 1

COMMITTED FAITH

Readings: Rom 3:21-30; Lk 11:47-54

A couple came to me for counselling. "I believe that my wife is a wonderful person; she loves me" said he. "But, father, his faith in me goes no further. He has come to ignore me lately. He spends less and less time with me. He has become more absorbed in another woman. So his faith is meaningless" she said. "But I do believe in your love." "But your faith is hollow." She was right. True faith translates itself into living commitment. St Paul says that we become righteous before God "through faith in Jesus Christ" (Rom 3:22). What he means by faith is our love and trust in Christ that tries to put his teachings into practice. Of course, such a committed faith will at times bring us persecutions, as it happened to many prophets. Jesus reminded the Jews: "You build the tombs of the prophets, whom your fathers killed" (Lk 11:47). But, our sufferings for the sake of faith will not go in vain. There is a reward of God's peace. This peace of God is Shalom, the well being of mind, heart and body. It can even exist in the midst of a war-torn community, and in the midst of unresolved problems. It is no easy peace, but it is everlasting for it comes from God.

FRIDAY – WEEK 28 / YEAR 1

"FEAR NOT"

Readings: Rom 4:1-8; Lk 12:1-7

Recently, a family travelling together on a vacation was involved in a serious automobile accident. While the husband and the two sons were not injured, the wife was severely hurt. Gail was rushed to the hospital, where for several days her life hung, by a thread. Gail survived the accident. But when later she recalled those days, she said that, as she lay in the intensive care unit, she could think only of her boys, her husband Sam and her God. As her condition worsened and her alertness dimmed in and out, she could think only of Sam and her God. Then as her energy dropped even more, in her weakest moment, all she could think of was God alone. Gail's experience brings to our minds the words of Christ about the concern of our heavenly Father for our welfare: "Even the hairs of your head are all numbered. Fear not" (Lk 12:7). Gail also reflects Abraham's absolute trust in God (Rom 4:3), with which he went ahead to sacrifice his only son Isaac as demanded by God. How often we have looked upon God as our last resource? Is it not our experience that when we went to him because we had nowhere else to go, the storms of life had actually driven us not upon the rocks but into the desired heaven?

SATURDAY – WEEK 28 / YEAR 1

THIS IS UNPARDONABLE

Readings: Rom 4:13, 16-18; Lk 12:9-12

However great our particular sin may be, we must not make it greater by imagining that Jesus can not forgive this one. "The blood of Jesus cleanses us from all sins" (1 Jn 1:7). Hence, to think that he is unable to forgive some sins is the cruellest of all sins. Why then, Jesus says, "he who blasphemes against the Holy Spirit will not be forgiven?"

(Lk12:10). Because those who blaspheme against the Holy Spirit are those who ascribe the Holy Spirit's activity to demonic agency. But, what if one were to repent of blasphemy against the Holy Spirit? Is there no forgiveness for the person who repents of this sin? The answer seems to be that the nature of this sin is such that one does not repent of it, because those who commit it and persist in it, do not know that they are sinning. They are like the Pharisees who knew in their hearts that Jesus was driving out devils by a divine power, but still maintained that he was doing it by the power of the devil. Their eyes were so tightly closed to the light that for them light had become darkness and good had become evil. The light is there for those who will accept it, but if some refuse the light, where else can they hope to receive illumination?

MONDAY – WEEK 29 / YEAR 1

GROWING RICH

Readings: Rom 4:20-25; Lk 12:13-21

Riches enlarge, rather than satisfy appetites. Accumulation of material wealth leaves us with perpetual craving. So Jesus warns us to be on guard against "covetousness, for a man's life does not consist in the abundance of his possessions" (Lk 12:15). We need to note that 'possession' does not mean only wealth. It could be other things as well. For example, friendship could become a possession and if we cling to our friends, we may lose them; but if we are not possessive in our relationships, we can make many more friends. Growing rich either with wealth, friends, fame or success can become an obstacle to growing rich in the sight of God. Therefore, we are called to develop those inner resources, those spiritual strengths, which enable us to appreciate God's love for us and to trust in God's care, as did Abraham. "No distrust made him waver concerning the promise of God" (Rom 4:20). We need therefore to attend to our spiritual growth. This attention can not be marginal. That is, it can not be confined to performance of some religious rituals. Rather, it has to do with the very core of our existence; it has to be transformative; it has to permeate every facet of our existence, including the mundane aspects of our lives.

TUESDAY – WEEK 29 / YEAR 1

ETERNAL VIGILANCE

Readings: Rom 5:12-15, 17-21; Lk 12:35-38

When a cupboard is full to overflowing and the doors are opened up, that which is within comes out tumbling and nothing can stop it. When floodgates are opened, the water rushes forth with tremendous power carrying all before it. So with the spiritual power, which is God's grace won for us by Jesus Christ's death and resurrection. Once this grace is received and released, nothing can stop the flow. It pours forth sweeping aside all negativity and disharmony, bringing with it peace, love and understanding. Is this grace available for us here and now? Yes. "If many died by one man's trespass, much more have the grace of God, in the grace of that one man Jesus Christ abounded for many" (Rom 5:15). That is, if sin is pervasive throughout the world, so the grace of Christ has pervaded it as well. But we must be watchful if we want this grace to enter into our lives. "Blessed are those servants whom the master finds awake when he comes." (Lk 12:37). Normally, we may expect the Lord to come with his grace while we are doing some spirituals. But the Lord can come at other unexpected times as well. Expect the Lord's visit today at any moment! Eternal peace can not ever be taken for granted. Its price is eternal vigilance.

WEDNESDAY – WEEK 29 / YEAR 1

REPLANTING

Readings: Rom 6:12-18; Lk 12:39-48

There is just so much that needs to be done: extra demands at home and at work; more time with the family; keeping up with our health exercise program; planning the next holiday; time out for friends; involvement in our children's school activities; completing that new management course. In these and many other ways, the busy round of life draws us into a myriad of activities, all-important but all demanding more of our time and energy. So we try to do more while our energies ebb away, and we become like uprooted trees. If we find ourselves in this condition, we need to plant ourselves again in a spiritually nourishing soil. This calls for change in our priorities and renewing of our inner strength through spiritual means. Time given to inner renewal is never wasted. It serves us at least in two ways. One is that it will help us "to yield ourselves to God as men who have been brought from death to life" (Rom 6:13). Second is that spiritual renewal will keep us always on alert to receive the grace of the Lord who comes "at an hour you do not expect" (Lk 12:40). Thus, constant attention to spiritual health is needed, not only because old tendencies tend to surface, but also because special moments of grace can come unexpectedly.

THURSDAY – WEEK 29 / YEAR 1

A WAR WITHIN

Readings: Rom 6:19-23; Lk 12:49-53

It strikes me that conflict is the principal feature of Christian life, this side of heaven. Jesus rightly declared, "I have come to bring division" (Lk 12:51). Obviously, what he meant was that following him might create conflict between us and those whom we love. But he must have thought also of the inner conflict the follower of Christ would face, namely, the tension between the freedom to hate and to love, between the freedom to obey God's will and to rebel, the freedom to do evil and to do good and so on. However, when we feel a war within us, it is a comfort to remember that it is an interesting phase of Christian experience. These inward conflicts show that we are spiritually alive. There is some life in the soul that hates evil even though it can not avoid evil all the time. But we have to take care not to loose the battle. We have to either overcome the evil or be overcome by it. Just recall the times you yielded to evil. "What return did you get from the things of which you are now ashamed?" (Rom 6:21). We can not let evil alone and evil will not let us alone. We must fight, and in the battle we must either conquer or be conquered. If you are to have peace with good, there must be war with evil.

INNER CONFLICT

Readings: Rom 7:18-25; Lk 12:54-59

War is an enormous crime. All battles are nothing but murder on a large scale. And yet there is so much of it in the world. In olden times, when there was a war, it was a human to human confrontation. Nowadays, it is much more terrifying, because a man in an office can push a button and kill millions of people and never see the human tragedy he has created. But all want to live in a peaceful world. How is it possible? If we learn "to interpret the present time" (Lk 12:56), as our Lord asks us to, we will realise that the conflict in the world has its origin in the conflict that goes on in every human heart. As St Paul puts it, "I do not do what I want, but I do the very thing I hate" (Rom 7:15). This internal conflict may take many forms. It can show itself through greed, hatred and thirst for power. Once the individuals are able to resolve this inner conflict and enjoy inner peace, global peace will be the natural result. Who will help us to resolve our inner conflicts and give us inner peace? If you ask a doctor, you might get a sleeping pill, which will give you some rest, not peace. If you go to a supermarket asking for peace, people will laugh at you. But there is one who can give us this peace, Jesus Christ.

TRYING HIS PATIENCE?

Readings: Rom 8:1-11; Lk 13:1-9

Even though there is no final answer to the mystery of evil prospering in the world, the overriding consideration that more than offsets everything else is God's unchanging love, care and blessings. Good when he forgives, supremely good. Even crosses from his hands are blessings in disguise. Even his judgements are always founded on his goodness. Just think only of the spiritual riches we Christians enjoy from the hands of God: Baptism, the Scriptures, Sacraments, especially the Eucharist and so on. Yet, for all the blessings we are receiving, there is much to be desired in our manner of response to God's infinite goodness. How can we go on enjoying the blessings of God, without showing adequate response in bearing enough spiritual fruits in our lives? God is patient, hoping we will repent and reform. He is like the owner of a fig tree which was not bearing fruit but was allowed to stand that it might bear fruit next year (Lk 13:9). There is no greater proof of the omnipotence of God, than his long patient suffering for our conversion, for it shows the greatest possible power of God to be able to control his anger which naturally must boil, and restrain a fury which otherwise must burn. But we must not try God's patience.

MONDAY – WEEK 30 / YEAR 1

"NOBILITY'S TRUE BADGE"

Readings: Rom 8:12-17; Lk 13:10-17

Compassion is mercy, and "sweet mercy is nobility's true badge", wrote Shakespeare. Compassion is a human quality. The compassion we see in the kind hearted is God's compassion, which he has given to us to protect the helpless. To a Christian, compassion is not only a human quality, but also one of the fruits of the Holy Spirit. Through the Spirit, we have received a new principal of life that not only places us in a new relationship with God, so that we can cry out to him "Abba, Father" (Rom 8:15), but also gives us new power to be merciful to others. It is this compassion that moved Jesus to heal a woman who "was bent over and could not fully straighten herself" for eighteen years. (Lk 13:11). But the Pharisees blamed Jesus because he healed her on a Sabbath. They had a heart for their donkey, but not for a human being. Are we insensitive to the suffering of others? There are people who lavish unstilted love and affection on their pet dogs and cats, but will not spare a kindly deed for a suffering human being. Many love animals because they can not love human beings. People are also animals, but animals are not people. Our dogs will love and admire the meanest of us, and feed our colossal vanity with their uncritical homage.

THERE IS SPRING

Readings: Rom 8:18-25; Lk 13:18-21

We try to accomplish many worthwhile things in our lives, striving to help others and to make this world a better place to live in. But discouragement begins to sap our energies. It seems that we often get to a point where we just don't care any longer, and our energy level falls to zero. At such moments, we need to remember with St Paul that a better future for ourselves and for the entire creation, is surely coming. Till then, "not only the creation, but we ourselves who have the first fruits of the Spirit" cannot but "groan inwardly" (Rom 8:22-23). When Jesus handed over his Spirit to the Church, it was not simply to save our souls but to set in motion the transformation of creation. This means, that the Spirit is working in every human being, especially in the baptised. It gives us the hope that the Kingdom of God, which began like "a grain of mustard seed" (Lk 13:19), will one day spread throughout the world, influencing every human being as "the leaven" (v.21), that influences dough. Therefore, we are advised to be patient. Winter is always a difficult season to pass through. But, as our hope lies in the magnificent flowers that will bloom in spring, so we hope for God to end the groanings of humanity in his own time.

THE NARROW DOOR

Readings: Rom 8:26-30; Lk 13:22-30

We are often urged to pray always. Is it possible? Yes, if prayer is rightly understood. Prayer is union of the soul with God. This means that even when our human faculties are engaged in other activities, we can pray, if we take effort to keep our soul united with God. This union is possible aided by the Holy Spirit. The Holy Spirit enables us not only to pray always, but also he turns all our groanings and pains into prayer: "He himself intercedes for us with sighs too deep for words" (Rom 8:26). The Holy Spirit is the agent of still something more. He enables us to enter into eternal life through the "narrow door" (Lk 13:24). But we have to cooperate with him as he takes us through it. How? Once I saw this cartoon: Charlie Brown stands inside his house staring at the door. He wants to get outside to ski, but he is too bundled up to get through the door. He shouts angrily, "Well, how am I going to get through the door?' Charlie's dilemma may be ours. If we are too wrapped up with the things of this world, how can we enter through the narrow door to heaven? Half of the confusion in our lives comes from our not knowing the difference between what we want and what we actually need.

THURSDAY – WEEK 30 / YEAR 1

GOD IS FOR US

Readings: Rom 8:31-39; Lk 13:31-35

As we move through life, we have high expectations such as: we will be successful in careers; have strong and satisfying marriage; raise good and responsible children; enjoy deep and abiding friendships and so on. Instead, though, our career may falter, marriage may be disappointing, children frustrating, friendships breakdown. When these hurts emerge, let us remember that God, who is all love, is with us. "If God is for us, who is against us?" (Rom 8:31). We trust that God can take our losses, our failures, our disappointments, our imperfections, and even our sins, and use them as means for our new beginning. It was this trust in God, that gave strength to Jesus to move on to Jerusalem to be killed, ignoring the advice of some good-willed Pharisees, who warned, "Get away from here, for Herod wants to kill you" (Lk 13:31). It should be so with us. Of course, we are free to surrender ourselves into the loving care of God. That could be our problem. Often, we allow our freedom to be shackled by our own perversity, selfishness, and pride, with the result that we side-step God's open arms. We are old enough to know that we can become our own worst enemies. Indeed, human freedom is awesome, as it is wonderful.

FRIDAY – WEEK 30 / YEAR1

WHETHER WE LIKE IT OR NOT

Readings: Rom 9:1-5; Lk 14:1-6

I asked a missionary if he liked his work in Africa. He replied, "Do I like this work? No. I do not like dirt. I have reasonably refined sensibilities. I do not like crawling into the huts through goat refuse. I do not like associating with ignorant, filthy, brutish people. But is a man to do nothing for Christ because he does not like? No. We have a Gospel to preach and we go, whether we like it or not." Jesus did not like the Pharisees, for they were hounding him all the time. But he did not write them off. So when they invited him for a meal, he went (Lk 14:1), seeing in the invitation a golden opportunity to evangelise them right in their homes. St Paul did not like his own kinsmen, the Jews, for they did not choose to follow Jesus as he did. Yet, he had not only deep affection for them, but a continued sense of unity with them (Rom 9:3). Like Jesus, we too must not write off our opponents, and give up proclaiming the Gospel even in the face of cold indifference. Like St Paul, we too must show respect to a relative or close friend who may not practice the faith. It is a painful experience to see someone we love, not enjoying the benefits of the spiritual values that we hold dear. But we can not give up on them.

SATURDAY – WEEK 30 / YEAR 1

THE "OTHER"

Readings: Rom 11:1-2, 11-12, 25-29; Lk 14:1, 7-11

A desert father had said that judging others is a heavy burden, while being judged by others, is a light one. And yet, how often we judge others harshly who are different from us in colour, religion, sexual orientation or lifestyle? Why is it that strangers and people different from us stir up in us fear, discomfort, suspicion and hostility? I suppose it is because they make us loose our sense of security just by being 'other'. Also because we don't realise that, as God loves us unconditionally, so he loves other people as well. For example, many Jewish people whom God had chosen as his own, refused to accept the Good News preached by his Son Jesus. But God did not abandon them and St Paul affirms: "I ask, then, has God rejected his people? By no means" (Rom 11:1). In fact, God does not abandon anyone of sincere faith, no matter what his or her religion is. What is our own attitude towards people of other creed? Is it one of spiritual pride? If so, it is self-destructive. Jesus warns of exalting oneself (Lk 14:11). There is no place in the Kingdom for self-exaltation, spiritual or otherwise. Our Christian attitude towards other religious traditions should not be measured in terms of superiority but of service.

MONDAY – WEEK 31 / YEAR 1

THE ANONYMOUS GIVER

Readings: Rom 11:29-36; Lk 14:12-14

A businessman came and expressed his gratitude to the principal of a Catholic school, for all that it had done to his sons, and added: "I would like to establish an annual scholarship for some needy students." The principal was delighted and said, "Would you give us the honour of letting the scholarship bear your name?" He replied, "Give the scholarship any name you wish, but not mine. I would like the source of it to remain anonymous." His was a giving in the true Christian spirit, which does not expect any reward in this life, but in the next. Jesus said, "When you give a feast, invite the poor, the maimed, the lame and the blind" (Lk 14:13). What he meant was that, though we may not receive anything in return from these unfortunate ones, we will receive a reward from God, for "from him and through him and to him are all things" (Rom 11:36).When it comes to inviting the poor, some people run out of invitation cards. People normally invite for parties only friends and loved ones; In doing so, they already have a reward: the pleasure the company of the loved ones give and the prospect of reciprocal invitation. But the truth is that the more selfless our service to others is, the more effective a vehicle it will be for heavenly rewards.

ENDLESS POSSIBILITIES

Readings: Rom 12:5-15; Lk 14:15-24

The Church is Christ's body. My physical body is made up of millions and millions of cells, vivified by one soul, governed by a visible head, and presided over by an invisible mind; So too, all of us who have in any way become incorporated into Christ, are the cells in his mystical body. We are vivified by one soul, the Holy Spirit; we are presided over by the invisible head, Christ; and a visible head, the Pope, governs us. This Church is God's Kingdom on earth, though not yet perfect. We all have gifts. We are invited to use them to build up the body of Christ into a perfect Church. We must not refuse this invitation as those in our Lord's parable of the wedding banquet did, making some excuses (Lk 14:18). One may be able to offer warmth, while others contribute discipline; One may provide sensitivity, while others provide direction; Some are good managers; Others are creative; Some can provide stability, others openness and flexibility. Some dream, others lead; Some provide presence; Others possess a practical wisdom. Our gifts "differ according to the grace given to us" (Rom 12:6); but the possibilities are endless.

COUNTING THE COST

Readings: Rom 13:8-10; Lk 14:25-33

Who has not sung the mystery of love? Poets, philosophers, romantics? All have. Psychology, for example, defines it in terms of caring relationship and mutuality. St Paul counsels: "Owe no one anything except to love one another" (Rom 13:8). Jesus gave us his definition of love which was radical. He said, "Love one another as I have loved you." He calls for the sacrifice of one's own life for the sake of another. Therefore, loving is costly. Once, a cloudburst stranded a newlywed couple on a country road. They walked to a nearby farmhouse, where an elderly couple invited them in and gave them a room for the night. Next morning, the newlyweds got up early and prepared to leave quietly without disturbing the old couple. When they reached the living room, they found the old couple asleep in chairs. Their elderly hosts had given the newlyweds their only bedroom. That was the cost of loving. So, before choosing to follow Christ, we must count the cost of discipleship, like a man "desiring to build, first sits down and counts the cost" (Lk 14:28). Love will always have a fragile character. It can not be regulated or sustained by structures, rules, and committees. It can be only sustained by self-sacrifice.

THURSDAY – WEEK 31 / YEAR 1

INFINITE VARIETY

Readings: Rom 14:7-12; Lk 15:1-10

Break off an elm bough, three feet long, in full beat, and lay it on the table before you and try to draw it leaf for leaf. It is ten to one if, in the whole bough, you find one leaf exactly like another. Perhaps you will not even have one complete. Every leaf will be oblique or foreshortened or curled or crossed by another. Though the whole bough will look graceful and symmetrical, you will scarcely be able to tell how or why there is not one line of it like another. If such an infinite variety prevails in creation, we must also expect such variety among human beings. One person is not like another. Therefore, if we find someone different from us in belief, morals, or behaviour, we should not judge them wrong or right, bad or good. "Why do you pass judgement on your brother?" (Rom 14:10) asks St Paul. Even if a person is found behaving badly, we must never condemn that person as a lost case. To God, every individual, good or bad, is infinitely more precious than a "lost sheep" (Lk 15:4) to a shepherd, or a "lost coin" (v.8) to a housewife. God remains close even when a person falls. Even when a person is contemplating suicide, the Spirit of God within him calls him back from the brink.

FRIDAY – WEEK 31 / YEAR 1

THE ASTUTE CHRISTIAN

Readings: Rom 15:14-21; Lk 16:1-8

A friend of mine in my parish alighted from his car to open his garage. A stranger came to him asking him for direction to a certain locality. The information was quickly given, but before the stranger got away, my friend asked, "Brother, we may never meet again, and I should like to ask you: Have you a personal interest in the Lord Jesus Christ?" "No," replied the stranger; "but I would like to have!" Then, in that semi-darkness, a brief conversation followed; Jesus Christ was introduced to the stranger; and he accepted Jesus as his Saviour. The following year I baptised him. In today's parable of the steward, he is praised (Lk 16:8), not for his dishonesty, but for the initiative he took in exploiting the opportunities that lay before him, to secure a safe financial future. My friend, like the steward, but at a different level, was enterprising in exploiting the spiritual opportunity that came his way, to lead a stranger to Christ. My friend is a lay Christian. As Pope Paul VI said, "Lay people, whose particular vocation places them in the midst of the world, and who are in charge of the most varied temporal tasks, must for this very reason, exercise a very special form of evangelizaton."

SATURDAY – WEEK 31 / YEAR 1

KEEP LOVE FLOWING

Readings: Rom 16:3-9, 16, 22-27; Lk 16:9-15

In his book, *Man in Search of Himself*, the psychologist Rollo May says: "Dr Walton Cannon has shown in his study of 'Voodoo death', that primitive people might have been literally killed by being psychologically isolated from the community. There have been observed cases of natives who, socially ostracised and treated by their tribes as though they did not exist, have actually withered and died." Do we love with affection all the members of our Christian community or do we exclude some from our love? We can not do that. See how St Paul shows his love for his co-workers in the ministry, by calling each one by his or her name! (Rom 16:3). Money is a very useful thing, and yet Jesus asks us to use it wisely (Lk 16:9) for it is a tainted thing. We all may not have money, but all have something much more precious than money, namely, love. The more love you give to others in your community, the more love you draw to yourself. It is the law of love. Never be discouraged, if love is not returned to you immediately. Simply know, that sooner or later, it will be; and so keep love flowing; Love never takes "No" for an answer. Love is never defeated. Love is not like a snail. It never withdraws when it is rebuffed.

MONDAY – WEEK 32 / YEAR 1

TEMPTING CHRISTIANS

Readings: Wis 1:1-7; Lk 17:1-6

In the modern environment, the role of God is less to do with creating and sustaining all things, than providing comfort for people in need. If people can fix up their own comfort from somewhere else, then they don't seem to need God at all. This goes just opposite to what Wisdom urges: "Seek the Lord with sincerity of heart" (Wis 1:1). If we Christians who profess belief in God behave as though there is no God, we too add to the godless atmosphere of this world. In that respect, we scandalise others and Jesus cautions us against it: "Temptations to sin are sure to come; but woe to him by whom they come" (Lk 17:1). Temptation in this context has to be understood as scandal. One such scandal is that we Christians talk much, but no action. This is dishonesty, which adds to the godless atmosphere of our society, for God is Truth. How hard some non-Christians find the contrast between our mega spirituality of Sunday worship, and the pettiness of our Monday routine! Another scandal is our 'busyness'. The Church diary is crammed with meetings and the Christians are so swamped with commitments, that they have no time for prayer or for each other. So, where is love of God and neighbour?

PRECIOUS TEARS

Readings: Wis 2:23-3:9; Lk 17:7-10

During his four-day visit to Peru in 1985, Pope John Paul II made a special effort to visit the economically and socially deprived. During one such visit, he was moved deeply by a spokesperson for the poor who told him, "We are hungry; we live in misery; we are sick and out of work; our women give birth in tuberculosis; our infants die because of malnutrition; they grow weak and without a future. But despite this, we believe in the God of life. We have walked with the Church and in the Church, and it has helped us to live in dignity as sons and daughters of God and brothers and sisters of Christ." Indeed, God "like gold in the furnace tried them" (Wis 3:6). Today the whole effort of many people is to push away pain, establish a distance to it and place oneself outside of its zone. The pleasure principle alone matters. And yet, tears are not without value, provided one sees a purpose in their shedding. As the morning rose is the sweetest when embalmed with dew, so love is loveliest when embalmed in tears. Many a person sees God through tears more often than in sunlight. But it does not mean that those of us who are having a good time can remain unmoved by the tears of others.

GRATEFUL PEOPLE

Readings: Wis 6:1-11; Lk 17:11-19

God is pleased with gratitude, but he gets so little of it. He often has to complain, "Were not ten cleansed? Where are the nine?" (Lk 17:17) Helen Keller said, "So much has been given to me, that I have no time to ponder over that which has been denied." Do we thank God for so many of his daily gifts? "He himself made both small and great, and he takes thought for all alike" (Wis 6:7). Do we thank him enough for the flowers that bloom about our feet, for the tender grass so fresh and sweet, for the song of bird and hum of bee and for all things we hear and see? It seems that precisely because we receive God's blessings so often and so regularly, we forget to thank him. Do we sincerely say, "Thank you" to people from whom we receive so many kindnesses? People are often the channels of God's gifts. Feeling grateful is spiritually and emotionally healthy. It is the mark of a mature person. Gratitude is the opposite of being self-centred, indifferent and arrogant. Expressing gratitude to God and to others, is a way of widening our love and spreading our joy. One remarkable mark of grateful people is that they accept people just the way they are, for they spend their day counting up blessings not tallying up burdens.

THURSDAY – WEEK 32 / YEAR 1

ALL WILL BE WELL

Readings: Wis 7:22- 8:1; Lk 17:20-25

Long ago, I came to the conclusion that all life is six to five against, for there is so much of suffering. Communities as well as individuals suffer. All over the world, there are large groups of people who are persecuted, mistreated, abused and made victims of horrendous crimes. There are suffering families, suffering circles of friends, suffering religious communities, suffering ethnic groups and suffering nations. In these sufferings, Christians are called to recognise the pangs of the birth of God's new reign over evil, which is sure to arrive. Our sufferings are in imitation of Christ who had to suffer grievously and be rejected by his generation, before his resurrection (Lk 17:25). As we suffer in our own lives, and as we respond to the cries of the sufferings of others in the world, by working for peace and justice, we are not left alone. God is working with us. The breath of the power of God penetrates through all creation, "reaches mightily from one end of the earth to the other, and orders all things well" (Wis 8:1). When the day of the final reign of God arrives, the pervasive and invisible presence of the power of God, working silently in every creation, will become obvious to all, as clear as lightning on a stormy night.

FRIDAY – WEEK 32 / YEAR 1

LOOKING BEYOND

Readings: Wis 13:1-9; Lk 17:26-37

We are struck with awe at what computers can do. But remember that a human mind had to invent the computer and a human mind had to program it. Awe and wonder are owed to people behind the computers not to computers themselves. The same is true of all that is in creation. All the beauty about us in the rich ambience of nature, and the radiant vitality, which shines forth from million human faces, makes us look beyond the creatures to adore the Creator of them all. Wisdom reminds us that "from the greatness and beauty of created things comes a corresponding perception of their Creator" (Wis 13:5). His Son Jesus has revealed that this Creator is our Father, who has prepared for us a Kingdom that will never end. But our entry into that Kingdom will be preceded by the Last Judgement at the second coming of Jesus Christ, the day "when the son of Man is revealed" (Lk 17:30). That day will come suddenly. This suddenness of his coming demands that we must be always ready, living a life ever pleasing to God. This Last Judgement should not make us fearful. We should not scrupulously imprison ourselves by notions of harsh Judgement, for God's judgement will be one of mercy, not of condemnation.

SATURDAY – WEEK 32 / YEAR 1

PLEAD!

Readings: Wis 18:14-16, 19:6-9; Lk 18:1-8

If there be anything I know, anything I am quite assured beyond all doubt, it is that praying breath is never spent in vain. Importunate prayer is a pleading prayer and does not reckon you have prayed unless you have pleaded, for pleading is the very marrow of prayer. If you are sure it is a right thing you are praying for, plead with cries and tears, and spread out your case. Order your arguments. Back your pleas with reasons. Urge the Father in the name of his Son Jesus Christ and he will listen. That is the implied promise Jesus gives in his questions, at the end of the parable of the importunate widow: "And will not God vindicate his elect, who cry to him day and night? Will he delay long over them?" (Lk 18:7). Some mercies are not given to us except in answer to importunate prayer. There are blessings which, like fruit, drop into your hand the moment you touch the bough. But there are others, which require you to shake the tree again and again, until you make it rock with the vehemence of your exercise, for only then will the fruit fall down. By making us repeat our petitions, the Father wants us to achieve a more dearly won victory. To persevere, trusting in the hopes we have in the Father, is courage in a Christian; only the coward despairs.

MONDAY – WEEK 33 / YEAR 1

HOMELY PERSECUTIONS

Readings: Macc 1:10-15, 41-43, 54-57, 62-64; Lk 18:35-43

Persecution was not new to the Jews. They had experienced it in Egypt and later in Babylon. And today's first reading records the beginning of another persecution by King Antiochus who sentenced to death any Jew practising publicly his or her religion (1 Mac 1:57). We can say that often certain blindness comes over those in power; but unlike the blind man in the Gospel who wanted to see (Lk 18:41), they seem to have no such wish. But the truth is that we ourselves run the danger of being spiritually blind to the fact that we may be persecuting others. I am thinking of the persecutions that may be going on in some families. When some child is rejected subtly, nagged and criticised excessively, punished unrealistically, disciplined inconsistently, humiliated persistently by elders, that child is undergoing psychological persecution. When one of the spouses is found to be consistently unfaithful to the partner, that is marital persecution. Infidelity has been called the most universally accepted justification for divorce. Can we open our spiritual eyes to see whom else we are persecuting? We run carelessly into the precipice, after we have put something before us to prevent us seeing it.

STANDING FIRM

Readings: 2 Macc 6:18-31; Lk 19:1-10

Whoever excels in what we prize, appears a hero in our eyes. If we prize human values, we do not admire the one who is able to tear the scalp off an elephant, but is insensitive to others. If we prize religious values, then we admire persons like Mattathias and Zachaeus of today's readings. Why? Mattathias was an old man, just the kind of person the persecutors did not fear, and actually looked upon in contempt. But the old man showed a deep religious strength, when he preferred to die rather than make a pretence of eating the forbidden meat (2 Macc 6:22). Zachaeus was also a person looked upon with contempt, not only because he was a hated tax collector but also because he was small in stature. And yet, after his encounter with Jesus, he showed spiritual strength to change what was wrong in his life (Lk 19:8). Can anyone admire us for our strong Christian convictions? We may come across people who will pour cold water on our religious enthusiasm, laugh at our spiritual goals, ridicule our Christian hopes, and negate our destiny which we aspire after. One of the highest human responsibilities is also the easiest. It is that of encouraging others; sadly though, the world is full of discouragers! But, if we are spiritually strong, we will stand firm.

SERVING OUR PARISH

Readings: 2 Macc 7:1, 20-31; Lk 19:11-28

Our society encourages individualism. We are constantly made to believe that whatever we think, say or do, is our personal accomplishment. This is not true. For example, whatever we know about God, about Jesus, about our faith, is not our invention. It is the knowledge that has come to us through the people of Israel, the Evangelists, the Church, her traditions and her saints. Therefore our faith is a gift from the People of God, the community of believers. This means that we are indebted to this community and have a duty to love it and help it to flourish. See how the mother of Maccabees "encouraged each of her sons in the language of their fathers" (2 Macc 7:21) not to betray the traditions of their community, but die for its sake. That is the measure of love she inspired in her children for their community. For us, here and now, our faith-community is our Parish. How generous are we in our love and service for our Parish? Our personal talents and resources may be small, but still, the Lord wants us to put them at the service of our community. The man in the parable who did not put into use the one pound (Lk 19:20) reasoned that he had so little money that he could excuse himself from doing any work. Are we like him? Remember that little drops of water make the mighty ocean.

THURSDAY – WEEK 33 / YEAR 1

"HE WEPT"

Readings: Macc 2:15-29; Lk 19:41-44

Shakespeare has Julius Caesar say this: "There is a tide in the affairs of men which, taken at the flood, leads on to fortune; omitted, all the voyage of their life is bound in shallows and in miseries." It reminds us about the tragedy of missed opportunities. The city of Jerusalem missed its opportunity when Jesus was around and failed to learn from him to live in peace. So, Jesus "wept over Jerusalem" (Lk 19:41). Even today Jerusalem remains a place of dispute between Muslims, Christians and Jews. The city of Jerusalem is symptomatic of many cities around the world today. The divisions are widespread and apparent: between black and white, rich and poor, the honest and the criminals, the religious and the secular, and so on. Are we missing the countless opportunities that come on our way to bring peace in our families, neighbourhoods, cities, and into the world? Of course, peace starts with each of us. When we have inner peace, we can be at peace with those around us. When our community is in a state of peace, it can share that peace with neighbouring communities. When we feel love and kindness towards others, it not only makes them feel loved and cared for, but also it helps us to develop inner happiness and peace.

FRIDAY – WEEK 33 / YEAR 1

CLEANSING THE CHURCH

Readings: Macc 4:36-37, 52-59; Lk 19:45-48

To the people of Israel, the temple was where God had his dwelling in the form of shekinda. Hence they were horrified by its desecration by the pagan king. Its rededication was a most holy and joyful event (1 Macc 4:54), which is still commemorated as the feast of Hannuka, the festival of light. Some generations after the Maccabees, worthy priests no longer served the temple, but men who used this official position to line up their pockets. When Jesus drove out the money-changers from the temple (Lk 19:45), he risked the rage of the corrupt religious establishment. But he was not afraid. He had to challenge the temple corruption. Today, the modern temple is for us our Parish church; it too may run the risk of being overrun by a new breed of money changers, both priests and laity, who seem to have lost the sense of what makes a Parish church a temple where God dwells. In some Parishes, much time and energy are spent on raising funds, putting up buildings, improving the existing facilities, as though a church is an institution made by brick and mortar. These may be needed actions, but can't be undertaken to the neglect of building up the Body of Christ on the Word of God and the Bread of Life.

SATURDAY – WEEK 33 / YEAR 1

THE PROMISE OF RESURRECTION

Readings: Macc 6:1-13; Lk 20:27-40

Although death comes to us all, we rejoice in the promise of resurrection to eternal life. At death, for God's faithful people, life is changed not taken away. Since God "is not God of the dead, but God of the living, for all live to him" (Lk 20:38), we are children of the resurrection. Just as a person casts off worn-out garments and puts on the new, even so, at death, our embodied souls will cast off our worn-out bodies and take on the new. Hence the resurrection is the beginning of a new life out of death. If eternal life is our destiny, how can one spend all of one's time enjoying this life without a thought for the future life? No person would find it difficult to die who died every day a bit to evil, such as selfishness, pride, and greed, the chief sources of evil. If we don't heed this warning, we will be frightened of our death as King Aniochus was. After having lived an evil life, he recalled in his deathbed all the evil he had done in Jerusalem and died lamenting, "I am perishing of deep grief in a strange land" (1 Macc 6:13). May we then daily examine our conscience to see whether we are living as God's faithful people. May we be ready now to bear any affliction, rather than be burdened with evil conscience.

MONDAY – WEEK 34 / YEAR 1

THE THANKSGIVERS!

Readings: Dan 1:1-6, 8-20; Lk 21:1-9

How generous God is when he gives us his gifts! He gives us not just a flower, but a bouquet; not just a drop of water, but an ocean; not just a grain of sand, but a beach; not just a blade of grass, but a lawn; not just something to eat, but his own body and blood in the Eucharist. How generous are we when we give to God and his people in need? The poor widow in the Gospel, who put two small coins in the temple collection box was praised by Jesus, because "she out of her poverty put in all the living that she had" (Lk 21:4). It has been said that there are three kinds of givers: Grudge givers, Duty givers, and Thanks givers. Grudge givers say, "I have to give." Duty givers say, "I ought to give." Thanks givers say, "I want to give." Who are we, when it comes to giving to God and the needy? Do we give grudgingly, because, if we don't give, we will be criticised and penalised in some way? Do we give dutifully, namely, we would rather not give but feel obliged to do so? Or, do we give thankfully because we want to, in gratitude to God's generous gifts to us? The question is not, "How much is the most I have to give?" The question is, "How much dare I keep and live like a Christian?"

TUESDAY – WEEK 34 / YEAR 1

THE ENDURING KINGDOM

Readings: Dan 2:31-45; Lk 21:5-11

In modern times, kings are almost out, except to describe cigarettes; Royalty is really like little chicken whose head has been cut off; it may run about in a lovely way, but in fact it is dead. It is in the nature of the kingdoms of this world to come and go. Through Daniel, God wanted Nebuchadnezzar to know that his kingdom, however precious to him, would undergo destruction and desolation (Dan 2:43), and it did. The temple of Jerusalem was not only a place of worship for the Jews, but also a symbol of their political and social achievements. But Jesus foretold that it would be destroyed (Lk 21:6), and it was. But there is one Kingdom that endures. That is the Kingdom of God established in Christ. It endures because it is founded on the enduring values of truth, justice, peace and love. Our world today boasts of scientific and technological wonders, the products of human ingenuity and skills we could rightly be proud of. But we need to remember that the mistake of the Jews was that they identified themselves too closely with the temple and not sufficiently with the God of the temple. Our own world can make a similar mistake, if it identifies itself with the achievements of human beings so closely, that it ignores God who is behind the achievements.

WEDNESDAY – WEEK 34 / YEAR 1

THE HANDWRITING ON THE WALL

Readings: Dan 5:1-6, 13-14; 6:17, 23-28; Lk 21:12-19

A small business began to do so badly that bankruptcy was inevitable. One day, the owner reluctantly admitted that "the hand writing is on the wall." King Belshazzar literally saw the handwriting on the wall (Dan 5:5), and it was interpreted by Daniel as God's sign that the king had become spiritually bankrupt. In the Gospel, Jesus also spoke of signs, but of different kind. He said that when his followers would face persecution for his name sake, they should read it as God's sign calling them "to bear testimony" (Lk 21:13). Persecution is a legacy bequeathed by Christ to his followers. Hence it is not natural for Christianity to be popular. As Christians we are 'strangers' in this world. If we were not strangers, the hounds of the world would not bark at us. Apart from the large-scale persecution the Church may encounter, each Christian must be ready to face it in his or her personal life. For example, when we are pressurised all round us to give in to the values of a materialistic society, we are suffering from certain kind of persecution. We are called to bear such persecutions as an opportunity to practice patience, and to deepen our faith that will lead us to the eternal glory, the weight of which makes all persecutions light.

THURSDAY – WEEK 34 / YEAR 1

"ENOUGH, ENOUGH, ENOUGH"

Readings: Dan 6:12-28; Lk 21:20-28

Millions of graves are dug every year, but it is inspiring to think that one generation of Christians will cheat the undertakers, for they will be still living at the second coming of Christ. Listening to many Christian preachers, some time I wonder whether they are all flying on one wing, for they all preach only about the first coming of Christ. The description of terrible signs that Jesus says will accompany the coming of "the Son of Man in a cloud with power and great glory" (Lk 21:27), naturally stirs in us awe and fear. But Jesus did not mean to frighten us. He will come to recreate humanity and will declare: "Enough suffering, enough terror, enough death, enough injustice, enough hatred, enough sickness, enough poverty, enough, enough, enough." Of course, he will come also to judge and dispense to all what each one deserves. Therefore, as we await the Lord's return, we are not so much to watch the clock with fear and trembling, as to be diligent servants of the Lord, undaunted like Daniel by any obstacles to our faith. In the face of the greatest threat possible, Daniel remained undaunted, faithful to God (Dan 6:22). Since the Lord may come any day, it is well to be ready every day.

FRIDAY – WEEK 34 / YEAR 1

IT WILL ENDURE

Readings: Dan 7:2-14; Lk 21:29-33

Victor Frankl was a prisoner of the Nazis in World War II. One early morning, he and some other prisoners were digging in the cold hard ground. As he was struggling to find a reason for all his sufferings and slow dying, a light was lit in the distant farmhouse that stood on the horizon, as if it were painted there in the midst of miserable grey. At that moment, he says in his book: *Man's search for meaning*, that the words of the Gospel, "The light shines in the darkness and the darkness has never put it out", flashed into his mind. From that moment he was a different man for it gave him hope and dispelled his despair. The Word of God may at times seem unattractive, even lifeless, like a fig tree in winter. But as the same tree bursts forth into bloom with the first signs of spring, so the Word which is always vibrantly alive, can burst giving enlightenment to a believer when he or she least expects. The Word of God will endure in its purpose. "Heaven and earth will pass away" (Lk 21:33), but not the Word. Nothing has affected our human cultures and civilisations so deeply as the Word. That is why, a thousand times over, the death-knell of the Scriptures has been sounded, the funeral processions formed, but some how the corpse never stays put!

SATURDAY – WEEK 34 / YEAR 1

HE IS COMING!

Readings: Dan 7:15-27; Lk 21:34-36

The greatest evil and the deepest despair together can not baffle the power that was unleashed from the death and the resurrection of Christ, for it was that power, which defeated the evil kingdom. If there is anything in the entire world that ought to interest a human being, it is the paschal mystery of Christ, for it was the triumph of good over evil, fulfilling the prophecy of Daniel, that his "Kingdom shall be an everlasting Kingdom and all dominions shall serve and obey" him (Dan 7:27). Why then, we still have to suffer from sin and its evils? Because what Jesus accomplished is still being unfolded and will be completed only at his second coming. Till that day, we must keep struggling against evils. "Watch at all times, praying" (Lk 21:36), asks Jesus. We have to keep watch against every form of corruption, against sharp falls in ethical and moral standards. On 15 April 1912, the ship Titanic struck an iceberg and sank, taking 1500 lives. If you had been there when the Titanic was sinking, would you have spent your last minutes rearranging the deck chairs and beautifying the cabins? That would be strange. Likewise, it would be strange for anyone busying all the time with things of this world, but remain unprepared to meet the Lord.

Year 2

BEING ORDINARY

Readings: 1 Sam 1:1-8; Mk 1:14-20

When we feel that the day is dark and gloomy and the fog obscures our view, because we are not learned or gifted; when we feel that we are just one of those ordinary people who have no challenge waiting anywhere for them; when we feel that our life is empty and barren, going through the daily routine of grinding duty, we need not lose heart. Instead, we do the job that lies before us, and keep our courage one more day, for God is working in us to carry out his divine plan for us and our loved ones. Beneath the surface of ordinary things, great events are brewing as God is working through us. We are called to believe that God guides and directs our personal lives as well as world events. See how God acted on behalf of Hannah, the wife of Elkanah, who was barren for years (1 Sam 1:2), but became the mother of Samuel, the last of the Judges who ruled Israel in God's name, before the age of the Israelite kings. See also how Jesus chose his apostles who were only fishermen, in order to turn them into "fishers of men" (Mk 1:17) for his Kingdom. Hence, may we not worry for being ordinary. The greatest forces in the universe are never spectacular. Summer showers are more effective than hurricanes, but they get no publicity.

WHICH IS A WASTE OF TIME?

Readings: 1 Sam 1:9-20; Mk 1:21-28

Often, trouble and perplexity drive us to prayer, and prayer drives away perplexity and trouble. That is the power of prayer of petition. It is wrong to think that prayer is a waste of time; the truth is that without prayer, our work is a waste of time. You can look millions of miles into space through a telescope, but through prayer you get nearer to God in heaven than you can, assisted by all the telescopes in the world. That is why, prayer of petition is so powerful. In the Gospel, Jesus drives out an unclean spirit, without being asked (Mk 1:26). But normally, Jesus helped needy persons in response to a petition. Why? Because God wants to give us what we need in response to our faith we manifest in our prayer. God willed to send Samuel to govern and direct his people because they needed him. But God first wanted Hannah to pray for a son despite her apparent inability to bear a child. And she prayed (1 Sam 1:11). God does not need to be informed about our needs. Rather, he has willed that prayer be the normal channel for him to act in our favour. Therefore, prayer is not overcoming God's reluctance, but co-operating with his willingness. Prayer is our greatest privilege, greatest responsibility, and greatest power God has put into our hands.

WEDNESDAY – WEEK 1 / YEAR 2

"SPEAK, LORD!"

Readings: 1 Sam 3:1-10, 19-20; Mk 1:29-39

God wants to speak to us. When he does, are we able to say with Samuel, "Speak, for thy servant hears" (1 Sam 3:10)? Often, we listen to so many other voices – the voice of self-seeking, the voice of pleasures, the voice of ambition, of prestige and of pride. But how attentive are we to the voice of God? Perhaps we have difficulty in discerning the voice of God. One sure way to overcome this difficulty is meditative prayer. The Gospel says that "in the morning, a great while before day, Jesus rose and went out to a lonely place and there he prayed" (Mk 1:35). The more time we spend daily in being alone with God, communicating with him in the stillness of our heart, the more clearly we can discern God's voice when he speaks to us. In meditative prayer, we can discover a depth within us. When a deep pool of water is still and the sunlight strikes it, how lucid it shines! So too, when our heart is still in prayer and the divine grace penetrates it, our inner self becomes translucent and our inner ear opens to hear God speak. That is how, in meditation, we not only discover the depth of our own inner self, but also our spiritual capacity becomes alive to be in complete harmony with God.

A LUCKY CHARM?

Readings: 1 Sam 4:1-11; Mk 1:40-45

Some people seem to think that religion is like parachute – something to grab when an emergency occurs. That is what the Israelites did. When they saw the Philistines threatening to overpower them, they wheeled out the Ark of the Covenant to protect them (1 Sam 4:4). Perhaps they saw the Ark as a lucky charm that insured God's automatic protection. But it did not and they lost the battle, for their hearts had fallen away from God. Instead of seeking the God of the Ark, they sought the Ark of God. Our God is not a magical God and he will not be manipulated as an amulet. After healing the leper, Jesus warned him not to report that incident to anyone (Mk 1:44). Possibly, the Lord feared that people would place a political, economical or magical gloss on his Messiaship, as news of his healings became known. The temptation is always with us, too, to rely merely on some 'ritual', or on some 'language', or some 'words', as if they have magical power. That is superstition and superstition is the religion of feeble minds; it is a godless religion. We need to realise that Faith is not magic. Our relationship with the Lord cannot be a commercial one. Unless we think, feel and live as Jesus had taught us, he has become for us only a lucky charm.

TO MAKE A CHOICE

Readings: 1 Sam 8:4-7, 10-22; Mk 2:1-12

The difficulty in life is choice. What people want is simply independent choice, whatever that independence may cost. The Israelites chose to set up a monarchy like other nations and demanded from Samuel for a king. The demand displeased both Samuel and God (1 Sam 8:7), because their demand was an admission of national lack of faith in God as their only King. But, God is the respector of human freedom. He knows that if we were not free to sin, we would not be free to love. He knows that people must have the right of choice even to choose the wrong, if they ever learn to choose the right. So he granted them their demand, but warned them of the price they would have to pay. The rest of Israel's history relates the sad consequences of that choice. However, God forgave them every time they made a wrong choice and never abandoned them. It is this forgiving love of God that Jesus revealed in forgiving the sins of a paralytic (Mk 2:5). But we need to remember that God wants us to choose life, not death. And we will do that if our choice corresponds to God's will. It requires a great attentiveness to the death forces within us and a great commitment to let the forces of life dominate every aspect of our lives.

SATURDAY – WEEK 1 / YEAR 2

A CHRISTIAN VISIONARY

Readings: 1 Sam 9:1-4, 17-19; 10:1; Mk 2:13-17

Every vocation is great, if greatly pursued. Saul had the vocation to be Israel's first king. Every thing seemed to favour Saul to become a king (1 Sam 9:17). But though gifted, he proved not to be a man whom God could use as his fit instrument. Perhaps, ambition, self-confidence, envy and the rest blinded him. Matthew too was called to be an apostle of Jesus. His response to the call was prompt (Mk 2:14). It was decisive. He never went back on his decision. He remained faithful to Christ to the end. We too have our vocation to a Christian life. Vocation can be described as the road crafted by our vision. It calls us to a radical commitment and a conscious willingness to pay the price of our vision. The test of a vocation is the love of the drudgery it involves. It is never safe for a visionary to look into the future with the eyes of fear. If our vision is to become a perfect Christian, then we must daily work at it. A vision without a task is but a dream; a task without a vision is drudgery; but a vision with a task is the hope for a Christian world. The bravest are surely those who have the clearest vision of what lies before them, glory and danger alike, and yet, go out and meet it.

OBEDIENCE IS BETTER

Readings: 1 Sam 15:16-23; Mk 2:18-22

A man snubbed his local vicar at a cocktail party saying, "The Church is full of hypocrites!" "Why don't you join?" suggested the vicar. "One more won't make any difference," he argued. A believer's hypocrisy can appear in different settings. One is the church worship. It is dishonesty to come to the church, offer gifts at the altar, sing God's praises and go away to live as we like. King Saul had been commanded by God to wage a holy war against the Amalekites. Nothing of their possessions was to be spared. But Saul made the mistake, in good intention, of course, but in disobedience: he did not destroy the best of the sheep and oxen in order to sacrifice them to God. But Samuel reprimanded him saying, "to obey is better than sacrifice" (1 Sam 15:22). In the Gospel, Jesus speaks out against the Pharisees who demanded that his disciples should fast, a hypocritical fast that had become nothing more than a ritual, devoid of any devotion and obedience to God. To worship and to fast, is to quicken our conscience by the will of God, to feed our mind with the truth of God, to open the heart to love of God and to devote our will to the purpose of God. Otherwise, we slander God by our worship and fast.

GETTING ADJUSTED

Readings: 1 Sam 16:1-13; Mk 2:23-28

An electrician converted a gas stove to electricity, but he did not have time to adjust it. He had to do it the next day. So he took a piece of cardboard and wrote on it: "Converted but not adjusted." At Baptism we all get converted to the Spirit of Christ, but are we adjusted to the Spirit? Our spiritual life can not develop unless we remain in continual contact with the Spirit. David after being anointed with the Spirit by Samuel (1 Sam 16:13), co-operated with the Spirit and that is how he rose to power as to establish the kingdom of Israel. How do we remain in contact with the Spirit? It is through our faithful reception of the sacraments and religious practices. But we need to guard against a mechanical application of religious rules and rituals for that would detract us from contact with the Spirit. While referring to the external observance of the Sabbath (Mk 2:27), Jesus tells us that such religious practices should not become an end in themselves but vehicles for communion with the Holy Spirit who leads us to love God and our neighbour. We might as well try to hear without ears, or breathe without lungs, as try to live and grow in Christian attitude without regular communion with the Holy Spirit.

WEDNESDAY – WEEK 2 / YEAR 2

GRACE UNDER PRESSURE

Readings: 1 Sam 17:32-33, 37, 40-51; Mk 3:1-6

No passion so effectively robs the mind of all its powers of acting and reasoning, as fear. Fear is not an unknown emotion to us. "Fearlessness," said M.K. Gandhi, "is the first requisite of spirituality. Cowards can never be moral." David was a beacon of moral courage in face of Goliath. Though being a lean, young shepherd boy, he defeated the armoured giant with only a sling shot (1 Sam 17:50). Jesus in the Gospel demonstrates what moral courage means. He was aware of the wrath that his saving action for the man with a withered hand would invite, from the disapproving Pharisees and the scribes. But, casting aside all the fears, he healed the man (Mk 3:5). Both for David and Jesus, the source of their courage was their conviction that God was on their side, with his power and grace. We are called to confront the powers of evil in our society, either directly or in their effects, with courage, trusting that God is on our side. It takes moral courage to stand up and be counted. But it takes more courage to keep standing up, after you have been counted up. Courage is not the absence of fear, but the willingness to push on in the face of it. Courage is grace under pressure, for it is fear that has said its prayers!

ENVY IS VERY SMALL

Readings: 1 Sam 18:6-9; 19:1-7; Mk 3:7-12

There are many roads to hate, but envy is the shortest of them all. One of the saddest things about envy is its smallness; to be envious is to turn eternally like a caged rat within the tight radius of malice. In the Gospel, we see the enormous popularity of Jesus as a healer. Great crowds gathered around him (Mk 3:9), acclaiming him as the Son of God; but the Pharisees and the scribes were not among the crowd. They were so envious of Jesus' popularity that it grew into fierce hatred against him. We need to remember that envy shoots at others but wounds itself. In other words, the jealous person poisons his or her own banquet and then eats it. Saul became envious of David because of his success in the war against the Philistines (1 Sam18:8). But what did this jealousy do to him personally? As David's star rose, Saul's glory and sanity eclipsed. Obsessive jealousy consumed Saul, swaying his judgement as king and his prowess as a warrior. Are we jealous of those people who seem to have no regard for God or for neighbour, yet enjoy wealth and power in this world, when we who try to be faithful to God struggle to make ends meet? Envy can plague not only kings like Saul, but ordinary people like us.

LEAPING OVERBOARD?

Readings: 1 Sam 24:3-21; Mk 3:13-19

I have known people who have dropped out of the Church because a pastor treated them harshly. Of course, an insensitive pastor might hurt us. But could that be the reason for discontinuing the practice of one's faith? If it is so, it is like leaping overboard because we do not like one of the crewmembers on a ship. Saul might have been a bad person, but he was nonetheless God's chosen king (1 Sam 24:6). That was the reason why David forgave him and did not kill him when he could have. A pastor may be a bad person, but still he is God's anointed one to be the spiritual leader of the flock. Besides, as Christians we are messengers of God's forgiving love. Jesus who "appointed twelve, to be with him, and to be sent out to preach" (Mk 3:14), has also called us to go forth to proclaim God's forgiving mercy in word and deed. One way to fulfil our calling is to forgive our pastors for their shortcomings. Unforgiving persons can ask themselves: Is not my own life liberally spotted with falsehoods? Then, why can't I forgive falsehood in others? Am I not wanting in love and guilty of hatred and arrogance? Then, why can't I pardon any want of love, or hatred and arrogance in others?

SATURDAY – WEEK 2 / YEAR 2

BIG PEOPLE

Readings: 2 Sam 1:1-4, 11-12, 17, 19, 23-27; Mk 3:20-21

We are called to be big people. Small people love only their friends and those who are good to them. But big people are big lovers; they rise above the pettiness of human inclination to react in kind, namely, to hate those who hate us and to ignore those who ignore us. A man hurled a stone at his dog. So terrific was the blow that the dog's leg was shattered. Whining and limping, the wounded creature came sadly to the man, fell at his feet and licked the hand that had hurled the merciless stone. That is how a Christian lover forgives. David exemplified that sort of forgiveness. David forgave his enemy Saul (2 Sam 1:12), although the later persecuted him for so many years. Not only did David weep over the death of Saul but also composed an elegy, in which he remembered only the good qualities of Saul. Only petty people delight in evil that comes upon their enemies. Jesus set forth his own directive to bigness and greatness of love. He said, "Love your enemies." Such teachings and his self-sacrificing love for others, embarrassed even his close friends and relatives that they thought he had gone mad, and so they came to fetch him home (Mk 3:21). But what is madness for the world is true greatness for God.

MONDAY – WEEK 3 / YEAR 2

'THEY' AND 'WE'

Readings: 2 Sam 5:1-7, 10; Mk 3:22-30

Universal responsibility is the key to human survival. It is the best foundation for world peace. Every nation carries responsibility for the welfare of humanity and for the planet itself, because this planet is our only home this side of heaven. Survival of this planet depends on how all nations work together to become one family. Before David became king, Judah, the southern kingdom and Israel, the northern kingdom, had remained separated. Knowing the need for a united kingdom, David made Jerusalem the one capital of both (2 Sam 5:5). Nonetheless, the kingdoms later drew apart completely, each having its own king. And the result was that eventually both kingdoms fell to the Barbarians. Jesus rightly said: "If a kingdom is divided against itself, that kingdom can not stand" (Mk 3:24). The same can become true of the nations today. If they remain separated into self-contained units, every nation crawling into its own hole, hiding itself away and hiding away everything it possesses, there is a real danger. The more a nation keeps itself at a distance from other nations, the more deeply does it sink into self-destroying impotence. Hence, the concept of 'they' and 'we' should go; and we have to think of the entire human race as 'we'.

TUESDAY – WEEK 3 / YEAR 2

LIKE ONE HUNDRED PIANOS

Readings: 2 Sam 6:12-15, 17-19; Mk 3:31-35

The flowering of the woods in spring may seem haphazard, with each plant just doing its own thing. But botanists tell us that the process is carefully orchestrated as a symphony. Likewise, we may come to church to celebrate Mass, sitting or standing separately. But what orchestrates us into a community is our common agenda to do God's will, which makes us "brothers and sisters" (Mk 3:35) to Jesus Christ. As the people who carried into Jerusalem the Ark which represented the presence of God among them, singing and dancing together with king David (2 Sam 6:12), so we celebrate the presence of God at Mass, a God who unites us into his family through our faith in his Son Jesus. Therefore the source of our joy in singing and praising God as we celebrate Mass ought to be Jesus Christ. Has it ever occurred to you that one hundred pianos, all tuned to the same fork, are automatically tuned to each other? They are of one accord by being tuned, not to each other, but to another standard to which each one must individually bow. So too, if one hundred worshippers together are in heart and mind united to Christ, they become nearer to each other, which inspires them to celebrate their being brothers and sisters in Christ.

WEDNESDAY – WEEK 3 / YEAR 2

THE OLD IS GOLD

Readings: 2 Sam 7:4-17; Mk 4:1-20

At the sea, those who are carried away from the direction of the harbour, bring themselves back on course, by some clear signal. So too, the Bible guides those adrift on the sea of life, back to the harbour of God's bountiful riches. The Bible includes both the New Testament and the Old Testament. The Old Testament is an indispensable part of the Bible. Its books are divinely inspired and retain a permanent value. It reveals the unfolding of God's plan for the salvation of the human race. Take, for example, king David. He was eager to build a house for the Lord; but God told him that he himself would build a house (2 Sam 7:11); What he meant was the dynasty of David. It marks the beginning of a belief that God would send to his people a Messiah, born of the house of David. In fulfilment of this prophecy, Jesus our King was born of Mary, of the house of David. Thus the Old Testament is very important for us; It is the history of God's people. It is also a store house of sublime teachings on God and of sound wisdom on human life; It is much more: it is a wonderful treasury of prayers. Therefore, our heart must receive the words of the Old Testament as a good soil receives seeds (Mk 4:8). If it does, it will bring forth even a hundredfold.

TAKE COURAGE

Readings: 2 Sam 7:18-19, 24-29; Mk 4:21-25

The agnostics and sceptics would fold their hands in despair for their miseries and troubles; but persons who believe in Jesus Christ take fresh courage, because Christ has established in his Kingdom supremacy of good over evil. God made a promise to David saying, "I will build you a house" (2 Sam 7:27). This promise was fulfilled in Christ, not politically but in the realm of the Spirit. Christ's Kingdom is spiritual and therefore its forces are temporarily hidden which will be made known at the end. Nothing is kept secret "except to come to light" (Mk 4:22). However, its hiding does not mean that it is now devoid of power. Amidst the forces that seek to perpetuate evil, the forces of the Kingdom are at work to overpower them. It is the reason for a believer's optimism. Most fish and other sea animals that live in perpetual darkness at depth below about a thousand feet, make their own light. In some fish, light is produced by bacteria in certain parts of the body; Other fish have special cells that make light. Disaster can sometimes mark our world as dark as the ocean depths. To get through life's dark times, we can produce our own light from the conviction that the invisible forces of Christ's Kingdom are active within us.

AFFLUENZA

Readings: 2 Sam 11:1-10, 13-17; Mk 4:26-34

A king asked his sage, "How can I be happy?" The sage said, "Find the happiest man in your kingdom and wear his shirt." So, the king sent his courtier throughout the kingdom and found the happiest man. The courtier told the king, "I have found the happiest man, but he did not even own a shirt." Yes; the more of heaven there is in our lives, the less of earth we covet. But the more of earth we have, the less of heaven is in us, and the shocking consequence is that we don't fear God who is in heaven. In his poverty, when his pillow was only a stone and his curtain the cobweb of a cave, David the shepherd boy was pure, pious, strong. But when he was at the zenith of his glory with all the wealth and power to enjoy, he fell from grace. He committed adultery (2 Sam 11:4) and followed it with murder (v.15), for when sin drives, shame sits in the back seat. David's essential sin was not lust, but greed. His career had progressed so successfully that he began to try to play God by disregarding the covenant of Sinai. This is the danger of materialism. Materialists suffer from a strange sickness called, 'affluenza'. Oscar Wilde said: "In this world there are only two tragedies; one is not getting what we need, and the other is getting it!"

SATURDAY – WEEK 3 / YEAR 1

"PEACE! BE STILL!"

Readings: 2 Sam 12:1-7, 10-17; Mk 4:35-41

In the greatest difficulties, in the heaviest trials, in deepest poverty and in the gravest sin, God never abandons us. All God's giants have been weak men and women, but they did great things for God because they counted on his faithfulness. As we are tossed about in the sea of life by storms of trials and tribulations, we need to remember that Christ is with us helping us not to drown. He has simply to utter these words: "Peace! Be still!" (Mk 4:39), and we are safe. When the cold wind of sorrow blows, turn to Jesus. When the hot wind of passion blows, wake up Jesus. Even when we have gravely sinned, God never abandons us. David sinned. But he repented saying, "I have sinned against the Lord" (2 Sam 12:13), and he was forgiven. But it was at God's initiative that David repented when God sent Nathan to remind David of his sin. That is how God shows his special concern when we are in trouble. There is the Providence of God that is governing all our human affairs. There is no conceivable situation in which it is not safe to trust in God. Therefore St Augustine said, "Trust the past to the mercy of God, the present to his love, and the future to his Providence."

THE GREAT LIBERATOR

Readings: 2 Sam 15:13-14, 30; 16:5-13; Mk 5:1-20

The only things that some people can fix around their house are scotch
and whisky, and they always wake up at the crack of ice. A friend of
mine read in the *Reader's Digest*: "Drugs are bad for you." And so,
he gave up reading *Reader's Digest*. So many in our society are
tormented by addictions to harmful substances and evil habits. Addiction
torments not only the addict, but also the society in which he or she
lives. The Gospel speaks of a man tormented by many demons,
restlessly moving among tombs. He is a vivid picture of those who are
in bondage to addiction. If you have any such problem and are unable
to shake it off, even after a therapy, surrender yourself to Jesus, the
great liberator, as the demoniac prostrated at the feet of Christ (Mk
5:6). Jesus will deliver you because he has taken upon himself all the
evils in humanity and has died for them. That is the difference between
Jesus and king David. David sinned and hence had to suffer for it at
the hand of his son Absalom (2 Sam 15:30). But Jesus suffered death
not for his sins, but our sins, out of pure love for us. That is why, we
need not despair over the hopelessness of our addictions to any evil. In
Jesus we find our deliverance.

HIS LOVE IS CONSTANT

Readings: 2 Sam 18:9-10, 14, 24-25, 30-19:3; Mk 5:21-43

Once I noticed a weather vane that was topped by the words: "God is
Love". First I thought that a weather vane to be an inappropriate medium
for such a message, since weather vanes are changeable, while God's
love is constant, as a father's love is. But on second thought it occurred
to me: what the weather vane is telling us is that whatever way the

wind blows, God is Love. When Jairus, in the Gospel, begs Jesus to come and cure his sick child saying, "Come and lay your hands on her" (Mk 5:23), we see how a father's heart can ache when his child suffers. Absalom a child of David but now a grown-up man, who had turned against his father, was killed. But the news of his death did not give any joy to David because his enemy was gone. On the contrary, he wept bitterly over his death crying, "O my son Absalom, my son, my son Absalom" (2 Sam 18:33). Even when we have deeply wounded God with our sins, he still loves us with an affection greater than that David had for his son Absalom. We shall never be without a friend as long as there is a Father in heaven. He does not delight in picking flaws in us, rather he helps us to be our best; he only magnifies all that is excellent in us, overcoming our evils with his goodness.

WEDNESDAY – WEEK 4 / YEAR 2

A SHRINKING GOD?

Readings: 2 Sam 24:2, 9-17; Mk 6:1-6

In our world, how important is God to many people? In more ways than one, it looks as if God has become an incredibly shrinking God. Our world is putting the human being in the place of God. It attempts to confer the Creator's dignity on human being, made in God's image. The philosophers call it humanism that says, "If it is to be, it is up to me!" The Bible condemns this attitude of human self-sufficiency. The motive of David's census (2 Sam 24:2) was to secure political security, which solely relied on military might, without any recognition of the need for God. According to the Covenant God had made with his people, all people, including kings, were expected to look to God as their ultimate defence. But David did not and hence God punished his land with pestilence. Why was it that Jesus could not work any miracles in his own hometown? It was "their unbelief" (Mk 6:6); They could not believe that God could raise a prophet from a carpenter's family. Our lack of faith in the almighty power of God distances us from him, with the result that we begin to rely solely on our own powers. The flowering of humanity is possible only so long as the human persons are not cut off from their divine roots.

A TEACHING FROM DINOSAUR

Readings: 1 Kgs 2:1-4, 10-12; Mk 6:7-13

We need structures in the Church, but not to a size of a dinosaur. The dinosaur's eloquent lesson is that if some bigness is good, an abundance of bigness is not necessarily better. If you look into some parishes, you wonder whether the dynamics of structure, have overtaken the essential apostolic mission of every parish. What is this essential mission? It is to love God and neighbour, both in word and deed, and to bring the rest of the humanity to do the same. We know that in order to emphasise the importance of love, Jesus gave his commandment of love on the eve of his death, during his Last Supper. As king David was dying, he said to his son Solomon: "Be strong, keeping the Lord's command-ments" (1 Kgs 2:3). Are our parishes keeping at least the chief commandment of love that the Lord Jesus gave us? It is in order to preach this Gospel of love that he sent out his disciples two by two on a mission (Mk 6:7). This is our mission too, for today. It is a fatal mistake to sacrifice this mission, for the sake of structures. We need structures, but they ought to be servants of our mission. We have to do away with unnecessary structures, as we lop away superfluous branches that bearing boughs may live.

LEAVING A TRAIL OF LIGHT

Readings: Sir 47:2-11; Mk 6:14-29

One person can completely change the character of a country and the industry of its people, by dropping a single seed in a fertile soil. So is our influence on others. Our Christian life has its invisible effects for good or bad on the people of next generation. King David brought Israel to a dazzling height. That is the heart of the eulogy in the first reading from Sirach. Jesus too, born in the line of David, was another king but of a Spiritual order, and he too established his own unending community of believers. John the Baptist, who prepared the way of the Lord Jesus, was killed (Mk 6:16), as Jesus was on a cross. Though David and John were centuries apart, each has influenced our understanding of Jesus. The songs of David and the message of John live on in our liturgy. What is it that you and I do for Christ today, which is going to influence Christians of next generations? There must be something. The career of a truly great Christian always remains an enduring monument for the Kingdom of Christ on earth. He or she may die and disappear, but their thoughts and acts survive in those who come after them. In fact, the best effect of a fine Christian is felt after he or she has left the stage.

SATURDAY – WEEK 4 / YEAR 2

THE GIFT OF UNDERSTANDING

Readings: 1 Kgs 3:4-13; Mk 6:30-34

In this life, nothing can be loved or hated unless it is first understood. That is why, to people who are in search of understanding, all other glory of greatness has no lustre. We need to understand ourselves, so that we can bear ourselves with humility and self-esteem. We need to understand God, so that we can know his will for us. We need to understand others, so that we can relate to them with charity. That is why, when Solomon was asked by God what gift he wanted, Solomon said, "Lord, give your servant an understanding mind" (1 Kgs 3:9). An understanding mind is a gift from God, and it is normally given to those who gather themselves regularly to be alone with God. No wonder, then, that Jesus tells his disciples, "Come away by yourselves to a lonely place, and rest a while" (Mk 6:31). To be alone with God is not to be lonely, but solitude. To be lonely is to be isolated, cut off from others, and locked into ourselves; it is to feel loss, sadness and self pity. But to experience solitude is to experience God, in quiet meditation. Modern people's life is grossly abnormal for we have neither time nor opportunity for quiet. But where there is will, there is a way.

GET SUNSHINE IN

Readings: 1 Kgs 8:1-7, 9-13; Mk 6:53-56

I know a violinist. He is poor but possesses an instrument that never fails to charm by its soothing mellowness. Played as only he could play, it never fails to awaken responsive chords in the hearts of the listeners. I asked him to explain its charm. He held out his violin, and tenderly caressing its graceful curves, said, "Ah, a great deal of sunshine must have gone into this wood and what has gone in, comes out." How much of God's sunshine has entered into our lives? The answer depends on how much time we spend in the radiance of his presence. Is it difficult to find God? No. Enter into any Catholic church where there is Blessed Sacrament. In the Eucharist is Jesus, God made flesh who died and rose again. He is the same God who once made his presence in the Ark of the Covenant (1 Kgs 8:11), that was placed in the temple built by Solomon. Although Jesus is not present in the Eucharist in his mortal flesh so that we can touch him, as did the people of the land of Gennesaret (Mk 6:56), he is really present in his risen body and soul, as our sacrifice and our spiritual nourishment. If more of the Eucharistic God's radiance had entered into our souls, we should be better able to radiate peace and hope to the crowds around us.

EVERY BUSH IS BURNING

Readings: 1 Kgs 8:22-23, 27-30; Mk 7:1-13

An eccentric professor, thinking to have some fun with a small boy who was reading a Sunday school paper, said to him, "Tell me, my good boy, where God is and I will give you an apple." The boy quickly looked at the man and replied, "I will give you a whole barrel of apples, if you tell me where he is not." God is as present as the air.

The world is crowded with him. Solomon, though exultant about the temple, realised that it could not contain God whom "heaven and the highest heaven can not contain" (1 Kgs 8:27), for he is present in all his creations. Criticising the Pharisees who forbade people to eat with unwashed hands and feet (Mk 7:3), as though they are not God's creations, Jesus implicitly declared that all things are clean, for all things come from God and bear his creative presence. If God is actively present in every created thing, why is it that all our efforts to pray seem to have little or no connection with every day life? Is it not like riding a chainless bicycle? Why is it we often speak of the sacred and secular, as though they are separate realities? The truth is that there is nothing in existence that does not have the stamp of the supernatural. Everything is sacramental and every bush is burning.

WEDNESDAY – WEEK 5 / YEAR 2

IS MASS A SOUVENIR?

Readings: 1 Kgs 10:1-10; Mk 7:14-23

The Mass is not a souvenir. Going to Mass is not like going to Calvary where we chip away a piece of rock and say, "This is the souvenir of the place where Jesus died." Mass is an action. At Mass, Jesus offers himself to the heavenly Father as our sacrifice, in an unbloody manner; he offers his body and blood as our spiritual food and drink; And he speaks to us his Words of wisdom, as found in the sacred Scriptures. Why did he tell the people, "Hear me, all of you, and understand?" (Mk 7:14). It was because he is the eternal wisdom of the Father. The queen of Sheba travelled a very long distance to meet and hear king Solomon speak words of wisdom (1 Kgs 10:4). Sheba is probably the present Yemen, about 1500 miles away from Jerusalem. So, the queen undertook a journey of 3000 miles coming and returning together. In those days, journeys were difficult. She had to journey through deserts and wilderness, often under scorching sun overhead, and sands beneath burning. However she faced all the difficulties, fatigue, and dangers, to see Solomon and hear his words of wisdom. At Mass, Jesus the Wisdom itself speaks. What sacrifices do we make to go to Mass in order to meet Jesus and hear him?

THE GIFT OF FAITH

Readings: 1 Kgs 11:4-13; Mk7:24-30

Some say that faith is a gift from God. So is the air, but you have to breathe it; so is bread, but you have to eat it. Likewise, for faith to be of any use to the believer, he or she must respond to it. Look at king Solomon. He had received the gift of wisdom. But in his old age, instead of becoming wiser than ever, he allowed his foreign wives to turn his heart to gods other than the God of Israel (1 Kgs 11:4). In effect, he abandoned his faith in the true God. But look at the woman in the Gospel. She was a foreigner, a Syro-phoenician; but she responded to the gift of faith given her by God, and approached Jesus begging him to drive the demons out of her daughter (Mk 7:26). Jesus granted her request because of her faith. Such a faith in God sees the invisible, believes the incredible and receives the impossible. As you know, our God is one who delights in impossibilities. You do not test the resources of God until you try the impossible. Faith makes the uplook good, the onlook bright, the inlook favourable and the future glorious. God is not looking for great people like Solomon with fame and riches, but for people as ordinary and unimportant as the woman in the Gospel, who will realise the greatness of God, by their response to his gift of faith.

SO LONG AS

Readings: 1 Kgs 11:23-32; 12:19; Mk 7:31-37

It is not possible to invite all the poor of Asia to our dinner tables; but the rich among us, can at least open our ears to listen to the cry of the most oppressed among them, and be willing to give them a proportion from our overabundance. But Jeroboam, the servant of Solomon, a minister of state, did not have the heart to listen to the cry of the oppressed. Under Solomon, the tribes were required to supply food, labour and money for the state. They were overtaxed and over burdened. When the representatives of the North complained to Jeroboam, he only increased their burden by further punitive measures. With that insensitive act, the northern tribes broke away and the split would never again be healed (1 Kgs 12:19). But Jesus, in the Gospel, listens to the cry of an oppressed man, deaf and dumb and hence isolated from society, and heals him (Mk 7:34). How one wishes that the same Lord opens the ears of so many of us, to hear the cry of the poor and the destitute in our society. As Christians, if we identify ourselves with Christ, then, so long as there are poor, we are poor; so long as there are prisons, we are prisoners; so long as there are the sick, we are sick; so long as there is hunger, we are famished.

SATURDAY – WEEK 5 / YEAR 2

WHAT ARE OUR IDOLS?

Readings: 1 Kgs 12:26-32; 13:33-34; Mk 8:1-10

Through the ages, people have peered into the darkness, listened in the stillness, looked into the cold, silent depths of space and come away with a heterogeneous collection of definition of 'something' that they think is 'out there'. But we Christians believe that that 'something' is God, who is a person, the Creator of all things, who revealed himself to the people of Israel as the one true God. It is he who sent his Son Jesus to be our Saviour, a Saviour who continues to save us, especially through his presence in the Holy Eucharist. The multiplication of loaves by Jesus (Mk 8:8), foreshadowed his giving of himself in the Eucharist. But this one true God, was rejected by Jeroboam, the ruler of the northern kingdom of Israel, after the death of Solomon. Away from Jerusalem, he set up official places of worship within his territory (1 Kgs 12:31), thus paving the way for his people to sacrifice to idols. Not one of us will offer sacrifices to idols, but we may be tempted to sacrifice spiritual values, at the altar of the world's materialistic values. Today, an invasive materialism is imposing its dominion on us in many different forms, and with aggressiveness sparing no one. Can we stand firm for human being's spiritual values?

WE ARE TEA-BAGS

Readings: Jas 1:1-11; Mk 8:11-13

Christian life is not problem free. Jesus Christ has not promised his
followers skies always blue, flowers-strewn pathways all our lives.
Every Christian is either coming out of a storm or headed for one. But
when we are in difficulties, we are to believe, that life is hard, but God
is good; believe that life is unfavourable, but God is sovereign; believe
that difficulties provide a platform for God to display his power. This
faith can be a powerful sign for others to recognise God's presence in
human lives. This is the kind of sign that Jesus expected the Pharisees
to observe in his own pattern of life, but they were looking for a
different kind of heavenly sign in order to believe in him, which he
refused to give (Mk 8:12). There is another reason why we should
willingly accept trials in our lives. "The testing of your faith produces
steadfastness and let steadfastness have its full effect, that you may be
perfect and complete." (Jas 1:3-4). Is it not true? As storms make oaks
take deeper roots, so afflictions make us more sober and wiser. On the
contrary, a life freed from all difficulties would considerably reduce
all our potentials. We are a lot like tea bags; we don't know our own
strengths until we get into hot water.

BEWARE!

Readings: Jas 1:12-18; Mk 8:14-21

Opportunity knocks only once, but temptation bangs on the door for
years. Temptations are like bums; treat one nicely and it will return with
its friends. To accumulate material riches is one of the most attractive
temptations, like some television commercials: frequently deceptive and
frightfully costly. Where does this temptation come from? There are

two sources. One is the primal disorder we all carry within. As St James puts it: "Each person is tempted when he is lured and enticed by his own desire" (Jas 1:14). The second source is the persons and things around us. Jesus said to his disciples: "Beware of the leaven of the Pharisees and the leaven of Herod" (Mk 8:15). He was referring to their corrupting influence on the disciples. They demanded from Jesus to show himself as conqueror, so that they could take him for Messiah. They failed to understand that Jesus had not come to build a material kingdom of wealth and power, but one of truth, justice and love. We live among people who are setting all their affections on material things, trying them all in turn, until they are exhausted with inner emptiness. Beware of them! Unless we have within us that which is above us, we shall soon yield to that which is about us.

WEDNESDAY – WEEK 6 / YEAR 2

TRICK BIRTHDAY CANDLES

Readings: Jas 1:19–27; Mk 8:22-26

A policeman must maintain law and order, not disrupt it. A doctor should foster and uphold human life, not destroy it. A judge should seek and promote justice, not violate it. Likewise, as persons of faith, we should radiate the goodness of God, for our faith shows us, as in a mirror, as God's children. If we fail to radiate the goodness of God, we are like those who look at their features in a mirror, but go away, immediately forgetting what they looked like (Jas 1:24); and we would be worse than the blind man in the Gospel (Mk 8:22), for he at least had no possibility of knowing what his appearance was like. If we see ourselves as God's children, then our lives must reflect the qualities of God, especially his goodness. We can reflect God's goodness to others in many ways. One is to be kind to those who have hurt us. Those who forgive others and still love them, in spite of their repeated acts of hurts, are like trick birthday candles, which re-light when they are blown out. These novelty candles have wicks treated with magnesium crystals. The wicks retain heat so well that they rekindle themselves as soon as they are blown out. Like these unquenchable little candles, we too can perpetually rekindle the warmth of God's goodness.

GOD'S SURPRISE MOVES

Readings: Jas 2:1-9; Mk 8:27-33

Many are sincerely searching for God, but in wrong places. They search for him in dusty libraries, in old manuscripts and daring new slogans, but can't find him. They search for him in banks and in busy building societies, but can't find him. They can't find him even in guilded Cathedrals and in decorated Basilicas. But let them, for once, visit the shantytowns of Asia and Africa filled with basic tin and cardboard huts; they can find God there, and in those who minister to the poorest of the poor. God lives with the hungry and the oppressed, inspiring many to work for justice and peace. The way we think is not God's way, a lesson Jesus gives to Peter in today's Gospel (Mk 8:33). We favour the rich and ignore the poor. We take notice of the well-dressed man in church, but close our eyes on the poor (Jas 2:3). But God's way is different. Our God is a God of unexpected moves. It is those who are poor and unimportant in the eyes of the world, that he chooses to be recipients of his true riches, as Christ chose fishermen to be his Apostles. God gives special attention to those who have next to nothing in this life. So we must. We may be rich, full of knowledge and feel so worldly wise, yet we can miss God, if we don't reach out to the poor.

TO GET A NEW COAT

Readings: Jas 2:14-24, 26; Mk 8:34-9:11

If I throw away an old coat, it makes little difference if I did so because it is torn, or because it is spotted with soup, or because it is moth-eaten, or because it is faded. The only thing that matters is that I throw it away. And when I throw it away, I get a new coat. That is what happens when we renounce our very self to follow Christ. We bury our nature with Christ and get a new nature, one that partakes of the new nature of God. But this will call for taking up one's daily cross (Mk 8:34). Cross means pain: psychic, economic, even physical. Renunciation brings with it pains not because God enjoys seeing us suffer, but sin is so expensive and massive, that we can release ourselves from it only with great painful effort. Anyone who believes that we can be reborn in Christ as new creatures without self-renunciation, is one who has faith which is devoid of works; but "faith by itself, if it has no works, is dead" (Jas 2:17). Works without faith are like suite of clothes without a body, empty; but faith without works is a body without clothes, no warmth. A life of faith involves hard work, courage and discipline. You may as well separate heat from fire, as works from faith. Work is the incarnation of faith.

SATURDAY – WEEK 6 / YEAR 2

TONGUE ONLY APPEARS TINY

Readings: Jas 3:1-10; Mk 9:2-13

One day, a harsh word harshly said sped upon an evil journey; like a sharp and cruel dart, it pierced a fond and loving heart. It turned a friend into a foe, and everywhere brought pain and woe. But a kind word followed it one day, swept swiftly on its blessed way. Of course, it healed the wound and soothed the pain, and friends of old were friends again; it made the hate and anger cease and everywhere brought joy and peace. Yet, Alas! The harsh word left a trace that the kind word could not efface. Words have a force. They can whip a crowd into a frenzy, or turn a mob into a congregation. "So the tongue is a little member and boasts of great things" (Jas 3:5). As we control a cycle or a bus or a car by the steering wheel, we can control our whole self by controlling our tongue and can do a lot of good. On the contrary, as a small spark of fire can set ablaze a whole building, so, if we do not control our tongue, it can do a lot of harm. But remember, for our tongue to behave well, we need a transformation of our heart, something similar to the transfiguration Jesus had on Mount Tabor (Mk 9:2), since from the abundance of the heart the mouth speaks.

COMBINING THE TWO

Readings: Jas 3:13-18; Mk 9:14-29

At the close of our life, the question God will ask us is not how much we got but how much we gave, not how much we won but how much we did, not how much we saved but how much we sacrificed, not how much we were honoured but how much we had served. Jesus spent a lot of his time during his public life, in ministering to those who were hungry, sick and handicapped, as we see him in today's Gospel, curing an epileptic boy. One of the reasons for this was to instil into us the importance of serving others through works of charity. But we need to remember that our works of charity have to be supported by daily communion with God in prayer. In fact, some of our works of mercy will be effective, only if we support it with prayer. That is what he taught his disciples when he said, "this kind cannot be driven out by anything but prayer and fasting" (Mk 9:29). There is another reason for prayer to go with our works of charity. Our works will not only be ineffective, but also will become disordered, if we do not purify our hearts regularly in the presence of God. As we know, it is in our heart that "jealousy and self-ambition exist" (Jas 3:16). Therefore, may we combine work with prayer.

HOW TO BE FIRST?

Readings: Jas 4:1-10; Mk 9:30-37

Glamour is not greatness; applause is not fame; prominence is not eminence; the man of the hour is not apt to be the man of the ages. A stone may sparkle, but that does not make it a diamond. So, who is the greatest? Jesus answers: "If any one would be first, he must be last of all and servant of all" (Mk 9:35). Does not the world know that it is often what the unimportant do that really counts and determines the course of history? For example, the world would soon die but for the fruitful, loyal and consecrated servants whose names go unhonoured and unsung. Hence "Humble yourselves before the Lord and he will exalt you" (Jas 4:10), says St James. How does humility lift a person up? Humility gives us strength to bear up under loss and to fight the bitterness of defeat and weakness of grief. It enables us to be a victor over anger, to smile when tears are close, to resist disease, evil people and base instincts. It gives us courage to hate hate, to love love, and to go on when it would seem good to die, and to look up with unquenchable faith to something ever more to be. These are tests of true greatness. Only the humble can do these things and be great.

WEDNESDAY – WEEK 7 / YEAR 2

PERSPECTIVE COUNTS

Readings: Jas 4:13-17; Mk 9:38-40

The perspective from which we view things makes a big difference. For example, a horse looks much like a horse from ground level; but if you look at one from the top, a horse looks much like a violin. So is our perspective upon life. To make a successful living and to achieve our professional goals are not trivial pursuits. However, we should place them into the perspective of the larger purpose of life, as God has planned for each of us. In other words, our motto should be: "If the Lord wills, we shall live and we shall do this or that" (Jas 4:15). If we have such a large perspective, we will not live with the illusion that we will never pass away from this world, nor will we live all the time in the fear of death. If our perspective is as large as God's own, then we will also refuse to look down upon the good works that non-Catholics and non-Christians are doing; We would rather join them in their good works, saying, "he that is not against us is for us" (Mk 9:40). Therefore, we need to release our perspective from its narrow confines. Otherwise, we will take the limits of our own personal perspective, for the limits of God's perspective. Can you ever see a field well enough, standing from within the field? Not really.

FOR HUMAN RIGHTS TO TRIUMPH

Readings: Jas 5:1-6; Mk 9:41-50

No matter what country or continent we come from, we are all basically the same human beings. We have common human needs and concerns. We all seek happiness and try to avoid suffering. The dramatic changes in the recent past clearly indicate that the triumph of human rights is inevitable. There is a growing awareness of people's responsibilities to each other. This is encouraging, even though so much suffering is continued to be inflicted, because basic human rights are denied. For example, the utter misery and poverty of people who, in spite of hard work and earnest efforts, are forced to live such a life, is a serious breach of human rights. Apparently, similar injustices existed even among early Christians. And so, St James reprimands them: "Behold, the wages of the labourers who mowed your fields, which you kept back by fraud, cry out" (Jas 5:4). Jesus calls for much more than respect for human rights. He expects us to see and love his own person hidden beneath the veil of suffering humanity. That is what he implied, in effect, when he said, "Whoever gives you a cup of water to drink, because you bear the name of Christ, will by no means lose his reward" (Mk 9:41).

"ENOUGH IS ENOUGH!"

Readings: Jas 5:9-12; Mk 10:1-12

A woman who had been married twenty years filed for divorce. The judge asked, "Why?" She said, "Enough is Enough." In the USA, in 1900, one of every 20 marriages ended in divorce. In 1920, one of every 12; in 1940, one of every 6; in 1970, one of every 2. The statistics are startling. But we have to keep in mind that marriage has never been easy. After a man says, "I do", he discovers a long list of things he'd better not do, and so for the woman. Therefore, we can't judge divorcees harshly, and St James counsels: "Do not grumble against one another" (Jas 5:9). However, the Scripture's stand is that "What God has joined together, let not man put asunder" (Mk 10:9). Marriage is a covenant of love, a relationship of natural trust and fidelity to three essential values of marriage: well-being of children, enriching companionship between spouses, and the good of society at large. Unbroken fidelity in marriage demands heroic effort, no doubt. It involves a great deal of pain. It demands a recurrent process of reconciliation. But for Christian couples, that should not be a surprise. If Jesus Christ is God and died for love of us, then nothing so much enhances a good marital love, as to make sacrifices for it.

SATURDAY – WEEK 7 / YEAR 2

GOD IS OUR CRUTCH

Readings: Jas 5:13-20; Mk 10:13-16

A little boy was tugging at a big rock and doing his best to lift it. He was grunting and pulling but it did not budge. His father came along and asked him if he was having any trouble. He said, "Yes. I am trying and trying and can't move the rock." The father said, "Well, son; are you using all available energy?" The boy replied, "Yes, father, I think I am." Then the dad looked at him and said, "No, son, I don't think you are, for you haven't asked for my help." So it is with us. We think we are unable to overcome some trouble, but perhaps it is because we haven't prayed to God for help. St James asks us to pray for all needs and at all times: "Is any one among you suffering? Let him pray. Is any cheerful: Let him sing praise." (Jas 5:13). All prayer, whether petition or praise, is a way of expressing our complete dependence on God, as children depend on their parent. Hence, embracing little children, Jesus declared "to such belongs the kingdom of God" (Mk 10:14). Nothing is more desirable than to be released from an affliction in the leg; but nothing is more frightening than to be divested of a crutch. Our crutch is God. Our efficiency will turn out to be a deficiency, unless we have God's sufficiency.

THE APPLE OF HIS EYE

Readings: 1 Pet 1:3-9; Mk10:17-27

Who is the apple of your eye? Your grand child? Your son recently promoted? Your fiancée with those soft eyes and tender smile? Whoever is the apple of our eye, one thing is certain, namely, we love that individual with a fervent love. The person gives us joy indescribable. Each of us, baptised in Jesus, has become the apple of God's eye. Why? He has given us a new birth through our baptism, a birth that guarantees everlasting life. "Blessed be the God and the Father of our Lord Jesus Christ! By his great mercy we have been born anew to an inheritance which is imperishable" (1 Pet 1:3). This new life comes from an act of God's love, as marital love does; It is the same love of God that brought his Son Jesus from death to fullness of life in his resurrection. Thus, God's joy over us is understandable. Since God's love has brought us from death to life, his joy is like the rugged joy of a warrior returning home, or the admiral sailing into port flying colours of victory. Therefore, we need to fear nothing when God invites us to make even a supreme sacrifice, as Jesus asked the rich young man in the Gospel (Mk 10:21). It will be always to give us a higher life. If a sacrifice is supreme, the life it brings will be also supreme.

SURRENDERING ALL TO HIM

Readings: 1 Pet 1:10-16; Mk 10:28-31

Every longing in the human heart finds in Christ its complete fulfilment. In him, we have a love that can never be fathomed and a life that can never die; a peace that can never be understood and a joy that can never be diminished; a hope that can never be disappointed and a light that can never be darkened; a wisdom that can never be baffled and resources that can never be exhausted. The dawn of the era of Christ was the era that the prophets of old had said would be in fulfilment of God's promise. St Peter therefore tells us: "The prophets who prophesied of the grace that was to be yours, searched and inquired about this salvation" (1 Pet 1:10). Since Jesus is the fulfilment of every person's religious search, we must adjust our lives in such a way that it revolves around him. Jesus has to be the centre of our lives, and nothing else can take his place, neither "house or brothers or sisters or mother or father or children or lands" (Mk 10:30). There is a reward for those who have given up everything to follow him. The reward is the gift of Christ's presence, qualitatively superior to anything we have surrendered. May the presence of Christ in us be the joy of our life, the service of Christ be the business of our life, but the will of Christ be the law of our life.

WEDNESDAY – WEEK 8 / YEAR 2

IT IS UP TO US

Readings: 1 Pet 1:18-25; Mk 10:32-45

Some people literally see the world in a rosier light than others. Apples and rubies and fire engines look redder to them. And their eyes can distinguish even the slight variations in the shades of red between, say, two red shirts that look identical to others. Studies show that a difference just in one amino acid makes the difference in colour vision. Hence, how we see colours is determined by heredity that is beyond our control. But to see our life with optimism, whatever the circumstances, is up to us. It depends on our trust that we are precious before God, and St Peter gives the reason: "You were ransomed from the futile ways inherited from your fathers, not with perishable things such as silver or gold, but with the precious blood of Christ" (1 Pet 1:18). In the Gospel, James and John are concerned about their places in the Kingdom (Mk 10:37).They wanted preferential treatment. Such should not have been their concern, nor need it be ours. We ought simply to rejoice in the fact that we are precious in the eyes of God. It is so easy to let something like pain, fear, hatred, illness or even another person block our optimism. We must not allow this to happen. Why should anything control our hope-filled life?

EVERY THING IS NEW

Readings: 1 Pet 2:2-5, 9-12; Mk 10:46-52

Imagine that you are in a flight to New York. An American lady from an adoption agency, sits behind you on the plane. In her arms, she holds two Korean babies. They are so beautiful that you can't take your eyes off them. These babies have no idea of the life they are heading into. Within seconds of that plane landing, their lives would be turned upside down. They would have new names, new citizenship, a new culture and new identities. They would have a new father and mother, in fact, a whole new family. Old things would pass away. From that point, all things would be new. At our baptism, something similar happens. We can't fathom the new world into which baptism is leading us into. In Christ, we become adopted children of God with a new family of saints and, a new citizenship in heaven. From then on, we belong to "a chosen race, a royal priesthood, a holy nation, called out of darkness into God's marvellous light" (1 Pet 2:9). We need eyes of faith to see the Christian dignity to which we are raised at our baptism. If our eyes of faith have lost their sight, we must beg Jesus: "Master, let me receive my sight" (Mk10:51). Faith is to believe what we do not see; but the reward of this faith is to see what we believe.

LOVE IN GOD'S HOUSEHOLD

Readings: 1 Pet 4:7-13; Mk 11:11-26

Our society encourages individualism. We are constantly made to believe that every thing we think, say or do, is our personal achievement deserving individual attention. But as people, who belong to the family of God through baptism, we know that anything of spiritual value is not the result of individual accomplishment but the fruit of a communal life. Today's readings call our attention to those principles that preserve and promote communal life: "hold unfailing love for one another" (1 Pet 4:8), "practice hospitality" (v.9), "empty your gifts for one another" (v.10); and "forgive if you have anything against anyone" (Mk11:25). Such a relationship with our fellow Christians calls for our love for them to be something special. We are to go a second mile for our neighbour; but we are to go the third or fourth mile for those in the household of faith. That is why Jesus who asked every one to love the other as one loves oneself, wanted his disciples to love one another as he himself has loved us. We need to grasp how wide and long and high and deep is the love of Christ for us, so that we can at least attempt to love our fellow Christians in the same way.

SATURDAY – WEEK 8 / YEAR 2

SITTING ON A PROBLEM

Readings: Jude 17:20-25; Mk 11:27-33

A significant number of people just sit on their problems and never do anything about them. For example, a married couple who know that they are drifting apart, but lacking in sincerity and courage, may not sit down to talk things out together. The result is that they continue to drift and their problems quietly get worse and more difficult to solve. There is another example in today's Gospel. The Pharisees were actually sitting on a problem of eternal life or eternal damnation, by refusing to take a decision on whether Christ was the true Messiah or not. They knew the Scriptures, witnessed Christ's works, listened to his teachings all in fulfilment of the prophecies, and yet they could not accept him as the true Messiah. They were only interested in harassing him. So when they asked Jesus, "By what authority are you doing these things" (Mk 11:28)? Jesus sensing their insincerity, refused to answer their question. We confess that Jesus is the true Messiah, but have we really taken a decision to follow him? John Oxman wrote: "To every man, there opens A Way, and Ways and a Way, and the High Soul climbs the High Way and the Low Soul gropes the Low, and in between on the misty flats, the rest drift to and fro." Does it describe our own situation?

GOLD-MINE WITHIN

Readings: 2 Pet 1:2-7; Mk 12:1-12

A Christian soul is a gold-mine that invites us to grab a pick and dig for divine riches within. "God has granted to us all things that pertain to life and godliness" (2 Pet 1:3), starting with faith. That is to say, that the Kingdom of God is within us. Why, then, should we go on searching for God's Kingdom when he has put wonderful deposits of great resources, within our reach? It is useless to expect God's kingdom to come into our life like great chunks of rock on a conveyer belt. It is not like a prescription that you can get across. a counter. It has been already planted in each of us silently at our baptism. Hence God is calling us to roll up our sleeves and dig within us for all those riches he has given us. He is calling us to dig using all the means such as "virtue with knowledge, knowledge with self-control, self-control with steadfastness, steadfastness with brotherly love" (v.6). Of course, we are free to reject God's call, as did the people represented by the tenant farmers in the Gospel (Mk 12:8). But God made us free in order to make us worthy of our nature and divine happiness. Hence, we must use freedom positively and use it to dig into the gold mine of possibilities that is within us, namely, within God's vineyard.

THE CHRISTIAN DREAM

Readings: 2 Pet 3:11-1, 17-18; Mk 12:13-17

Martin Luther King was born in 1929. As leader of civil rights movement, he inspired hope for millions of Americans of all colours. He was both revered and reviled, but no matter on which side of the battle line you stood, there is no denying that Martin Luther had a dream, which he elucidated in one of the most stirring and memorable speeches made in the twentieth century, called, "I have a dream". We all need to dream. As Christians, what ought to be our dream? It is the "new heavens and a new earth" (2 Pet 3:13), which Christ would fully establish at his second coming. How will he do it? Not by annihilating all the good that humanity has achieved, and much of what Christians have done for the world, is too valuable to disappear in smoke. Hence, God will preserve them all, but purify them as to become part of his new Kingdom. But we must hasten the arrival of that Kingdom, by our Christian conduct according to what Christ has taught us. He is the one who truly taught the way of God (Mk 12:14). Let us, therefore, not simply dream the Christian dream, but live that dream now. Only those who dream and do, will one day enter the gates of the new heavens and the new earth.

WEDNESDAY – WEEK 9 / YEAR 2

IN ALL SEASONS

Readings: 2 Tim 1:1-3, 6-12; Mk 12:18-27

It is easy to witness to our faith, when it is easy. We wake up to a bright day brimming with possibilities and spiritual energy, singing as we breeze out the door and giving our smile and "God bless you" to everyone we encounter. This is witnessing 'in season'. Then, there are "out of season" days. Our shoulders shag, our hearts feel dry and we wonder if God has abandoned us, and before the day hardly begins, we write it off. But St Paul counsels us to "take your share of suffering for the Gospel in the power of God who saved us and called us with a holy calling" (2 Tim 1:8-9), and "to rekindle the gift of God that is within you" (v.6). We are encouraged to witness to the power of God within us, in and out of season, with the hope of immortal life after death, for our "God is not God of the dead but of the living" (Mk 12:27). Yes; we strongly believe in the resurrection after death, and resurrection is not mere resumption of the earthly existence, as the Pharisees thought (v.23), but an entirely new life. May we then be faithful to God also in difficult times; God is pleased with gusty faith and tough love, and is glorified when we push through the doldrums, shake off the fog, and shine in his love.

LOVE ENNOBLES ALL

Readings: 2 Tim 2:8-15; Mk 12:28-34

On the walls of an insane asylum were scrawled the following words by some unknown inmate of the institution: "Could we within the ocean fill, and were the skies of parchment made, and every blade of grass a quill, and every man a scribe by trade; to write the love of God to man, would drain the ocean dry." We who believe in God's immense love for humankind are called by the Lord to respond to that love by loving God "with all your heart" (Mk 12:30). But our love of God to be true, "you must love your neighbour as yourself" (v.31). It is not so much a question of loving God and loving our neighbour, but rather loving God–in-our neighbour as a single thing. But loving our neighbour demands sacrifice. St Paul was willing to make that sacrifice, and so he wrote: "I endure every thing for the sake of the elect" (2 Tim 2:10). Our notion of sacrifice is wringing out of us something we do not want to give up, full of pain and agony. But the Bible idea of sacrifice is that in sacrifice I give as a love-gift the very best thing I have, and love turns any sacrifice sweet. As Elizabeth Browning wrote, "The sweetest lives are those to duty wed, whose deeds both great and small, are close-knit strands of unbroken thread, where love ennobles all."

FLAWLESS LIKE SILVER

Readings: 2 Tim 3:10-17; Mk 12:35-37

Silver often takes back seat to its richer brother gold. But silver has a greater attraction. It is cooler, purer and shinier than gold, which looks as if it has got all kinds of junk in it. This is why the Psalmist compares the Word of God to silver: "The words of the Lord are flawless like silver refined in a furnace of clay" (Ps 12:6). They are flawless because it is God who is pure who inspired the words in Scripture. It is true not only of the New Testament but also of the Old, and hence Jesus alludes to "what David himself, moved by the Holy Spirit declared" (Mk 12:35). The words of God are compared to silver rather than to gold because God is less interested in the attractiveness of his Word than of its purity. One unusual quality of silver is its ability to kill bacteria when it comes into contact with it. It is as if bad things can not survive in silver or around it. So too, the Word of God has the ability, when applied by faith, to make the reader to become changed, holy and pure. That is why St Paul states: "All scripture is profitable for teaching, for reproof, for correction, and for training in righteousness" (2 Tim 3:16). The purity of God's Word should make us treasure it highly. More importantly, it should make a change in our lives for the better.

SATURDAY – WEEK 9 / YEAR 2

LIMITED RESOURCES?

Readings: 2 Tim 4:1-8; Mk 12:38-44

Do you ever feel as if you can do only so much, especially in the face of some pressing need? We can all find excuses to side step a problem. We can say that we are the wrong people for the job, that we can't do it alone, that we have other priorities, that God has not called us to meet the need or we can use the ever-ready excuse, "I only have limited resources." In this, we are influenced by the world that measures a person's value by his or her human gifts or possessions. But in the eyes of God, our value as a person lies in the generosity of our heart. So Jesus valued the poor widow more than the Pharisees, because the two small coins she offered was all that she had (Mk 12:44), while many Pharisees put in out of their abundance. We are called to possess not everything that the world can offer, but to be generous with whatever we have, in the service of others. St Paul too inspires us to such generosity, when he says, "I am already on the point of being sacrificed" (2 Tim 4:6). Hence, may we not excuse ourselves from serving others, because of limited resources. God laughs in the face of limited resources. In fact, he often uses limitations of our resources to strengthen and test the generosity of our heart.

IN HIM WE TRUST

Readings: 1 Kgs 17:1-6; Mt 5:1-12

An old monk said to his disciples: "Trust in yourself, and you are doomed to disappointment; trust in your friends, and they will die and leave you; trust in money, and you may have it taken from you; trust in reputation, and some slanderous tongue may blast it. But trust in God, and you are never to be confounded in time or eternity." Trusting in God alone, during the great three-year draught in Israel, Elijah did what the Lord asked him to do, namely, he "went and dwelt by the brook Cherith, and the ravens brought him bread and meat" (1 Kgs 17:5-6). As a matter of fact, Elijah lived according to the Beatitudes even before Jesus proclaimed them. All Beatitudes add up to one call: Be "poor in spirit" (Mt 5:1), and the chief mark of the poor in spirit is that they trust in God. No matter how challenging or threatening a situation may be, they trust in God. During an earthquake, the inhabitants of a small village were very much alarmed. But one old woman was surprisingly calm and joyous. When asked for the reason, she said, "Because I know that I have a God who can shake the world." Yes; God is in control of all events. If we doubt, we don't trust; if we trust, we don't doubt.

LOVING AND BEING LIGHT

Readings: 1 Kgs 17:7-16; Mt 5:13-16

It is in our nature to love light. When the grey skies of winter are finally breaking apart, and the bright sunshine of spring is bursting through, touching our cheeks and caressing our shoulders, how grateful are we for the light and its warmth! If it is our nature to love light, it is our calling to be light for others. "You are the light of the world. Let your light shine before men" (Mt 5:14,16). What Jesus meant by 'light' is our goodness. Every Christian shares in the goodness of God, not only because we are created in the image of God, but also because we have become adopted children of God through Christ Jesus. We are called not to hoard this goodness of ours, as if it were a lamp to be stowed away in a closet. We are called to be generous in our good works for others, even when we ourselves have only limited resources. We think of the poor widow in the first reading. She was in a dire situation herself, expecting to die due to the famine over the land; Still, she went out to share her frugal meal with a hungry Elijah, and her generosity was rewarded by God who saw to it that her jar flower did not go empty until the famine ended (1 Kgs 17:16). It is in the nature of light to heal and nurture, to warm and soothe. So be our goodness to others.

WEDNESDAY – WEEK 10 / YEAR 2

GOD IN A CRADLE

Readings: 1 Kgs 18:20-39; Mt 5:17-19

On the cover of one of the issues of the European *Time* magazine, were the following words: "God is dead; Marx is dead; and I'm not too well myself." It is right; for without belief in God, there is nothing left for us to survive in this life. But today, many people have problem not believing in God, but believing in the God whom Jesus has revealed as the true One. They are like those people who worshipped Baal as their God, in preference to the true God of Elijah. And the true God had to send down fire to set ablaze the water-soaked offering upon the altar (1 Kgs 18:38) built for Baal. God may not repeat a similar miracle, in order to convince modern non-believers. The reason is that God has already given us the greatest miracle possible to win all people's loyalty to him. That miracle is Jesus Christ, his Son, God in flesh. In all history, there is nothing like the Christmas event. If you stroll through cities around the world, you will see imposing monuments to outstanding men and women. But have you ever seen a statue of a famous person as an infant? You never see Napoleon portrayed in a stroller. It would be silly. But it is not silly to honour Christ as a baby, for he is the Lord of the universe, made flesh.

GOD-SIZED WONDERS

Readings: 1 Kgs 18:41-46; Mt 5:20-26

If we make a list of all the great creative works God has done for us, what would be on it? Our list would definitely include galaxies, black holes, solar system, the law of thermo-dynamics, and the atmosphere, the asteroid belt, constellation and photosynthesis. All of them are God-sized wonders of his love for humankind. Think about all the intricate inventions with which we surround ourselves: our timed dishwashers, our CD players, our video cams, and cars. Now think of the way God keeps running the universe- everything from DNA to weather patterns, from magnetic fields in space to ants in your backyard. Our belief in God's actions for us should motivate us to be faithful to him. But king Ahab was not. Both the draught and its conclusion marked by heavy rain were signs to Israel of God's sovereign power; but the king did not learn the lesson and allowed his pagan wife Jezebel to turn him against God (1 Kgs 10:45). Our response to God's love for us should inspire us to great generosity towards God and others, his children. We often hear about people with no religion, but who lead very good lives. But Jesus told us his followers that our "righteousness must exceed" (Mt 5:20) that of those who do not share our faith.

SEVERE PRESCRIPTION

Readings: 1 Kgs 19:9, 11-16; Mt 5:27-32

In one movie, some shipwrecked men are left drifting aimlessly on the ocean in a lifeboat. As the days pass under the scorching sun, their ration of food and fresh water run out. The men grow deliriously thirsty. One night, while others are asleep, one man ignores all previous warnings and gulps down some seawater. He quickly dies, for ocean water contains seven times more salt than human body can safely ingest. When we lust, we become like this man. Lust is a desperate thirst for what is sexually immoral. And if we yield to it, it may not kill our body, but it kills us inside, setting rot in the bones. Hence, when it comes to lust, God prescribes a severe operation: "If your right eye causes you to sin, pluck it out and throw it away" (Mt 5:29), and so with hands. That is because if we don't deal severely with lust, then a glance becomes a gaze; something which we would dare not touch before, becomes something we brazenly handle, for lust and reason are enemies. Putting away lustful thoughts is painful. Turning our eyes away from sensual images is incredibly difficult. Slamming the door on an unhealthy relationship seems impossible to do. But it must be done, for the unspeakable peace and joy that follows.

SATURDAY – WEEK 10 / YEAR 2

MINDING THE LITTLE FOXES

Readings: 1 Kgs 19:19-21; Mt 5:33-37

A decision to follow Christ ought to be a turning point where I say good-bye to the past and get charged up about the future. It has to be a radical and total commitment; any half-hearted dedication will only drag us away and away from the Lord. When Elijah called Elisha to succeed him as God's prophet, "by casting his mantle upon him" (1 Kgs 19:19), Elisha was at first somewhat reluctant; but soon repenting for his hesitation, he accepted Elijah's call. His slaughter of the oxen and his burning of the plough, marked his complete break with his old manner of life. At baptism, we promised to be committed witnesses to the truth of Christ. In the Gospel Jesus tells us to be truthful. "You shall perform to the Lord what you have sworn" (Mt 5:33), he says. We are called to a radical commitment to truthfulness. Even in small things we are not to make any compromise with falsehood. We are usually on guard against the big falls in our lives; but it is the little foxes, namely, the little lies that spoil tender grapes. Little faults kill good intentions, intentions that are tender and young, like the new little grapes on the vine that haven't had a chance to mature. It is the tender fruits, which are most susceptible to ruin.

VENGEANCE IS HIS ONLY

Readings: 1 Kgs 21:1-16; Mt 5:38-42

Once, I noticed a sign on a factory bulletin board with the words: "To err is human; to forgive is not company policy." These days, not to forgive does seem to be not only company policy, but also general human policy. And yet, forgiveness is better than revenge, for forgiveness is the sign of a gentle nature, but revenge is of a savage nature. So, Jesus counsels us not to take "an eye for an eye and a tooth for a tooth" (Mt 5:38). In his dealings with us, God does not take revenge, but he always shows mercy and forgives us. King Ahab unjustly seized the property of Naboth, after he was stoned to death by his pagan wife Jezebel (1 Kgs 21:16). But later in the story, God relented in the punishment due to Ahab because he repented. God has given us many good gifts: gifts of health, wealth, food, work, friends and especially the gift of himself in Jesus his Son. His gifts overflow in abundance, meeting all our needs. There is one thing, however, that God has not given us. That is revenge. God says, "Vengeance belongs to me alone." He reminds us to keep hands off when tempted to avenge a wrong. And there is a good reason why we should forgive the offender. How can I get ahead of anyone, as long as I am trying to get even with him?

LOVING THE ENEMY

Readings: 1 Kgs 21:17-29; Mt 5:43-48

How often we hear people wishing their enemies dead! On his deathbed, when asked by a priest if he forgave his enemies, a man replied: "I do not have to forgive my enemies; I have had them all shot." But Jesus tells us: "Love your enemies, and pray for those who persecute you" (Mt 5:44). In this, Jesus wants us to be perfect, as our heavenly Father is perfect (v.48). King Ahab was guilty of murder and injustice towards Naboth. And yet God so loved this wicked man that he delayed his sentence, giving time to get his life in order; and when he did repent, God forgave him saying, "I will not bring the evil in his days" (1 Kgs 21:29). It is not easy, of course, for us human beings to love our enemies as God loves even wicked people. But perhaps we consider this: My enemies tell me what they don't like in me rather than the things they do like. Thus, they provide me an object of love, outside the small circle of my selfishness. They rub off the artificial varnish and make me see my natural complexion. Their mirror of biting sarcasm and scathing rebuke reveals to me myself. And so we can love our enemies. But if we hate them, we are giving them power over us: power over our sleep, our appetites, and our blood pressure.

WEDNESDAY – WEEK 11 / YEAR 2

HIS GRACIOUS PULL

Readings: 2 Kgs 2:1, 6-14; Mt 6:1-6,16-18

For a long time God dealt with his people chiefly through his prophets. And so, when Elijah died, God saw to it that Elisha took his place. As God's sign of the prophetic role passing from Elijah to Elisha, the Jordan river divided to right and left (2 Kgs 8) when Elisha struck it with the cloak of Elijah. God can act in any way he chooses, but for the most part he wishes to communicate his truth and love through human beings, which we can see in his Church. He communicates through bishops, priests, and deacons; even through a lector who proclaims God's words and through a special minister who gives Holy Communion. You may be a very ordinary instrument in the hand of God and your ministry may be so insignificant that it goes unnoticed by others. But you must trust that "your Father who sees in secret will reward you" (Mt 6:4). But we who are called to be ministers of God, have to remember this: However learned, popular and eloquent a minister may be, he or she is nothing without the Holy Spirit. The bell in the steeple may be well hung, fairly fashioned and of soundest metal, but it is dumb until the ringer makes it speak. So too, our ministry is ineffective until the divine Spirit gives it a gracious pull.

OUR FATHER

Readings: Eccl 48:1-14; Mt 6:7-15

A king sits with his council deliberating on high affairs of state involving the destiny of the nation. Suddenly, he hears the sorrowful cry of his little child who has fallen down or been frightened by a bee. He rises and runs to his relief, assuages his sorrow and relieves his fears. Is there anything unkingly here? Does it not even elevate the monarch in our esteem? Yes it does. And yet, we at times think it dishonourable for God, the King of kings, to consider the small matters we bring to him in prayer. Remember, Jesus asked us to address him "Our Father" (Mt 6:9). He is indeed the Father of Jesus and our Father. Elijah was great; "As in his life he did wonders, so in death his deeds were marvellous" (Eccl 48:14). But, even he knew God only as the Creator of heaven and earth; he had no revelation that God is actually a father. It was left to Jesus to reveal to us that God is our Father. Therefore, we can bring to our heavenly Father all our concerns big and small, great and trivial. There is no parental abuse in the character of God's Fatherhood. We need to see our circumstances through God's love, instead, as we are often prone to do, of seeing God's love through our circumstances.

FIRM GRASP WOUNDS

Readings: 2 Kgs 11:1-4, 9, 18-20; Mt 6:19-23

We are not to hold earth's treasures with too firm a grasp. Our losses would not be half so sharp, if we always viewed our worldly possessions as being lent to us. A man does not cry when he has to return a tool that he has borrowed. Yes; this world is important, but it is passing. So Jesus tells us: "Do not lay up for yourselves treasures on earth... but lay up for yourselves treasures in heaven" (Mt 6:19-20). Only heavenly treasures will last, something Athalia, King Jehoram's wife forgot. She expected that her son Ahaziab would become king of Judah. When he was assassinated, Athalia violently usurped the throne of Judah. Her treasures were power and the luxury. However, since they were only earthly treasures, she could not hold them long, for after seven years, she was overthrown and was "slain with the sword at the king's house" (2 Kgs 11:20). May we then set our hearts on lasting heavenly treasures, such as humility and simplicity? Humility makes us look to God as the source of all life and holiness. Simplicity makes us realise that lasting values are found in goodness, in love and in unselfishness. It is sad to see some people who know the price of everything, yet seem to know the value of nothing.

SATURDAY – WEEK 11 / YEAR 2

"TWO MASTERS?"

Readings: 1 Chr 24:17-25; Mt 6:24-34

The Robin said to the Sparrow: "I should really like to know why those anxious human beings rush about and worry so much!" The Sparrow said: "Friend, I think that it must be that they have no heavenly Father like the One who cares for you and me." Our Lord tells us: "Do not be anxious about your life" (Mt 6:25) because there is a heavenly Father who will provide for us. Perhaps we do rely on God, but then, we also find it difficult not to worry about our material needs. Thus we are constantly pushed to serve "two masters" (v.24). In this we are somewhat like Joash. He wanted to be the king of Judah and that meant that he was to be totally dedicated to the God of Israel. But he also wanted to please the powerful princes who were pagans at heart. As a result, he became so attentive to the princes that he began to despise God (1 Chr 24:20). We need steadily to overcome this tension between anxiety for material needs, and reliance on God. We can overcome it by doing what we can to earn our livelihood, while trusting in the divine Providence which continues to work on our behalf. There are no worries for those whose trust is buried in the Providence of God. Whoever falls from God's right hand, is caught into his left.

JUDGE NOT!

Readings: 2 Kgs 17:5-8, 13-15, 18; Mt 7:1-5

While my friend and I were eating in a fast-food restaurant, discussing some parish affairs, we overheard a couple at a nearby table having a heated argument. "You, dumbbell," the woman hissed, "why don't you ever listen to me?" I mentally slammed down the gavel and pronounced the woman guilty. The nerves of her talking like that! But Jesus tells us: "Judge not, that you be not judged" (Mt 7:1). Yes; we ought to weigh between right and wrong. Yes; we should hold our brother or sister accountable to Christian standards. But we are not to close the book on any individual. God's grace is operative in every person's life at each moment and we can not predict the result of its mysterious chemistry. Further, we can't fully comprehend the life experiences that made an individual the type of person he or she has become. Lastly, our snap judgement can be wrong. In truth, judging others is like measuring another's coat on our own body; we want others to be as we are! We judge ourselves by our best intentions and others by their worst faults. Is it fair? As the saying goes, "There is so much good in the worst of us, and so much bad in the best of us, that it hardly becomes any of us, to talk about the rest of us."

THE MOST COMFORTING HYMN

Readings: 2 Kgs 19:9-11, 14-21, 31-36; Mt 7:6, 12-14

One of the most comforting hymns I have ever heard begins with these words: "What a friend we have in Jesus, all our sins and griefs to bear! What a privilege to carry everything to God in prayer!" Hezekia, the ruler of Judah did exactly this. After subduing the southern kingdom of Israel, Senuacherib, the king of Assyria, was about to invade Judah.

Hezekia knew that Judah was no match to Assyria. It would be like an infant trying to defend himself against a giant. So he did the best of all things. He turned to God in earnest prayer: "O Lord, the God of Israel! Incline thy ear and hear, open thy eyes and see" (2 Kgs 19:16). And God heard his prayer. That night, the Assyrian army was devastated by a freak plague and Judah was saved. The best thing we can do when we have insurmountable difficulties is to spread them before the Lord. Let us ask for his help and guidance. He will do what is needed. Our prayer will at least help us to yield to God's will, but bringing with it into our hearts that inner peace, which surpasses all understanding. Hence, the same comforting hymn concludes: "Oh, what peace we often forfeit; Oh, what needless pain we bear; all because we do not carry everything to God in prayer."

WEDNESDAY – WEEK 12 / YEAR 2

A SOUND TREE

Readings: 2 Kgs 22:8-13; 23:1-3; Mt 7:15-20

A Peach tree, for example, may be strong and healthy looking, and you might think that it would produce more fruit than the tree that may appear inferior to it. However, the real result may be different, namely, it might produce less fruit than the one which appeared inferior. As Jesus says, "Every sound tree bears good fruit, but the bad tree bears evil fruit" (Mt 7:17). When applied to Christian believers, it means that it is not one's appearance that counts, but what he or she actually does as one dedicated to our loving God. Of course, complete dedication to God depends on the strength of our belief that God has already made a new Covenant of love with us and has sealed it with the blood of his Son Jesus Christ. When the "Book of the Law" which contained the Old Covenant God had made with Israel was discovered in the temple and presented to Josiah, the king of Judah, he felt that he had received a fortune by inheritance. Hence, he promised to the Lord to keep his statutes with "all his heart and all his soul" (2 Kgs 23:3). How convinced are we that God's Son died for us and established us in a new loving relationship with God our Father, the Creator of the universe? The stronger this conviction is the more good fruits we will bear.

RELIGIOUS INSIGNIA NOT ENOUGH

Readings: 2 Kgs 24:8-17; Mt 7:21-29

A father warns his child time and again to stay away from those containers underneath the sink. But one day Dad walks into the kitchen and sees his little boy pale and unconscious on the floor. Somehow the boy managed to pry the lid off that old bottle of insecticide. Doctors report that the boy will be permanently impaired. Similarly, when we knowingly disobey God's will, we bring upon ourselves disastrous consequences. See what happened to Judah. It was a religious kingdom; namely, the king was not merely a political figure, but the representative of God. However, the spiritual foundation of the kingdom was lost, for its king and his people lived lives as if there were no statutes given by God. The result was that Judah fell under the Babylonians (2 Kgs 24:16). The saying of the Lord came true: "Not everyone who says to me, 'Lord, Lord', shall enter the kingdom of heaven, but he who does the will of my Father" (Mt 7:21). Pretending to be a religious country without doing God's will is to be like the corrupt kingdom of Judah. To be a Christian nation implies a great deal more than the insignia of religion, prayer in schools, religious mottoes, hymns at inaugurations and prayerful invocations at public dinners. It means doing God's will.

SAVED!

Readings: 2 Kgs 25:1-12; Mt 8:1-4

Saved! What a sweet sound it is, to the one who sees the vessel going down, but discovers that the lifeboat is near and will rescue him from the sinking ship! But to be rescued from sin and death is a greater salvation still and demands a louder joy, for it is being reconciled to God our Father. God never abandons us when we go astray from him.

This we know from the history of the people of Judah. The devastation and the captivity which they suffered twice at the hands of the king of Babylon (2 Kgs 25:7), were the consequences of their blatant infidelity to God. Yet God did not abandon them, but was calling them to return to him repentant. The hope of humanity for getting reconciled with God was realised in Jesus Christ, sent by God for that purpose. As a sign that Jesus had come to heal the world of the wounds of sin, he healed many sick people, as he healed the leper mentioned in today's Gospel (Mt 8:3). Yes. Jesus is the Saviour of all. We will sing it in life and whisper it in death and chant it throughout eternity. Saved by the Lord! I heard someone saying, "Oh, I would give my eyes for salvation!" But I said to him, "Give your heart to Jesus Christ, and take his salvation free!"

SATURDAY – WEEK 12 / YEAR 2

YOU MATTER TO GOD

Readings: Lam 2:2, 10-14, 18-19; Mt 8:5-17

"God sits above, scattering galaxies and exploding supernovas. He sets stars and suns spinning in motion, ladles out rivers and puckers up mountain ranges. He is lofty and is magnanimously absorbed in matters of the universe. He is happy up there. But we are down here drowning in misery. Does he care?" We know he does, because we know his Son Jesus. The Son, the image of the invisible God, went about healing people such as the servant of the Roman Centurion (Mt 8:13) and Peter's mother-in-law (v.5), mentioned in today's Gospel. God's mercy is always willing to lift us up from the mire of the troubles and problems, which we often bring upon ourselves by our infidelity to God. The first reading gives a striking but sorrowful picture of a shattered people drowned in the sea of afflictions. But in the middle of this national grief, there is a firm faith that God is with them and hence the prophet urges the people: "Cry aloud to the Lord! O daughter of Zion" (Lam 2:18). God our Father, for all his grandeur and loftiness, stoops down to those who cry for his mercy. I asked a famous preacher: "If you could say one sentence to a secular audience, what would you say?" He answered, "You matter to God."

NEITHER THIRSTY NOR DRUNKEN

Readings: Amos 2:6-10, 13-16; Mt 8:18-22

Increasing affluence has not made people friendlier towards one another. They are better off; but that new-found wealth has not resulted in a new sense of community. You get the impression that affluent people are more preoccupied with themselves and have less time for one another, than when they did not possess so much. Affluence gives us less room for God's peace, than the absence of it. Affluence can also make for self-protection, an unwillingness to surrender what one possesses. Sometimes, self-protection can go as far as the exploitation of the poor. Amid the affluence of the northern kingdom of Judah, there was so much corruption that "they sold the righteous for silver and the needy for a pair of shoes" (Amos 2:6). God warned them that their injustice and oppression of the poor made a mockery of their faith in God. "The son of Man had nowhere to lay his head" (Mt 8:20), for he wanted to identify himself with the poor. Can we at least go for moderation in wealth and possession? Moderation is the silken string running through the pearl chain of justice and peace. It is better therefore to rise from life as from a banquet, neither thirsty nor drunken. Moderation leaves a surplus wealth, made available for the poor.

IT IS FIFTY-FIFTY

Readings: Amos 3:1-8; 4:11-12; Mt 8:23-27

Have you seen the picture of Jesus with hair parted down the middle, surrounded by cherub-like children and bluebirds? Every where this Jesus walks, strains of organ music sound! This is a very sentimental notion of Jesus. "He speaks and the sound of his voice is so sweet that the birds hush their singing" is a hymn that is also sentimental. Why do we prefer a sentimental picture of Jesus or of God? Because it requires nothing from us, neither conviction nor commitment. But God wants to convince us that while he loves us, he also expects us to respond to that love by committing ourselves to him. For example, God had entered into a covenant love with his chosen people, but they were expected to respond in kind, which they did not do. So God lamented "Do two walk together unless they have made an appointment?" (Amos 3). Likewise, Jesus was looking for a return of faith from his apostles for all the signs of love he had manifested. But it was not forthcoming, in the midst of a storm on the sea, and the disappointed Jesus exclaimed: "O men of little faith!" (Mt 8:26). Our relationship with God has to be like marriage. It is a fifty-fifty proposition, a two-way street. It cannot be just sentimental.

WEDNESDAY – WEEK 13 / YEAR 2

OUR SOLEMN CELEBRATIONS

Readings: Amos 5:14-15, 21-24; Mt 8:28-3

A Christian king in medieval Europe was making a tour of his kingdom. When he came across a very elderly man working in a vineyard, "How old are you?' he inquired. The man replied, "Your majesty, I am four years of age." The king laughingly protested that this was impossible; so the man explained: "Your majesty, I count only those hours when I have faithfully served the Lord." It was an inspiring reply. But, what is faithful service to the Lord? Is it when we spend hours-attending worship services, saying prayers and offering sacrifices? Not really. God says, "I take no delight in your solemn assemblies" (Amos 5:21), "but let justice roll down like waters" (v.24). This means that our liturgical celebrations, though good in themselves, become irritating to God, if after celebrating, we fail to practice justice towards others. Does this disturb us? The people who witnessed Jesus exorcising two demoniacs were also disturbed, probably because they saw the Lord as a threat to their ungodly way of life in which they had settled. And so "they begged him to leave the neighbourhood" (Mt 8:34). Have we got accustomed to only the outward form of religion, with no justice flowing in our relationship with others?

APPEARANCE CAN MISLEAD

Readings: Amos 7:10-17; Mt 9:1-8

St John Vianney, the Curé of Ars, performed so poorly in his priestly studies that his seminary officials seriously questioned if he were intelligent enough to be ordained. The pastor to whom he was assigned after ordination, considered him too stupid to preach. Yet, as the years passed, people came to Curé from all over Europe to seek his advice and confess to him. On some days, he spent up to 14 hours in the Confessional. We look at the outward appearance but God looks at the heart. Amos was despised by Amazia because he was only a shepherd and a dresser of sycamores (Amos 7:14). Yet, God had chosen him to be his prophet. Jesus was only a carpenter and hence when he forgave the sins of the paralytic, he was accused of blasphemy (Mt 9:3). A priest appears to be only a human being and in fact he is so; but God uses him to forgive sins of people. What appears to be bread and wine are really the body and blood of Jesus upon the altar. God can use any ordinary substance, any insignificant event, any poorly looking person as a vehicle for his presence. In the world, persons and things are valued, not for what they are but what they seem to be, as if people are saints because they use holy water. But God's value is different.

HONESTY STILL THE BEST POLICY?

Readings: Amos 8:4-6, 9-12; Mt 9:9-13

Diogenes was a Greek cynic philosopher, who was said to have gone about the market streets of Corinth in broad daylight with a lighted lantern, looking for an honest man! Even today, honesty in business is thought to be old-fashioned. Of course, many still believe that honesty is the best policy, but strange to say, that some people can not afford the best! God condemns dishonesty especially in our dealing with the weak. If we are accustomed to cheat the poor and the vulnerable, we are called to repentance. When Amos condemned those Israelites who were cheating in business deals and took advantage of the poor, "dealing deceitfully with false balances" (Amos 8:5), God, in effect, was calling them to repentance. Matthew, a tax collector, made his living by overcharging his fellow countrymen, rich or poor. When Jesus told him to follow him and "sat at table" with him and with similar tax collectors, he was calling them too to repentance. A doctor warns a patient that his way of living is so injurious to his health that if it were not stopped, it would prove fatal. So too, through Amos and Jesus, God is warning those of us who may be unfair towards others, to repent before our dishonesty becomes fatal.

SATURDAY – WEEK 13 / YEAR 2

GOD IS NO MISER

Readings: Amos 9:11-15; Mt 9:14-17

In return for some good work done, an old miserly man, carefully unties the strings of a small money bag, reaches in for a tiny coin which he places very carefully in the worker's hand saying, "Now, don't spend this all in one place." Some of us imagine God to be like this miser, which is wrong. God is generous beyond our powers to imagine. Although the message of Amos was one of impending doom, his vision pierced beyond the coming darkness, to a time of abundant light and restoration, which the generous God would bring about. He was not talking about the economic and political restoration of Israel, but the resurgence of her spiritual power. The doom Amos predicted came a generation later. The restoration of the great outpouring of God's love, described by Amos in terms of agricultural abundance (Amos 9:13), came six centuries after, when Jesus died and rose again. God is not miserly in giving. When Jesus spoke of "old wineskins" (Mt 9:11), he was in effect telling us not to limit God by the old wine skin of our miserly image of him. The new wineskin of God's love is infinite. He is more forgiving than we suspect, more generous than we hope, and more loving than we can possibly know.

A FOUNTAIN OF LOVE

Readings: Hos 2:16-18, 21-22; Mt 9:18-26

If a man could know that he was loved by all his fellow human beings, if he could have it for certain that he was loved by all the angels, yet that love would be like a drop that could not compare with the ocean of God's love for him. That God's love for us is like that of a husband for his wife is revealed in what he told Israel: "You will call me 'My husband'" (Hos 2:16). We get a better picture of God's love by observing the actions of Jesus Christ who is God in flesh. We see his concern for the synagogue leader whose daughter had died (Mt 9:18); we see how he heals the woman with a haemorrhage (v.20). God's love appreciates human problems, both critical ones like the death of a little girl, and less serious ones like the illness of the woman. Do we need to be healed of some malady in body, or mind or soul? Let us reach out to God. We have to be at least willing to touch the tassel of Jesus' garment and make a move towards the throne of God's mercy. If we make the slightest movement in the Lord's direction, he will extend his hand to us, for his love for us is a fountain of love. Remember that this fountain of love has its spring in itself, not in you, nor in me, but in God's own gracious and infinite heart of goodness.

CRUEL TO BE KIND

Readings: Hos 8:4-7, 11-13; Mt 9:32-38

In Shakespeare's play, when Hamlet admonished his mother, Queen Gertrude, for her immorality, she complained about his cruelty with bitter tears. Hamlet replied, "I am cruel only to be kind." God seems to say the same when he sends us some afflictions. He who once poured out his love for Israel by saying, "I will betroth you to myself for ever"

(Hos 2:19), later pronounced severe warning through the same prophet: "They sow the wind and they shall reap the whirlwind" (Hos 8:7). And yet, his words of warning were motivated by nothing other than love. Only the hand of love inflicts the hardest blow that God ever lays upon us. Jesus went round "healing every disease and every infirmity" (Mt 9:35). But there were times when the same Jesus put out severe warnings and condemnation of improper practices among people. Even on those occasions, Jesus was no less loving than he was when healing diseases. In our lives, when everything seems to be going wrong, it is difficult to believe that there is a loving God. But our knowledge of how God dealt with his chosen people and Christ's own actions, should convince us that God loves us even in our afflictions.

WEDNESDAY – WEEK 14 / YEAR 2

HE NEVER GIVES UP

Readings: Hos 10:1-3, 7-8, 12; Mt 10:1-7

When stomachs and pocketbooks are full, warnings fall on deaf ears. The northern kingdom of Israel was prospering. The more fruitful their orchards were, the more altars they built for false gods; and more productive their fields were, the more pillars they erected for pagan idols. Hosea warned them to reform and if they did not, punishment would descend upon them (Hos 10:10), and it did. The northern kingdom was destroyed by Assyrian armies within ten years. But God never gives up on his people. In the Gospel we see Jesus choosing his twelve apostles and sending them to recover "the lost sheep of the house of Israel" (Mt 10:6). By most standards, we live today in an affluent culture. Are we aware of the dangers of too much affluence? – Mammoth productive facilities with computer minds, the cities that engulf the landscape and pierce the clouds, planes that almost outrace time – these are awesome, but they can not be spiritually inspiring, if material prosperity is made an end in itself. In the absence of any moral purpose, we ourselves become smaller as our works and machines bigger. But God has not given upon us. He intends to protect us from the dangers of affluence, provided we are prepared to listen to his Gospel.

DOMESTICATING OURSELVES

Readings: Hos 11:1-4, 8-9; Mt 10:7-15

Joseph Stalin's daughter, Svetlana Allilvyeva, wrote a book called *Twenty Letters to a Friend.* In it, a letter from her father contains this excerpt: "You don't write to your little pap. I think you have forgotten him. Never mind. I kiss you. I am waiting to hear from you." Stalin, though a cruel tyrant, unknowingly revealed a heart for love because he too had been created in the image of God who is love. God revealed his fatherly love when he said to his people, "It was I who taught Ephraim to walk; I took them up in my arms" (Hos 11:3). But the more God loved Israel, the more they rejected him and made him angry. Still, because of his love, he promised: "I will not execute my fierce anger" (v.9). It is this fatherly love of God which Jesus revealed as he sent out his disciples on a mission saying, "Heal the sick, raise the dead, cleanse the lepers, cast out demons" (Mt 10:8). Our own love for others has to reflect God's tender love for us. God's Kingdom is one of love. Kingdoms founded on force will not last. Most ferocious animals are not safe. If someone meets a cobra, he kills it. If instead he meets a domestic animal, he is not afraid. The security of pet animals lies in their mildness. We should domesticate ourselves with love and meekness of God, and spread them around.

HANG ON TO IT!

Readings: Hos 14:2-10; Mt 10:16-23

Some believers say that God cares so much for us that he would never want any hurt or heartache to touch us. "If we really trusted in God," they reason, "he would go to any length to release us from our pain." But is this so? Not really. The Scripture indicates that God allows sufferings to wound us, but that never means he does not care for us when we are wounded. God certainly cared for Israel when they suffered at the hands of the Assyrians, and hence he protested: "I will heal their faithlessness, I will love them freely; I will be as the dew to Israel" (Hos 14:4-5). Therefore, as we go through a difficult phase of life, we must trust that we are still in the protective hands of God. Our difficulties may not be the same as those of the disciples about which Jesus warned: "You will be hated by all for my sake" (Mt 10:22). Difficulties and trials are different for each of us; but whatever they are, God still cares for us in them. But the focus of God's care will normally be the welfare of our souls. And the expression of his care will be peace and contentment. It is God's beautiful promise that he cares for you whether you are ill for weeks, bedridden for months or struggling within your marriage for years. Grab hold of this truth and hang on!

SATURDAY – WEEK 14 / YEAR 2

HE IS ALL HOLY

Readings: Is 6:1-8; Mt 10:24-33

As the light of the moon is swallowed up by the brightness of the sun, so the shining achievements of men and women are swallowed up by the glory of God. The glory of God refers primarily to who God is, not to what he does. God is infinite; outside of him there is nothing but nothing. The infinity of God is not mysterious; it is only to us that it is unfathomable. A reverent and Godly Christian sees the infinite God first in his transcendent glory, majesty and holiness, before he sees him in his love, mercy and grace. When the great prophet Isaiah saw the glory of God in a vision and heard angels chanting, "Holy, holy, holy is the Lord of hosts; the whole earth is full of his glory" (Is 6:3), he became instantly conscious of his unworthiness to stand before God. We are called to approach God with the simplicity and confidence of a child. But we must never forget that he is God. We can not make him less than he is. For example, when we come to Eucharistic celebration and ask for God's mercy at the start of the

Mass, how truly are we conscious of God's holiness and our unworthiness? To God, holiness is not just an attribute; it is his very essence. When we see even a small glimpse of God's holiness, we will bow in worship.

MONDAY – WEEK 15 / YEAR 2

RITUALS CAN BE LIES

Readings: Is 1:10-17; Mt 10:34–11:1

The husk of worship becomes worthless, when the worm of selfishness has eaten out the kernel of love. As the dress is hideous which no longer covers a living body but covers a merciless heart, so the sweetest voice is only hateful, that utters no concern for a neighbour's plight. God warned his people against being hypocritical in their religious worship, an attempt to deceive him by means of a display of a ritualised religion, while under the surface, exploiting the vulnerable: "What to me is the multitude of your sacrifices?" – "Cease to do evil, learn to do good, seek justice, correct oppression" (Is 1:11,17). Our worship is not meaningful when we are indifferent to the needy among us. In order to encourage us to make our worship meaningful by caring for the weak in society, Jesus went so far as to promise a reward to one who would give even a cup of cold water to a needy person (Mt 10:42). If our life is corrupt, our prayer is corrupt; if our lives as God's people are lies, our rituals are lies. What is needed is not so much liturgical reformation as personal transformation. What is of urgency is not so much the dutiful observance of august ceremonies, as the filling up of the social and economic gap between the rich and the poor.

MY INVISIBLE TORMENTOR

Readings: Is 7:1-9; Mt 11:20-24

A doctor would be doing a great disservice, if he were to pretend that we are in good health when actually we are not. He will be truly kind if he tells us the truth. Isaiah was a good spiritual doctor. He told king Ahaz that God was deeply disturbed about the spiritual decay of Israel, and if things did not change for the better, "all the lands would be briers and thorns" (Is 7:23). Jesus, the Divine Physician was normally kind and gentle; but he also gave people occasional stern warnings, especially to those who would not believe even after witnessing his miracles. "Woe to you, Chorazin! It shall be more tolerable on the day of judgement for Tyre and Sidon than for you" (Mt 11:21-22), was one of his warnings. How do we know that God is warning us of something about us, right now? Let us examine our conscience. Does it feel guilty of something? The greatest tormentor of a human soul is a guilty conscience. If I am disturbed in my conscience, God is calling me to repent and begin to enjoy a clear conscience. There is no pillow so soft as a clear conscience. We need to remember that once we assuage our conscience by calling an evil a necessary evil, it begins to look more and more necessary, and less and less evil.

THE ESSENTIAL VICE

Readings: Is 10:5-7, 13-16; Mt 11:25-27

The essential vice, the utmost evil, is pride. Unchastity, greed, and drunkenness are mere fleabites in comparison. Temper, for example, is what gets most of us into trouble and pride is what keeps us there. Assyria was a great military power bent upon conquering all neighbouring nations. Assyrians were haughty, and in their pride, they attributed their victories to their own power (Is 10:13). Isaiah had to remind them that they were but an instrument in the hands of God to purify the sinful Judah, and warned them that God would in time humble their pride, which he did. Jesus in the Gospel gives praise to his Father for his love of the simple and the humble: "I thank thee Father," he says, "that thou has hidden these things from the wise and the understanding and revealed them to babes" (Mt 11:25). Jesus does not condemn intelligence; what he condemns is intellectual pride. Even the most unlettered among us could understand the mysteries of God's kingdom, if we are humble of heart and mind, before God and others. A Bible scholar told me this in good humour: Moses spent forty years thinking he was somebody; then he spent forty years on the backside of the desert realising he was nobody; finally, he spent the last forty years of his life, learning what God can do with nobody!

THURSDAY – WEEK 15 / YEAR 2

WHAT IS A YOKE?

Readings: Is 26:7-9, 12, 16-19; Mt 11:28-30

What is a yoke? It appears to be a weighty burden, but it makes the workload light for the animal. A plough or a coal drag would be intolerable if it were attached to the oxen in any other way. But when we work an animal by means of a yoke, the weight the animal has to pull does not harm it. The load becomes light. Jesus says, "Take my yoke upon you and learn from me for I am gentle and lowly in heart, and you will find rest for your soul" (Mt 11:29). Yes; Jesus wants us to take his yoke of righteousness, of gentleness and of humility, promising that such a living will give us peace of soul. Isaiah foretold: "The way of righteousness is level; thou dost make smooth the path of the righteous" (Is 26:7). A yoke is not a contrivance to make work hard. It is a gentle device to make hard work light. A yoke is meant not to give pain but to save pain. Burdens are inevitable in our lives. But we have a choice either to drag our workload under our own strength or put on the yoke of Christ. We will find a deep, sweet, peaceable rest even in the midst of our labours, when we put on the yoke of Christ.

FRIDAY – WEEK 15 / YEAR 2

FORGIVING MERCY

Readings: Is 38:1-6, 21-22, 7-8; Mt 12:1-8

In one of my former parishes, my parish priest was an unusually kind and forgiving person. One day a shabby street person approached him. The man told a wildly improbable tale of woe but the priest gave him £5. After the panhandler left, I said to him, "You should not have given that man any money. His story could not have been true. He just made it up." "Yes," he replied, "but imagine how it would feel to be so desperate that you had to make up a story like that." That was mercy, and mercy often goes with forgiveness. We are called to be merciful to others as God is towards us. See God's mercy and compassion to king Hezekiah. The king deserved to die because of his sins; God could have dealt with him in stern justice; However, in answer to the fervent prayer of the king, God allowed him to live longer, saying "I have seen your tears; behold I will add fifteen years to your life" (Is 38:5). Our Lord reminds us in the Gospel of what God had said: "I desire mercy, not sacrifice" (Mt 12:7). Is there anyone in our life whom we won't forgive? If so, we are not imitating our merciful heavenly Father. Unforgiveness is a form of power over another person, a way to manipulate, control and diminish another.

SATURDAY – WEEK 15 / YEAR 2

FOR JUSTICE SAKE

Readings: Mic 2:1-5; Mt 12:14-21

Once a man complained to me: "Sometimes, I would like to ask God why he allows poverty, injustice and oppression of the poor, when he could do something about it." I said, "Well. Why don't you ask him?" "Because," he replied, "I am afraid that God might ask me the same question." Indeed, God does ask you and me what we do to right oppression perpetrated on the poor by the rich. Prophet Micah attacked the wealthy landowners of his time who had been dispossessing the poor by illegal means (Mic 2:2). In our own time, there are other kinds of bullying the poor: employment with minimal wages, exacting a very high rate of interest, violence, terrorism, dacoity, hijacking, bribe and the rest. God asks us what do we do to remedy the situation. Some of us are naturally afraid of the painful consequences that we may have to suffer while trying to right the wrong. But Jesus himself could not avoid persecution because he spoke against the bullying Pharisees who "went out and took counsel against him, how to destroy him" (Mt 12:14). Martyrdom for justice's sake is part of Christian discipleship. David Barret, a Christian author, writes that 41 million Christians have been martyred from the dawn of Christianity.

MONDAY – WEEK 16 / YEAR 2

A MATTER OF QUITTING

Readings: Mic 6:1-4, 6-8; Mt 12:38-42

A Sunday school teacher asked the class what the word 'repentance' meant. A little boy put up his hand and said, "It is being sorry for your sins." A little girl also raised her hand and said, "It is being sorry enough to quit." She was right. But what is the true sign of quitting sinful ways? Despite all that God had done for them, the people of Israel had realised that they had been unfaithful and hence they repented. But when it came to prove their repentance, they made a mistake. They thought that if they offered to God tons of sacrifices, thousands of rams and rivers of oil God would be appeased. But God answered that he did not want more liturgy, for the issue was not a ritual one. As the sign of their repentance he wanted them "to do justice, to love kindness and to walk humbly" (Mic 6:8) before him. This admonition had been the constant message of the prophets. When the Pharisees asked Jesus for a special "sign" (Mt 12:38), Jesus, in effect, told them to follow the teachings of the prophets, such as Jonah, especially their call to repentance and prove it by quitting their sinful ways. Therefore, it is not enough to say "I am sorry and I repent", and then go on from day to day just as I always went.

FOR THE GOOD OF THE WORLD

Readings: Mic 7:1-15, 18-20; Mt 12:46-50

According to a Mexican proverb, none but a mule denies his family. However, our blood family is not the only family we must be concerned with. There was once a man who was busy building a home for himself. He wanted it to be the nicest, cosiest home in the world. Someone came to him asking for help because the world was on fire. But it was his home he was interested in, not the world. When he finally finished his home, he found that he did not have a place to put it on. Yes; It is impossible to have security for our blood family, without also working for the welfare of our world family. Our work for the good of the world consists mainly in doing God's will for our world, and doing God's will makes us children of God and brothers and sisters of Jesus Christ, as Jesus himself had said (Mt 12:50). The prophet Micah saw God as a warm hearted shepherd who "does not retain his anger for ever for he delights in steadfast love" (Mic 7:18). It is this love that is poured into all those who become part of God's family by doing God's will. But doing God's will can not be reduced to an itemised list of some specific religious observances. It means collaborating with God's plan for the welfare of the human race.

WHETHER GOOD OR BAD

Readings: Jer 1:1, 4-10; M 13:1-9

Winter seasons are notorious for their lack of romance. The deepest lakes thicken their icy crust. The wintry wind bites with fury. As creatures of comfort, we easily interpret such harsh circumstances as God's punishment. And pleasant skies and pleasant living are seen as God's favour. But Jeremiah whom God had consecrated to be his prophet before he was born (Jer 1:5) took with equanimity both good and bad days. The first part of his ministry occurred during the reign of the devout king Josiah and hence Jeremiah's words were like the seeds that "fell on good soil" (Mt 13:8) yielding a rich harvest. But after the death of Josiah, corruption among people abounded. So the prophet became sad and preached repentance, but much of his words were like the seeds that fell on "thorns" which grew up and choked them (v.7). But Jeremiah did not give up his prophetic work. When we face difficult situations, we need to remember that God does not order the events of the universe just to fulfil the desires or deservedness of a single person; he has a whole world to take care of. It is true that God orders all our circumstances. But whether they become for us celebrations or crises, depends upon our humble submission to him.

THURSDAY – WEEK 16 / YEAR 2

"YOU ARE MY BELOVED"

Readings: Jer 2:1-3, 7-8, 12-13; Mt 13:10-17

Marriage is not a finished affair. No matter to what age you live, love must be continually consolidated. But this was not to be when God united Israel to himself as in a marriage. It was a great beginning of a spiritual marriage when God delivered Israel from Egypt and shaped them into his own people. The honeymoon did not last forever. After entering into the promised land, they began to worship idols, so that God grieved: "I remember the devotion of your youth, your love as a bride" (Jer 2:2). We know that, through Christ, we ourselves have entered into a more intimate spiritual marriage with God. So the time of Jesus on earth was an exceptional time for the people of God, which Jesus referred to when he said "Truly I say to you, many prophets and righteous men longed to see what you see and did not see it, and to hear what you hear, and did not hear it." (Mt 13:17). Many voices compete for our attention. One says, "Be sure to become successful, popular and powerful." Another says, "You'd better be ashamed of yourself." Still another says, "Nobody really cares about you." But underneath all these often noisy voices, there is a still small voice that says, "You are my beloved; my favour rests on you." That is the Lord's voice.

FRIDAY – WEEK 16 / YEAR 2

HEARING HOMILIES

Readings: Jer 3:14-17; Mt 13:18-23

Some preachers would make good martyrs: they are so dry they would burn well. But we also need to note that even a well-preached homily will not be effective, unless it is also heard well. The seed "along the path" (Mt 13:19) in our Lord's parable, may refer to those hearers for whom the beginning of a homily is the sequel to turn out, sink into reverie or doze. Such people have concluded a priori that sermons are useless interludes. The seed "on the rock" (v.20) which have no roots, may refer to those who expect homilies to stir their emotions, set the hearts to flutter, bring tears to the eye, all with a message that escapes them. They come to hear oratorical fire works. The seed "among thorns" (v.22), may refer to those who are engaged in a running debate with the preacher. They mentally contradict, correct and argue with the homily. However, there is a "good soil" (v.23) that tries to hear the Word of God, despite the dryness and the accent of the homilist. If the Word of God, even when well delivered does not sink into the hearts of some hearers, it might be they are not convinced about the value of God's Word for their lives. The Word of God can redirect our will, cleanse our emotions, enlighten our mind and quicken our whole being.

SATURDAY – WEEK 16 / YEAR 2

A HORSESHOE ON THE WALL

Readings: Jer 7:1-11; Mt 13:24-30

Few of us acknowledge our superstitions. A man had a horseshoe on his wall. I asked him why. "Of course, I don't believe in it. But I understand it brings you luck whether you believe in it or not" he replied. Some people in Jeremiah's time had their superstition. Simply because they possessed a temple in Jerusalem, they believed God would favour them. Their trump card was: "This is the temple of the Lord, the temple of the Lord, the temple of the Lord' (Jer 7:4). God's response was "Amend your ways and your doings, and I will let you dwell in this place" (v.3). Religion is superstition if it does not bring forth acts of justice, love and charity. Material temples should help us to build ourselves into spiritual temples. It is better to have a community of pious, upright and truly charitable people dwelling in huts, than to have whole streets of splendid palaces with a church in the middle, but inhabited by self-indulgent, proud people indifferent to one another. At the harvest time of God's Judgement, the weeds will be burned while the good wheat will be gathered into the barns (Mt 13:30). We will be gathered into the loving arms of God, not because of our religious superstitious practices, but because of our practical love for God and our neighbour.

MONDAY – WEEK 17 / YEAR 2

THE CORRUPTION OF THE BEST

Readings: Jer 13:1-11; Mt 13:31-35

Corruption is like a ball of snow: when once set a-rolling, it must increase. It is what happened to the people of Israel. They were expected to cleave to God. But unfortunately, decay began to set in their relationship with him and God lamented: "This evil people who refuse to hear my word shall be like this waistcloth, which is good for nothing" (Jer 13:10). But God's plan can not be thwarted by human corruption. With the coming of Christ, he made all things new. The renewed presence of God's love and life in and among us, started with Jesus and his small band of followers. It was a small beginning, as tiny as a "mustard seed" (Mt 13:31), but it has spread throughout humanity. And yet we realise that we are not still immune from corruption in our society, such as injustice, irreligion, greed, cruelty, and the rest. Therefore, our life in God is a constant challenge to be a "leaven" (v.33), to be a means not for corruption but for purification. Israel was the best nation, for God had chosen them as his own, and we are the new Israel. We need to resist every temptation to become corrupt, for the corruption of the best is the worst.

TUESDAY – WEEK 17 / YEAR 2

ANY BLACK HOLE?

Readings: Jer 14:17-22; Mt 13:36-43

Many people live with an emotional 'Black Hole'; when parents, spouses, children or friends fail, as humans inevitably will, they suffer deep and painful anguish. Too many people experience tear-soaked pillows, pain-wracked nights, broken relationships and revolting divorces. During life's tribulations such as these, we need to desist doing what the people of Judah did. During their own time of adversity of war and drought, some of them simply gave up on God; others decided to excuse themselves for the misfortunes, but put the blame on others; still others sought someone other than God to help them. But Jeremiah acted differently. First, he acknowledged the people's own responsibility for their calamities, for human beings are never perfect. And then he turned to God for he is the source of all hope. And so he cried out "Are thou not he, O Lord, on whom we set our hope?" (Jer 14:22). Like Jeremiah, we also need to lookup to God in our sufferings, for he alone can provide us what we deeply and authentically need. We must also be patient for God, in his own time, to remove "the weeds" (Mt 13:38) from our lives. Simply wait on him. So doing, we will be directed, supplied, protected, corrected and rewarded.

WEDNESDAY – WEEK 17 / YEAR 2

THE HIDDEN TREASURE

Readings: Jer 15:10, 16-21; Mt13:44-46

You see a field that is bleak, like a sandlot with broken bottles and old tires scattered here and there. But once you know that the scrubby field contains a treasure, the whole picture changes. The empty scrap of land suddenly brims with possibilities; and like the man in our Lord's parable (Mt 13:44), you sell all that you have and buy the field.

The treasure in the parable is Jesus Christ, for he is the totality of God's love and life. But in order to possess this incomparable treasure, one has to be faithful to God till the end and in all circumstances, pleasant or unpleasant. This is the lesson Jeremiah learnt through a hard way. During his ministry, which became very difficult to bear, he felt abandoned by God who had given him his mission. And so he protested: "Why is my pain unceasing, my wound incurable, refusing to be healed" (Jer 15:18)? God did not take away his pains but renewed his promise to strengthen him. As time went on, Jeremiah, began to experience the treasure of God's strength hidden in his pain. At that moment he realised that any sacrifice was worth remaining loyal to God. Are we prepared to invest all that we are in God's service, in order to possess Jesus Christ, the treasure of God's love and life?

THURSDAY – WEEK 17 / YEAR 2

IN THE POTTER'S HANDS

Readings: Jer 18:1-6; Mt 13:47-53

Too often, God is viewed as a 'bulldozer', who moves straightforward towards an objective. If God says that something will happen, it will happen. While this idea has some basis in the Bible, it can be taken to extremes and lead to a fatalistic view of life: "God is going to do what he is going to do, and so it does not matter what I do." Through Jeremiah, God reveals himself not as a bulldozer but as a potter. He says, "Behold, like clay in the potter's hand, so are you in my hand" (Jer 18:6). If the vessel that the potter was making is spoiled in his hand, he works it into another vessel. So also, God works with circumstances as they emerge. God may intend to make a vase out of me, but events may cause God to make a cereal bowl instead. But one thing is certain: We are continually being shaped into more perfect persons. All types of persons join the Church. So Jesus compares it to a "net thrown into the sea and gathers fish of every kind" (Mt 13:47). Whatever an individual's motive to join the Church, God intends to mould him or her into a more and more perfect image of Christ. But to be shaped by God, we must be pliable in his hand; and if we are so today, we will be a bit different tomorrow, from what we are today.

FOR BEING A PROPHET

Readings: Jer 26:1-9; Mt 13:54-58

Prophets were spokespersons for God. God conveyed his message for his people through prophets like Jeremiah. There are special times when our own words spoken at the right time, in the right place, to the right person and in the right manner, become God's words to another human being. Then in a small but special way, we become prophets. But we have to immediately add that in doing so we must be ready to suffer like all other prophets. Jeremiah warned the people of inevitable destruction, unless they turned from their suicidal public policies and lifestyle, towards covenant living with God. The result was that "all the people laid hand on him saying, 'you shall die'" (Jer 26:8). Jesus too preached repentance but with little of Jeremiah's harshness, for his message was overlain with love. And yet, he too met with rejection and rebuff from his own town people who "took offence at him" (Mt 13:57). For being a prophet in your own small way, you may find yourself the brunt of gossip in your office; neighbours may whisper behind your back; people may smile stiffly at your words of witness; you may be left out at parties. When it happens, don't fret or feel intimidated. That is the price we all have to pay for being a prophet.

EACH TEAR IS LISTED

Readings: Jer 26:11-16, 24; Mt 14:1-12

In our world, evil appears to triumph and good to be defeated. Jeremiah, a good man, dedicated to God and to his people, called them to repent and return to God. But their response was to persecute him and eventually to exile him from his homeland (Jer 26:11). John the Baptist tried to turn the rich and the powerful king Herod from his evil ways;

but the result of his efforts cost him his head (Mt 14:11). Jesus, despite the fact that he did nothing but good throughout his life, was crucified on the cross. In our own time, the poor who consciously work hard get only poorer, when the lazy rich get richer. Many of us strive to please God in everything, but some of us suffer more than the godless and the worldly. In spite of our efforts to live a life of truthfulness, justice and goodness towards others, how many times we have cried from hurts, disappointments, emotional and physical pains! You may have thought that in those moments of pain no one noticed your red eyes. Not so. God noticed them, and he will give you indescribable glory for your grief, not with a general wave of his hand, but in a considered and specific way. Each tear has been listed and will be rewarded for embracing and living by God's values.

MONDAY – WEEK 18 / YEAR 2

WANTS AND NEEDS

Readings: Jer 28:1-17; Mt 14:13-21

There is a great difference between our wants and needs. A child cries for some 'junk food' to eat. But her mother insists that her child eats only good and substantial food, for that is what it needs. God is like this mother. He always gives us what we need, though not always satisfying our wants. Zedekia, the king of Judah wanted to hear that he would soon defeat the king of Babylon. Hananiah, the false prophet, gave the word that the king wanted to hear. But the Word of God the king needed to hear came from Jeremiah: "I have put upon the neck of all these nations an iron yoke of servitude to the king of Babylon" (Jer 28:14). As a prelude to the institution of the Eucharist, Jesus multiplied five loaves and fed five thousands (Mt 14:21). The Eucharist is not nearly as palatable as the dinner we eat at home. Some of us would wish that Jesus could have given us a gift of food different from the Eucharist, a food that could have made our life more comfortable. But Jesus knew what we really need is his own Body and Blood as our spiritual food. Therefore, whenever God does not answer our prayer of wants, it is good to recall what C.S. Lewis said: "If God had granted all the silly prayers I've made in my life, where would I be now?"

TUESDAY – WEEK 18 / YEAR 2

A PEOPLE OF HOPE

Readings: Jer 30:1-2, 12-15, 18-22; Mt 14:22-36

Some time ago, on a particular day, I read in a daily paper the headlines referring to conflicts and killings in Rwanda and Burundi, Bosnia and Chechinia, Israel and Palestine, North Korea, Kashmir and Haiti. Closer to home, there are dreadful statistics about increasing incidents of violence, child abuse, and crimes. Our world seems to be in great turmoil. But we are fundamentally a people of hope, for God is in control of everything. So, Jeremiah held out a hope to his people in the face of military forces that were bent on destruction. Their hope was to be found only in God who could "restore the fortunes of the tents of Jacob" (Jer 30:18). In order to demonstrate that God has power even over the dark mysterious depths of the ocean, the great primal force which can bring death, Jesus walked on the waves of the sea (Mt 14:25). Therefore, whenever we feel as if all elements are conspiring against us and the fatal waters of calamities are about to engulf us, let us hope in the almighty power and infinite mercy of God that can save us. Unbelievable as it may seem, it is possible for a person to live up to seventy days without food and nearly for ten days without water. But it is impossible to live even a single day without hope.

WEDNESDAY – WEEK 18 / YEAR 2

ALL-INCLUSIVE LOVE

Readings: Jer 31:1-7; Mt 15:21-28

George Elliot once asked, "What do we live for, if it is not to make life less difficult to each other?' However, most of us who can find ways to be kind to our family members, friends, and colleagues, can't be kind to those whom we dislike or to those who have hurt us by words or deeds. Jesus constantly preached that love ought not to be exclusive, and he exemplified it with his own actions. Jews considered the Canaanites to be a sinful race that embodied all that was wicked and hence deserved to be exterminated. Yet, Jesus showed love and compassion to a Canaanite woman by curing her daughter who was sick (Mt 15:28). The woman stands for anyone who we may dislike or hate. Our love for others has to be all-inclusive. Jesus asked us to love even our enemies. The present world requires new witnesses to this power of love over hate and of forgiveness over animosity. Can we stand up and show that we are Christians by our love even for our enemies? For one thing, hating people is like burning down your own house to get rid of a rat, for we hurt ourselves by hating others. The fire of hate compressed within our hearts would soon burn fiercer and burst into flames, consuming not only ourselves, but also engulfing the world.

THURSDAY – WEEK 18 / YEAR 2

TOWARDS A HAPPY ENDING

Readings: Jer 31:31-34; Mt 16:13-23

Everyone loves a happy ending. We see a movie in which a boy meets a girl, they fall in love, but then they are separated. We all react by saying, "Oh, no!" God too wants a happy ending. Through Jeremiah who was normally a prophet of doom, God painted a rosy picture of a new age to come, the age of a new covenant between him and his people, with the promise, "I will put my law within them and I will be their God and they shall be my people" (Jer 31:33). And Jesus came to establish that new covenant. Jesus' own life would arrive at a happy ending, but only through death on the cross, which shocked St Peter who said: "God forbid, Lord! This shall never happen to you" (Mt 16:22). He did not understand that in the grand plan of God, his own Son would go through rags to riches, from death to life. We too want a happy ending to our lives. That will come when we enter into eternal glory. But our happy ending has to pass through trials and difficulties in life. We can't be like the boy during the World War II, who said, "I would not mind going to war and being a hero, if I knew I would not get hurt." At times, the Lord has to break us so that he can rebuild, wound us so that he can heal, make us walk in darkness so that we can see his light.

THE PAPER TIGER

Readings: Nah 2:1, 3; 3:1-3, 6-7; Mt 16:24-28

Two friends met in one street. One said to the other, "Did you know that Sam died?" "Is that right; Did he leave anything?" "Yeah, everything!" There is no fear like the fear of death, for in death, we leave everything. Most people die in wars or because of wars, and wars are being waged from the dawn of history. As the prophet Nahum foretold (Nah 3:6-7), Assyria, the persecutor of Israel was destroyed by the combined forces of Babylon and Media. The Jews thought that that was the end of their misfortunes, which was not to be. Again, Babylon and later Rome conquered them. It was like the Second World War that followed the First. Following the Second World War, conflicts in Korea and Vietnam followed. War is terrible but death of each of us is inevitable by any manner. However, Jesus proclaimed a message of hope to our death-obsessed humanity: "Whoever loses his life for my sake, will find it" (Mt 16:25). The world is a very dangerous place, yes. You never get out of it alive, yes. But to a Christian who believes in the resurrection of Christ from the dead, death is but a paper tiger. It is but a temporary inconvenience that separates our smaller living here on earth, from our greater being in heaven.

PRAYER OF FAITH

Readings: Hab 1:12-2:4; Mt 17:14-20

Faith is the master key of the Christian life. "If you have faith as a grain of mustard seed, nothing will be impossible to you" (Mt 17:20). But what is faith with which we must pray to God? It is not the assurance that whatever we ask of God, will be granted to us. Rather, it is our certainty that God's will, will be done to us. Our faith may not always get for us what we want, but it will get what God wants us to have. In the Gospel a man begs Jesus: "Lord, have mercy on my son, for he is an epileptic" (Mt 17:15) and his prayer is answered with what he prayed for. But the prophet Habakkuk could not understand why God would allow Judah, in spite of her faith in him, to be punished by her enemies, who were more sinful than Judah. "Why are you silent when the wicked swallows us up?" (Hab 1:13), he pleaded. The reason might be that God wanted to teach Judah to want what they needed. Prayer is true only when it is within the compass of God's will. The marvellous and supernatural power of prayer consists not in bringing God's will down to ours, but in lifting our will up to his. Every true prayer is a variation on the theme, "Thy will be done." We ask what we think to be the best, but God gives what he knows to be the best.

MONDAY – WEEK 19 / YEAR 2

THE INDWELLING GOD

Readings: Ezek 1:2-5, 24-28; Mt 17:22-27

God's presence can not be limited to any one place. He is present as the air. Within his circling power we stand; on every side we find his hand. Prophet Ezekiel saw the glory of God in the form of "fire with brightness round about" (Ezek 1:28). But remember that he had this vision in the land of Chaldeans, a pagan land far from the temple in Jerusalem. And so God can be present in a special manner even among unbelievers. But when God took human flesh, Jesus Christ became the true temple of God, for Jesus is God's Son, equally divine with God. It is to this unique Sonship that he made reference, when he asked St Peter. "From whom did kings of the earth take tribute? From their sons or from others?" (Mt 17:26). Now, we ourselves, the baptised, are the temples of God, for in Christ we have become God's adopted children. Hence, God dwells in each of us. A little boy, whose father was away from home most of the time, looked at his dad's picture on the wall and said to his mother, "Mother, I wish that father would come out of that frame." We God's children need not say anything like this about our heavenly Father. He is not like a picture on the wall, wonderful to look at, but still in a frame. God is within us. We are his temples.

TUESDAY – WEEK 19 / YEAR 2

BITTER-SWEET

Readings: Ezek 2:8-3:4; Mt 18:1-5, 10, 12-14

One of my friends had seven children who had come in rapid succession. He was hard working and well spoken of. His children were asleep when I went to visit him. When I expressed the pleasure the sight of their peaceful faces gave me, the father said, "Yes, these are fine times for them; they don't need to worry about anything." The same should be said of all true children of God our Father. Our trust that he will provide us with everything, if only we please him in all things, should take away every worry from our minds. Jesus commands us: "Unless you become like children, you will never enter the kingdom of heaven" (Mt 18:3). If only we could absorb the meaning of this command as Ezekiel did, it will taste sweet. Ezekiel's eating of the scroll (Ezek 3:3), which represented God's message of warning, was a sign that he had accepted God's word and hence it tasted sweet as honey. But when he proclaimed it to his people, they could not accept it and hence it tasted bitter to them. Likewise, the command of Jesus to become like children will be sweet to those who are willing to be submissive to God; but it will be bitter for those who want to live their lives on their own, with no reference to him.

WEDNESDAY – WEEK 19 / YEAR 2

THE HOPE OF THE WORLD

Readings: Ezek 9:1-7; 10:18-22; Mt 18:15-20

Most people can see no farther than their noses. But Ezekiel could read far into the future; he could almost read into the mind of God aided by heavenly visions. In one of his visions, he saw the city of Jerusalem being destroyed because of the appalling sins of its people (Ezek 9:5-6). Yet, there was also in the vision a sign of God's good will, that the innocents would be spared marked with an 'X', which is the last letter of the Hebrew alphabet. It may be that the use of the last letter of the alphabet was intended to mean that the innocent would find redemption on the Last Day, when the Kingdom of God would be fully established. In the mean time, however, the Kingdom of peace, harmony and love has already arrived and moving towards its completion. But we must also work towards the realisation of that Kingdom, especially by seeking reconciliation with each other (Mt 18:15), and through community prayer (v.20). Reconciliation calls for humility to acknowledge our own faults, and gentleness towards those who have hurt us. Community prayer, where Jesus is present, unites us in love. So, we Christians have a task. A vision without a task is only a dream, as a task without a vision is drudgery. But a vision and a task together, is the hope of the world.

THURSDAY – WEEK 19 / YEAR 2

"FORGIVEN"

Readings: Ezek 12:1-12; Mt 18:21-19:1

In a cemetery, I saw a headstone engraved with a single word: "Forgiven". The message is simple, unembellished. There is no date of birth, no epitaph. There is only a name and a solitary word: "Forgiven". But that is the greatest word that any dying person would want to be engraved on his or her headstone. God indeed forgives us every time we repent. His patience and repeated forgiveness are meant to give us time to change. Even when he punishes us for our wilful wrongs, his punishment is only medicinal and not an act of revenge. For example, when God warned people through Ezekiel that he would send them to exile, which the prophet acted out, God gave the reason for this punishment. "It is a rebellious house, who have eyes to see but see not, who have ears to hear but hear not" (Ezek 12:2). In this way, he hoped that an exile would teach them a lesson. God like a good mother never punishes us for his own satisfaction, but that we may become better. God keeps no grudge against any of us. Are we ready to forgive those who have hurt us or do we still keep our resentment green? Jesus asks us to forgive others "seventy times seven" (Mt 18:22), meaning "always". When we forgive others, we give them a chance to improve.

IN GOD'S VOCABULARY

Readings: Ezek 16:1-15, 60, 63; Mt 19:3-12

With so many divorces happening today, you would think that when a lot of people were married, they were mispronounced man and wife. But Jesus commanded, "What God has joined, let no man put asunder" (Mt 19:6). In God's plan, when a man and woman get married, their union is forever. One reason why Jesus condemned divorce is that Christian marriage is the human expression of God's love for his people. And God has been always faithful to his covenant of love. Once there was neither charm nor appeal in God's people. But God said, "Live and grow up like the plant of the field" (Ezek 16:7), and they did and became beautiful people. Then forgetting from where their beauty came, the people gave themselves to pagan idols. And yet, God did not abandon his people. Divorce is not in his vocabulary. It is true that there are marital difficulties in remaining faithful to the end. But Christian couples are encouraged to face up to the pain of marital life and deal with its causes, rather than run away. Where God commands, he will always provide resources to enable compliance. Besides, divorce is never the easy way out that it often appears to be. It brings more pains than expected, for a marriage can never be over.

CHILDHOOD APOSTLES

Readings: Ezek 18:1-10, 13, 30-32; Mt 19:13-15

We find delight in the beauty and happiness of children that turn our heart too big for our body. As Aldous Huxly wrote, "Children are remarkable for their intelligence and for ardour, for their curiosity, their intolerance of shams, the clarity and the ruthlessness of their vision." Indeed, childhood brings down something of heaven into the midst of our rough earthiness. But the ancient Jews did not think so. They had a proverb: "The fathers have eaten sour grapes, and the children's teeth are set on edge" (Ezek 18:2), which meant that children inherit the sinful ways of their fathers. But God rejected this proverb through his prophet, for like any grown-up person, a child too is born with an innate power of freedom to choose between good and bad, and that is their dignity. Besides, unlike many adults, children are humble and simple, qualities that are required to be the citizens of God's kingdom. Hence, Jesus said, "Let the children come to me, for to such belongs the kingdom of God" (Mt 19:14). We have to have a positive attitude towards children. Children too are God's apostles sent to 'preach' love, hope and peace. Every child is born with a number of potentialities. We have to take those potentialities and guide them in the right direction.

MONDAY – WEEK 20 / YEAR 2

HAPPINESS IS LIKE A BUTTERFLY

Readings: Ezek 24:15-24; Mt 19:16-22

Some people are never going to be happy. I am not being cynical, because the very folks about whom I am writing would agree. A man saves for a very long time to buy the most expensive car of his dream. But after buying it, deep down, he has to admit that an automobile could not give him the happiness that his heart yearns for. A youth marries a very beautiful girl, but later he complains of their dead-end marriage. She gets a very well paid job, but starts complaining about the constant irritations of her superior at work. We need not be surprised at this, for dissatisfaction is the nature of all material possessions. As the prophet Ezekiel's wife died (Ezek 24:18), so all must one day die. Even before death, we can taste only the impermanence of material joys. These joys are only gifts from God and we can't substitute the gift for the giver. God is the ultimate source of true happiness. "What good deed must I do to have eternal life?" (Mt 19:16) asked the rich man. In effect, Jesus asked him to free himself from dependence on material things and turn his life over to God. Happiness is like a butterfly; the more we chase it, the more it will elude us. But if we turn our attention to God, it comes and softly sits on our shoulders.

TUESDAY – WEEK 20 / YEAR 2

ARE THEY BETTER?

Readings: Ezek 28:1-10; Mt 19:23-30

Salvador Dali is a modern painter. At the age of 20, Dali was unknown and starving. At 70, he was famous and a millionaire. His paintings hung in 41 museums around the world. One sold in New York for $250,000. Yet, through his rise from rags to riches, Dali managed to keep his perspective. He never let fame or wealth blind him or distort his spiritual vision, as they did to the prince of Tyre. Because of his reliance on wealth he had accumulated, together with the assumption that his success was due to his charm and power, the prince had developed a fatal perspective. His vice was not his material success, but the deification of that success. So God warned him: "I will bring strangers upon you; they shall thrust you down into the Pit" (Ezek 28:8). When Jesus said, "It will be hard for a rich man to enter the kingdom of heaven" (Mt 19:23), he was not praising poverty as an intrinsic good; he was only asking us to have the spirit of detachment from material riches, as a necessary condition to possess the greater riches of everlasting life. If we have something we can't do without, we don't own it; rather, it owns us. How deep is our attachment to the world's superfluities? Just because people are better off, it does not mean that they are better.

WEDNESDAY – WEEK 20 / YEAR 2

"THE NERVE OF GOD!"

Readings: Ezek 34:1-11; Mt 20:1-16

God shows compassion to whomsoever he wants. Some times, we don't like that. We seem to blame God mentally saying, "The nerve of God to save that child abuser, to reach out to that rapist on death row, to show compassion to that drug pusher!" Some of us feel a stab of resentment when God wipes the slate clean for somebody whom we would rather have wiped off the face of the earth. The parable of the owner of a vineyard calls us to let God be generous to anyone he wants. And so, when those who came early to work complained about the owner giving the same wages to the latecomers, Jesus makes the owner say: "Am I not allowed to do what I choose with what belongs to me?" (Mt 20:15). God's generosity should inspire us to be generous with our neighbours, rather than provoke us to complain about it. The reason why Ezekiel condemned the kings and princes of Judah, was that, as representatives of God, they were expected to reflect his generosity towards their subjects; but, instead they thought only of filling their own pockets (Ezek 34:3). Therefore, when we hear of a serial killer returning to Christ, or about the deathbed conversion of a tyrant, let us not become envious; but be motivated to be generous as God is.

THURSDAY – WEEK 20 / YEAR 2

LOVE TURNS VIOLENT

Readings: Ezek 36:23-28; Mt 22:1-14

The uman heart yearns for love. The tragedy is that much violence comes from a demand for love. Driven by search for love, kissing easily leads to biting, caressing to hitting, looking tenderly to looking suspiciously, listening to eavesdropping and surrendering to raping. The human heart longs for love without conditions, limitations and restrictions. But no human being is capable of offering such unconditional love except God. In fact, God invites us to a union of such love with him. In olden times, God compared this union to that of husband and wife. Through Ezekiel, God proclaimed, "A new heart I will give you" (Ezek 36:26); and a heart is a symbol of love. The Gospel speaks of a wedding banquet. Many marriages, even now, are arranged marriages in which freedom of love is taken away from the spouses. But God does not force his love on us. We are all invited to the banquet of his love. We have been given the wedding garment of baptism. But are we willing to come into the banquet of God's love? If we don't, we would look more foolish than the people in the parable who refused to come to the banquet (Mt 22:5), for they at least did not yet possess the wedding garment.

SPRINGING INTO NEW LIFE

Readings: Ezek 37:1-14; Mt 22:34-40

A closely sealed vase was found in a mummy pit in Egypt. In it were discovered a few peas, old, wrinkled and hard as stones. They had lain sleeping in the dust of a tomb for almost three thousand years. But they were planted carefully under a glass, and at the end of thirty days, they sprang into life. This is a faint illustration of our mortal body putting on immortality, when we will rise on the Last Day. In his vision, Ezekiel saw the bones joining together and flesh coming over them. When God breathed his Spirit on those who had died, they came to life again (Ezek 37:10). This vision prophesied that Israel will one day be freed from bondage in Babylon. But it also hinted that the restoration promised by God would be fully realised for all people of faith, in the general resurrection at the end of time. Those who love God and their neighbour, as Jesus taught us to (Mt 22:40), will be raised body and soul to the fullness of new life. This doctrine of the resurrection offers great comfort to the bereaved. It clothes the graves with flowers and wreathes the tomb with unfading laurel. The sepulchre shines with a light brighter than the sun. Who of us would like to lose this glorious risen life forever, for want of generosity in loving God and our neighbour?

DISPOSABLE BABIES?

Readings: Ezek 43:1-7; Mt 23:1-12

There are about 50 million abortions performed a year world-wide. In 1991, there were 179,522 in England and Wales, more than seven times the figure of 1968. Since the 1967 Act was passed, there have been 3.7 million deaths from abortions, in Britain alone. And yet, no child is a mistake in God's eyes and even unborn babies are made in the image of God. Those who abort babies in the womb are taking human life in their own hands, as if they are the creators of human life. It is not we, but God who is the source of human life. The image of the flowing water, which Ezekiel saw in his vision (Ezek 43:2) is the sign of God's gift of life to a people who were near extinction. It is also a call to us to look up to God as the source of all life. When Jesus said, "Call no man your father on earth" (Mt 23:9), Jesus was not objecting to a child calling his male parent 'father'. What he objected to was an attitude that denies God as the Father of us all. Our society is making a serious mistake in wantonly destroying human life through abortion. To eliminate the scourge of illegitimate children, what is required is more self-control than abortions. It is only a short step from disposable babies to disposable people.

MONDAY – WEEK 21 / YEAR 2

RELIGION, A GAME OF RULES?

Readings: 2 Thess 1:1-5, 11-12; Mt 23:13-22

Some bureaucrats in our society tend to apply a law blindly, with no respect for the purpose of the law. Involving innumerable legislations, increasing red tape, sticking hard and fast to unbending legal procedures, is how they seem to play the oppressive role of Pharisees, making life for the ordinary and innocent people unnecessarily burdensome. Jesus roundly condemned such legalistic abuse in the religious leadership of the Pharisees, and for this, he called them "hypocrites" and poured on them "woes" (Mt 23:13). Jesus was harsh on those who were harsh and intolerant of those who were intolerant. To him, the heart of religion is love for God and neighbour. It is true that law is needed and practice of it is necessary, for law makes love practical and love that is unexpressed dies. But, to say that God is satisfied with our attempt to obey a moral code is a lie. Law is needed only as love's eyes, for it is love that makes the law enjoyable. Law without love makes religion a game of rules, and to force this game on others is very cruel. Religion is a loving response to a loving God. "Love God and do what you will" said St Augustine. If we love God, every thing will fall into place. On the contrary, if we don't love God, even a million rules won't help.

ACTIVE WAITING

Readings: 2 Thess 2:1-3, 14-17; Mt 23:23-26

A preacher once asked some friends, "Do you think that Christ will come tonight?" One after another said, "I think not." When all had given the answer, he solemnly repeated this text: "The son of Man comes at an hour you think not." The Lord would return on the Last Day, but when that day would be, we don't know. In the mean time, without getting hysteric about his coming, we believers have to actively await his coming. What is active waiting? St Paul answers: "Hold to the traditions which you were taught by us" (2 Thess 2:15). Tradition one: Live in the trust that God our Father loves us and in his mercy has given us eternal consolation and hope. There is no conceivable situation, when it is not safe to trust God. We need never be afraid to entrust an unknown future to a known God. If sorrow makes us to shed tears, trust in the love of God that dries them. Tradition two: "Comfort your hearts and establish them in every good work and word" (v.17). We need to be Christlike in our good works. A Christian is expected to be a mind, through which Christ thinks; a voice, through which Christ speaks; a heart, through which Christ loves; and a hand, through which Christ helps.

ATTENTION TO THE PRESENT

Readings: 2 Thess 3:6-10, 16-18; Mt 23:27-32

Observe a mason building a wall. He does not rush. He picks up a rock, brushes off the dirt, turn it over in his hands and lines it up this way and that, trying to place it just right; he pays attention to just what he is doing at the moment. That is how we too have to live our pilgrim life on earth. Our past need not control our present, as it did that of the

Pharisees. Jesus lamented that they could not get rid of the past from their minds, when he said, "You build the tombs of the prophets and adorn the monuments of the righteous" (Mt 23:29). We waste tremendous amount of energies living in our past, past mistakes, regrets and painful experiences. Nor must we allow the future to control the present. Preoccupation with the Second Coming of Christ led some early Christians to fail in their duties for the present. Many of them became too lazy to work for their livelihood and so St Paul had to remind them: "If anyone will not work, let him not eat" (2 Thess 3:10). Excessive thinking about the future leads to a general social enervation in the present. In fact, Jesus' return as Judge requires a vibrant missionary zeal, to transform and change our present world, in preparation for his coming. Hence, may the past and the future revolve around the present.

THURSDAY – WEEK 21 / YEAR 2

CHRISTIAN OPTIMISM

Readings: 1 Cor 1:1-9; Mt 24:42-51

What is optimism? It is a cheerful frame of mind that enables a teakettle to sing, though in hot water up to its nose. A man had lost a leg in an accident and when he discovered what had actually happened, he said to those around him, "Thank God, it was the leg with arthritis." That is optimism. St Paul was an optimist. He was calling the Christians in Corinth to right practice, and Corinth was a city known for moral decay. But while writing, he began on a note of optimism, based not on the ability or goodness of the Corinthians, but on the grace of God. "Our Lord Jesus Christ," he wrote, "will sustain you to the end guiltless" (1 Cor 1:8). In spite of their living in a sin-city, he was convinced that they could become like "the faithful and wise servants" (Mt 24:25), spoken of in today's Gospel. Am I living a life dull and dispirited, emotionally and spiritually empty? Are defeat, discouragement and depression my daily companions? Do I feel as though I am simply going through empty motions each day? Then, this is the time to stir up my spirit of optimism, and ask God for his grace, a grace that can perform spiritual wonders. God's adequacy can overcome our inadequacies and God's strength can take over where our strength fails.

BITTER AND SWEET

Readings: 1 Cor 1:17-25; Mt 25:1-13

Some things are bitter and sweet at the same time. Certain kinds of fruit can be sour yet sweet. How about a woman giving birth to a baby? She is in pain, yet she feels joy. Yes, A person can experience two different emotions at the same moment. The crucifix of Christ is both bitter and sweet. It is bitter because it challenges us to a sacrificial living, but it is sweet as well, for the reward of our sacrifice is a share in the risen life of Christ into eternity. That is why St Paul boldly went to preach Christ crucified, even to those Corinthians who in their worldly wisdom rejected the cross of Christ as a folly. He said to them, "To us who are being saved, the word of the cross is the power of God" (1 Cor 17:18). We too, like St Paul, are convinced that the crucified Christ is our Saviour. But are we acting upon this conviction? Our actions today have consequences for our future. Even our inaction has its consequences, as it was for the five foolish maidens of the parable. They could not enter into the wedding hall because they came late after the bridegroom had arrived (Mt 25:10).If we are convinced in the power of the cross, we should start living a sacrificial life for God and others without further delay.

OUR VIPS

Readings: 1 Cor 1:26-31; Mt 25:14-30

The label: 'VIP', applies only to those who are considered to be prominent and very important citizens. But it is not that way, with God. In an expensive restaurant, the private table goes to those people who give the headwaiter a handsome tip. But it is not that way, with God. St Paul makes it quite clear that God favours the weak and the lowly, and adds that "God chose what is weak in the world to shame the strong" (1 Cor 1:27). The reason is that the weak and the lowly are in a better position, to realise that they completely depend upon God, unlike the rich and the powerful, who think that they do not need God and can get along very well by themselves. But the truth is that all that we are and have, comes from God, a point illustrated by the man in the parable, who "going on a journey, called his servants and entrusted to them his property" (Mt 25:14). While receiving everything from God, how can one boast that he or she does not depend on God? That is sheer conceit, and conceited persons never really get anywhere, because they think they are already somewhere. Be humble and you are a 'VIP' in God's eyes. Humility is not denying the power we have, but realising that power comes not from us, but through us from above.

MONDAY – WEEK 22 / YEAR 2

SOME ROOM FOR FAITH

Readings: 1 Cor 2:1-5; Lk 4:16-30

When a rich man lay dying, he called his children around him and said, "I am about to leave you all my earthly possessions. There is one more thing I would like to leave you, namely, Christian faith. If I could leave you that and nothing else, you would be rich indeed. If I would leave you everything else, and not the faith, you would be poor indeed." God says the same thing to us. He asks us to have faith above everything else. For example, Jesus was only a carpenter (Lk 4:29). If he had had better credentials such as wealth, grandeur, and prestigious parents, the people of his town probably would not have rejected him. As it was, everything was simple about him and hence it called for faith to accept him as the Son of God. St Paul was only a tent maker who spoke a simple message, relying not on lofty words and human wisdom, but on the power of the Spirit (1 Cor 2:1). Hence, only those who had faith could accept his message. The reason why God prefers a simple and an unassuming approach towards us, is because that approach leaves some room in us for faith. Faith is not so much a leap in the dark, as a leap out of darkness into the light. Faith puts God between our circumstances and us, so that our life is safe in any circumstance.

TUESDAY – WEEK 22 / YEAR 2

THE ALL-PERVASIVE ONE

Readings: 1 Cor 2:10-16; Lk:31-37

Jesus possessed the power of the Holy Spirit and had authority from God. Power without authority, always looks dangerous and authority without power always looks comical. Jesus had both, to confront evil. To show that the kingdom of God is mightier than that of Satan, Jesus rebuked the evil spirit: "Be silent and come out of him" (Lk 4:35) which he did. The evil spirit is around the world so pervasively, that we can almost hear the beatings of his wings anywhere. A gentleman told me that his mother was a witch, and so he left her. The evil spirit can enter a nation sowing the seeds of division, and feeding on the blood of innocent victims. The evil one can enter even some of the most astounding modern discoveries, such as the Press and TV. The Pope speaking on a World Communication Day, urged people to simply shut off television, because it glorifies sex and violence, and is a major threat to family life. Satan has attacked us all, so that all human beings are in a sense evil, and will declare so, when occasion is offered. I myself, when I am good, I am very good; but when I am bad, I am better. But those who are always united to Christ need not fear the evil one, for Christ has conquered evil.

WEDNESDAY – WEEK 22 / YEAR 2

UNITED IN JESUS

Readings: 1 Cor 3:1-9; Lk 4:38-44

In a green field, there is normally a variety of vegetation, plants, trees, grass and so on. The field would look monotonous if there were only one type of plant. So too, in the field of God's Church, there is ample room for every type of peoples, institutions, and gifts. However, what is important is that there be unity in the Church. St Paul had noticed that factions had developed among the Christians at Corinth. The reason was that each became attached to a particular minister of Christ, some saying, "I belong to Paul" others, "I belong to Apollos" (1 Cor 3:4). The religious 'groupies' were more dazzled by the procession of messengers than by the message they brought, with the result that the one who sends out messengers, namely, Jesus, was left out. If we find similar disunity in our own Christian community, we need to bring Jesus to its centre. Even the demons driven out by Jesus confessed: "You are the Son of God" (Lk 4:41). Jesus being the Son of God can reconcile our differences. The Son of God left his purse to Judas, his body to Joseph of Arimathea, his mother to St John, his clothes to the soldiers, his Gospel to the world, but his presence with those who come together in his name. Our differences will melt away in the presence of Jesus.

THURSDAY – WEEK 22 / YEAR 2

WISDOM FROM ABOVE

Readings: 1 Cor 3:18-23; Lk 5:1-11

An executive from the aircraft industry watched a small plane, full of passengers, being prepared for take-off. He went to the pilot and said, "Surely, you are not going to take off in this dreadful weather, are you?" "Of course, I am", said the pilot. "But you won't make it", said the man. "I am the one who flies it and I know I can", said the pilot. "I come from the firm that built the plane," said the man, "and I say you can't." Not long after the plane had taken off, it crashed and killed everybody on board. God who created us knows best how we should live our lives. If we refuse to live by his wisdom we are in danger. When Jesus asked Peter to throw the net again early in the morning, human knowledge made Peter protest, "Master, we toiled all night and took nothing" (Lk 5:5), but obeyed. The reward of following divine wisdom was a big catch of fish. God's ways are not our ways. St Paul insists that "the wisdom of this world is folly with God" (1 Cor 3:19). Scripture nowhere condemns our acquisition of knowledge. It is the wisdom of this world, not its knowledge, that is folly with God. True wisdom is found in the will of God and hence it must be sought from above. If you lack knowledge, go to school; if you lack wisdom, get on your knees.

BECOMING NEW

Readings: 1 Cor 4:1-5; Lk 5:33-39

Never believe those who say, "Once a thief, always a thief." The
Christian claim affirms that even the worst of us can become new in
Christ; and, indeed, we are entitled to become ever new persons, because
our Master Jesus Christ was and is, in every way new. His teachings,
his way of life, his actions, his attitudes were all new. However, in
order to become new in Christ, one must shed off his or her old nature
to put on the new garment of Christ, since "no one tears a piece from a
new garment and puts it upon an old garment" (Lk 5:36). Christ is also
the new wine and "no one puts new wine into old wineskins" (v. 37).
Can we ever put off our old nature and put on the newness of Christ?
Yes, we can, because the grace of God has power to regenerate life. It
makes little difference what my old nature was. If I throw away an old
coat, it makes little difference if I did so because it is torn, or spotted
with soup or moth-eaten or faded. The only thing that matters is that I
throw it away. And when I throw it away, I get a new coat. The
difference is that by putting on the newness of Christ, we do not throw
away something external; we bury our old nature in Christ. We do it
because we get a new nature, one that shares in the nature of God.

TO KEEP A BALANCE

Readings: 1 Cor 4:6-15; Lk 6:1-5

When it comes to religious law, it is very difficult to keep a balance
between rigidity and laxity. A couple once said to a priest who had just
preached a sermon condemning the evils of our times: "That was
powerful sermon, father; we are glad it was nothing personal." Like
this couple, some of us favour rigidity as long as we are not personally

affected. Some others may favour laxity when they do have something personal at stake. In order to keep these two extremes in check, authority is needed in the Church. Jesus exercised such authority. The Pharisees complained that his apostles were violating the Sabbath rest by pulling off the grain heads, shelling them and eating them. But Jesus, after telling, in effect, that a law must be interpreted with compassion, excused the apostles' action (Lk 6:5). St Paul demonstrated similar authority. He corrected the Corinthians (1 Cor 4:15) who were led astray by pretentious preachers whose authority did not come from the Lord. Today, the Pope exercises such authority in the name of Christ, to preserve unity, by keeping a balance between extreme forces in the Church. The corpse of the Pope takes no more room than his sacristan's; but he has his authority entrusted to him by Christ.

MONDAY – WEEK 23 / YEAR 2

A PRIME MOVER

Readings: 1 Cor 5:1-8; Lk 6:6-11

The sex instinct is one of the three or four prime movers of all that we do and are and dream. Hence, if sex is desecrated, civilisation is demeaned. It appears that what Malcolm Muggeridge wrote is becoming true: "Orgasm has replaced the cross as the focus of longing and the image of fulfilment." There is sex for money and sex for free, the difference between the two being, that the former costs a lot less! St Paul came to know a Christian in Corinth living with his step-mother and so he angrily charged: "There is immorality among you, and of a kind that is not found even among pagans" (1 Cor 5:1). Sexual immorality jeopardises the relationship between man and woman, by confusing love with lust, generating guilt-feelings. Guilt whether conscious or unconscious will introduce an inner conflict that brings pain. The basic principle underlying an enjoyable lifestyle is self-control. Long-term gain is only available in a short-term pain, that is, a willingness to forgo immediate pleasure for a long-term reward. Sex can only be positive and life-giving experience, if it is a part of a life-long relationship in marriage. Sex as an end in itself becomes boring, demeaning and soul destroying, whether within or outside marriage.

CHRISTIAN DIGNITY

Readings: 1 Cor 6:1-11; Lk 6:12-19

Two sisters had been living in different cities. They came home on a visit. While away from home, one of the girls had become a Christian. After a few days, the other girl said, "I do not know what causes it; but you are a great deal easier to live with than you used to be." Yes; when Jesus comes in, it should make a difference. At baptism, Jesus himself, speaking through the baptising minister, calls each of us by name, as he called his twelve apostles (Lk 6:13), to become his follower and be a witness to him in the world. What an exalted dignity it is to be called by the Son of God himself! A Christian is a walking mystery for the triune God has come to dwell within. Christians are not just nice people; they are new creations, for the living God actually comes to rule their minds. Do we have a proper sense of our Christian dignity and recognise that dignity in others too? St Paul was saddened to see that this was not the case with some Christians in Corinth. They dragged one another into court over squabbles (1 Cor 6:1), instead of settling them between themselves in charity. When we fail to act with Christian dignity, we hurt Christ more than non-Christians do. Enemies within the fort, are more dangerous than those without.

OUR HAPPY FORTRESS

Readings: 1 Cor 7:25-31; Lk 6:20-26

God is a happy fortress, and to be happy is to be blessed. Our blessed God is always exultant and joyous, radiant and rapturous; he is not a threatened deity starving for attention. He is not easily angered, touchy or out of sorts on bad days. He is not biting his nails when the world goes awry. He is always happy and the source of happiness. Therefore anyone who seeks and serves God, is in union with the source of happiness, unequalled by any joy the world can offer. Jesus declared that those are blest who are poor, hungry, sorrowful and hated (Lk 6:20-26), precisely because the people in such conditions are those who turn to God as the source of their happiness. It does not matter whether one is married or celibate. "Are you bound to a wife? Do not seek to be free. Are you free from a wife? Do not seek marriage" (1 Cor 7:27), because either state is good, as long as we are single minded in seeking and serving the Lord, the source of our happiness. If we are in trouble, God had better not be. If we are miserable, it would do us no good to go to someone who is himself miserable. People in deep distress need to reach out to a strong and happy anchor. God is just that: a happy foundation and a blissful rock.

THURSDAY – WEEK 23 / YEAR 2

GOD, A POLICEMAN OR SANTA CLAUS?

Readings: 1 Cor 8:1-7, 11-13; Lk 6:27-38

To some, hell is a place of punishment and heaven a place of reward. Some look on God as a policeman, who tries to catch us when we make a mistake and sends us to prison; others think of him as a Santa Claus, who counts up all our good deeds and puts rewards in our stockings at the end of the year. God however is neither a policeman nor a Santa Claus. God is love and perfect love. In God there is no hatred, desire for revenge or pleasure in seeing us punished. God wants to forgive, heal, restore, show us unending mercy and see us come home. Jesus asks us to reflect God's perfect love in our dealings with others. "Love your enemies, do good to those who hate you, bless those who curse you, pray for those who abuse you" (Lk 6:27). Of course, we are not God and so can't love others as perfectly as God does. Even in a family, no father or mother can love their children perfectly, no husband or wife can love each other with unlimited love. There is no human love that is not broken somewhere. When our broken love is the only love we have, should we despair? No. We can still live our broken love as a partial reflection of God's perfect love, forgive each other's limitations and enjoy together the love we can offer.

FRIDAY – WEEK 23 / YEAR 2

A SPIRITUAL BATTLE

Readings: 1 Cor 9:16-19, 22-27; Lk 6:39-42

Years ago, a neighbour near my study, persisted in practising flute. He bored my ears as with an auger and rendered my mind almost an impossibility to think. Up and down his scale, he ran relentlessly, until even the calamity of my temporary deafness would almost be welcome to me. Yet, he taught me a lesson on how I must also practice my discipleship to Christ, as rigorously as he did. "Every athlete", says St Paul, "exercises self-control in all things. They do it to receive a perishable wreath, but we an imperishable" (1 Cor 9:25). How indefatigable did Paul labour, with what vehemence did he pray! Slander and contempt he bore with utmost patience. Scourging and stoning had no terror for him. Death itself, he defied, all for the eternal reward. Every Christian is called to fight against evil in themselves and against an ensnaring world, a corrupt flesh and a busy devil. We know that the front lines in a battle are risky, but the battle prize is great. To some, the front line of the good fight may be drawn against an extra minute or two of an indecent TV program or when we battle a surge of self-pity, or of immoral thoughts or words that hurt others. We have to choose our own spiritual weapon, for our warfare is spiritual but real.

SATURDAY – WEEK 23 / YEAR 2

WE ARE ONE BODY

Readings: 1 Cor 10:14-22; Lk 6:43-49

It seems that there are five kinds of parish churches. Museum style – where you go only as a spectator. Hairdresser style – where they split every hair four ways. Service station style – where you go just to be filled up. Sleeping car style – where the passengers don't want to be disturbed. Refrigerator style – where the icy chill drives out any new arrival. Do any of these styles fit in with the vision of the Church Jesus had when he instituted it? St Paul compares the Church to a living body. "We who are many are one body" (1 Cor 10:17). As different parts of the body are united to the head and work for the welfare of one another to keep the whole body healthy, so members of the church are expected to be united to Christ and work for the good of each other. If we do not actively care for the concerns of one another, especially the most vulnerable among us, and still go to Mass as a church, the Lord will be saddened to repeat his words: "Why do you call me 'Lord, Lord', and not do what I tell you" (Lk 6:46). Being indifferent to one another and allowing factions to spread within the church, can we still call ourselves united in love? You may tie the tail of a cat and a dog together by a rope and have union, but you surely have no unity.

MONDAY – WEEK 24 / YEAR 2

"I AM UNWORTHY"

Readings: 1 Cor 11:17-26, 33; Lk 7:1-10

The Eucharist is the Sacrament of sacraments, for it brings on the altar our Lord Jesus Christ himself. However, as Thérèse of Lisieux said, "Our Lord does not come from heaven every day to stay in a golden ciborium. He comes to find another heaven, the heaven of our soul in which he loves to dwell." Truly worthy souls have experienced heaven in them after Holy Communion. "Yesterday", wrote St Gemma Galgani, "on approaching the Blessed Sacrament, I felt myself burning and I had to withdraw. I am astounded that so many receive Jesus and are not reduced to ashes." If we always feel nothing special after receiving Holy Communion it is possible that we come unworthy to receive the Lord. The Christians in Corinth were quarrelling among themselves, ate and drank too much, so greedy that they would not share anything with others. Hence, to such unworthy recipients of the Eucharist, St Paul wrote, "When you come together, it is not for the better, but for the worse" (1 Cor 11:17). We must all acknowledge our unworthiness as we come to the Eucharist and pray the words of the Centurion, "Lord, I am not worthy to have you come under my roof, but say a word and I shall be healed" (Lk 7:7).

TUESDAY – WEEK 24 / YEAR 2

TO BE HIS INSTRUMENT

Readings: 1 Cor 12:12-14, 27-31; Lk 7:11-17

"Lord, make me an instrument of your peace; where there is hatred, let me sow love; where there is injury, pardon; where there is doubt, faith; where there is despair, hope; where there is darkness, light; where there is sadness, joy." Obviously, St Francis was inspired to pray this prayer, by the ministry of Jesus, all of which had one purpose: to bring new life to those who appeared to be dead. And that we see at its most dramatic, in his raising a dead boy to life and comforting a widow's grief (Lk 7:15). It is our ministry too. As St Paul puts it, at baptism "by the one Spirit we were baptised into one body" (1 Cor 12:13). The same Spirit has endowed each of us with different gifts and we are called to use that gift in order to bring hope, faith and love into people who seem to have lost them. God has someone in mind he wants to touch today. He has grace available for this person. At the same time, God is looking for another person to serve as his conduit. What does he do next? He crosses, say, your path. He puts two of you together in a grocery check line, on a golf course, at choir recital, in a parking lot or at a telephone booth. What happens next is up to you. Would one miss such an opportunity to bring new life into another?

WEDNESDAY – WEEK 24 / YEAR 2

LOVE IS PRACTICAL

Readings: 1 Cor 12:31-13:13; Lk 7:31-35

How we delight in the love of Christ! Travelling to Bethlehem, we see Love incarnate. Tracking his steps as he went about doing good, we see Love labouring. Visiting the house of Bethany, we see Love sympathising. Standing by the grave of Lazarus, we see Love weeping. At Gethsemane, we see Love sorrowing. Passing on to Calvary, we see Love suffering, bleeding and dying. All the qualities of love that St Paul mentions, such as, "Love is patient and kind; Love endures all things" (1 Cor 13:4-7) are found in the love of Christ for us. Only those born in the Spirit as God's children can understand the depth of the love of Christ, the wisdom of the Father. Truly "wisdom is justified by all her children" (Lk 7:35). Now it is through us believers that Christ wants to love every human being. He wants to love with our hearts, embrace with our arms, and to serve with our hands. True love is practical; it is not something that is stored up in our hearts. It must be expressed. Bouquets of flowers, a kiss, words of tenderness, gestures of affection, are nothing in comparison with love to which they bear such humble witness. But what would love be without them? To love is to perform love-deeds.

THURSDAY – WEEK 24 / YEAR 2

WOUNDED WE COME

Readings: 1 Cor 15:1-11; Lk 7:36-50

One reason why sin flourishes is that it is treated like a cream puff instead of a rattlesnake that can kill. We all sin. We are like the moon, for we all have a dark side. Some sins we have committed, some we have contemplated, some we have desired, and some we have encouraged. In the case of some, we are innocent only because we did not succeed. To sin is human. Yes; but why don't we repent for it when we have committed it, and seek God's forgiveness? Perhaps it is because, when sin drives, shame sits in the back seat. Do we know what happens to us when we repent for our sins and the Lord forgives us? We are reborn as children of God and our right to heaven is restored. This is made possible by the death and the resurrection of Jesus. When St Paul preached about Jesus "raised on the third day" (1 Cor 15:4), he was placing the death and resurrection of Christ at the very heart of the Christian message. Jesus forgave the sins of a woman as reported in the Gospel (Lk 7:47).What he did for the woman, he does for all of us, in the power of his death and resurrection. When we have sinned, let us repent and come to the Lord wounded. If we can not come to him wounded, let us come to him so that he may wound us, and make us whole.

FRIDAY – WEEK 24 / YEAR 2

UNITED TO THE LIVING CHRIST

Readings: 1 Cor 15:12-20; Lk 8:1-3

We go to the train station to await the arrival of a loved one. We look down the track with eagerness and we see the light of the engine in the distance. We cry out, "Here she comes", for we know that if the engine is arriving, the coaches would be right behind. The resurrection of Christ is like the arrival of an engine, because if we believe in the resurrection of Christ we ought to believe in the forgiveness of sins, in our own resurrection and in the eternal life. St Paul insists: "If there is no resurrection of the dead, then Christ has not been raised" (1 Cor 15:13). But we have to remain united with Christ in life and in death, in order to rise like him into eternal life. If a coach gets detached from the engine as it is running, how can it reach its destination? The risen Lord is with us. Touched by the power of his risen presence, so many people have been following him down the centuries, as several of those who were healed by him during his earthly ministry did (Lk 8:2). Ashoka, once emperor of India, distributed Buddha's ashes, in minute portions to 84,000 Indians. One wonders whether Buddhism is centred on the worship of the ashes of the dead founder. But Christianity is not. It centres on its living Lord.

SATURDAY – WEEK 24 / YEAR 2

AMAZING TRANSFORMATION!

Readings: 1 Cor 15:35-37, 42-49; Lk 8:4-15

It happened that a little acorn was buried in the process of covering a grave. During the months that followed, the seed sprouted and the tender shoot found its way up through the crevice between two of the stones. Years passed and the small shoot grew into a sapling, then into a huge oak tree. It burst asunder the clamp of iron binding the stones, pushing aside the rocks that could never be moved otherwise. Our bodily resurrection will be similar to this. Following the parable of Jesus about some seeds that "fell into good soil and grew and yielded a hundredfold" (Lk 8:8), St Paul writes: "What you sow is a bare kernel, but God gives it a body" (1 Cor 15:37-38), and then compares it to our dying and rising. Nourished by water and soil and energised by the sun, the seed undergoes an amazing transformation. So too, nourished by God's life giving Spirit at baptism, energised by the body and blood of the Lord at the Eucharist, we are able to rise completely transformed. Even now we can have a foretaste of that risen life. If we die to our selfishness, he will renew our inner self. To those who give their all to the Lord, he will give his all. Indeed, to renounce all for the Lord is to gain all; to descend is to ascend and to die is to live.

MONDAY – WEEK 25 / YEAR 2

POSTPONING KINDNESS

Readings: Prov 3:27-34; Lk 8:16-18

A man's car simply went dead on a busy street. He raised the hood and began a fruitless search for the problem. Motorists swerved around him blowing their horns and hurling verbal unpleasantries at him. The man insists that he counted over hundred cars that passed him by, before someone paused, rolled down his window and asked if he needed help. The Proverb says, "Do not withhold good from those to whom it is due, when it is in your power to do it" (Pro 3:27). Perhaps, many were too busy to stop, but the Word of God goes on to say, "Do not say to your neighbour, 'Tomorrow I will give' – when you have it with you" (v.28). Implying that each of us is like a lamp, Jesus says, "No one after lighting a lamp covers it with a vessel" (Lk 8:16). Jesus wants us not to hide the lamp of our goodness, but let it shine before others, in response to God's goodness to us. A small board hangs on the wall of a social worker's house with these words on it: "My life shall touch a dozen lives before this day is done; shall leave countless marks for good or ill before sets this evening sun; so this is the wish I always wish: let my life help the other lives it touches by the way." We can't do a kindness too soon, for we never know how soon it will be too late.

ACTIONS MATCHING WORDS

Readings: Prov 21:1-6, 10-13; Lk 8:19-21

A wife at times will complain to her husband, "You never say you love me anymore." The husband usually responds, "You know I love you. I work hard at my job for you and the kids. That shows that I love you." And yet, the wife quite rightly would like to hear it in words. On the other hand, the situation is much worse when a man uses words of love which are hollow, because he does not back them with actions. The people of Israel who worshipped God, but failed to live up by God's commandments were often admonished by the prophets by words such as "To do righteousness and justice is more acceptable than sacrifice" (Prov 21:3). Jesus had much the same idea in mind when he said, "My mother and brethren are those who hear the word of God and do it" (Lk 8:21). Sometimes we try to justify our disobedience to God's word with a show of religion. For example, one may remain in an evil trade thinking that he can then give more to the Lord. A child is practising on the piano during the hour when she ought to do her chores. The mother reminds her of her duties, but the child continues to fill the house with the melody of praise: "Jesus loves me!" Songs of praise lose their meaning when offered out of disobedience.

A PRAYER OF BALANCE

Readings: Prov 30:5-9; Lk 9:1-6

A wealthy industrialist leaped from a ninth-story room of a city hotel leaving behind this note: "I am worth ten million dollars as men judge things, but I am so poor in spirit that I can't live any longer. Something is terribly wrong with life." He was right. Something was terribly wrong with 'his' life, for he had relied on his riches for happiness. His wealth made him proud and forgetful of God as if he had no obligation to God. When Jesus sent his disciples on a mission, he said, "Take nothing for your journey" (Lk 9:3). In effect, he wanted them to learn dependence on God, rather than on all kinds of provisions. This does not mean that God wants us to live in utter destitution, so that we have to literally wonder where our next meal is coming from. And so the author of the Proverb prays: "Give me neither poverty nor riches" (Prov 30:8), because, if we become very wealthy we might forget God, but if we become extremely poor, we may be forced to steal and thus turn away from God. It is a prayer of balance. 'Enough' must be our motto: health enough to make work a pleasure; wealth enough to support our need; strength enough to battle with difficulties; grace enough to acknowledge our dependence on God.

THURSDAY – WEEK 25 / YEAR 2

ALL IS VANITY?

Readings: Eccl 1:2-11; Lk 9:7-9

To a pessimist, there is no meaning or purpose in life; everything is utter disaster. He is one who foresees calamities, suffers them twice over. He looks both ways before crossing a one way street. A cynic is not merely one who reads bitter lessons from the past; he is one perpetually disappointed in the future; Cynics are only happy in making the world as barren to others, as they have made it for themselves. Was the person who cried, "Vanity of vanities! All is vanity" (Eccl 1:2), a pessimist or cynic? He could be both. However, if he meant that life without God is vanity, we agree with him and the life of God is available even now in Jesus Christ. Herod asked, "Who is this Jesus about whom I hear such things?" (Lk 9:9). Indeed, Jesus is the Son of God who makes human life fulfilling to any one who believes in him. To a believer, death is not an end but a door opening to eternal life. Therefore there is meaning and purpose in life, for those who strive after a loving relationship with God in Jesus. Do we tend to be pessimistic and down on life because everything seems to be getting worse? The earlier we get away from such pessimistic outlook, the better for us, for when we get used to pessimism, it becomes as agreeable as optimism.

FRIDAY – WEEK 25 / YEAR 2

TIME SCHEDULE

Readings: Eccl 3:1-11; Lk 9:18-22

If we do love life, then we can't squander time, for that is the stuff life is made of. We say that time flies; Yes; but we are its navigators. "For everything there is a season and a time for every matter under heaven" (Eccl 3:1). There is a time to work, for it is the price of success; a time to think, for it is the source of power; a time to play, for it is the secret of youth; a time to enjoy friends, for it is the source of joy; a time to relax, for it refreshes body and mind; a time to laugh, for it is the music of the soul. But there must be time also to be alone with God in prayer, for he is the source of happiness. We will never find time to pray, indeed to do anything, unless we make it. If we have a time and place for everything and do everything in its time and place, we will find enough time for God. Always hurrying about, as if trying to overtake what has been lost, is not going to give us time to be with God. Jesus, in a relatively short time, founded the nucleus of his Church, managed to make at least St Peter, the future head of the Church, recognise him as the "Christ of God" (Lk 9:20), and indeed accomplished the salvation of the world. Our time too is short and counting time is not nearly so important as making time count.

SATURDAY – WEEK 25 / YEAR 2

THE WORLD'S OLDEST WISH

Readings: Eccl 11:9-12:8; Lk 9:43-45

We live in a 'disposable' age. People use a paper plate and a plastic knife and fork at a picnic, and then throw them away. Many drinks come in disposable bottles to be used once and never again. After a disposable item has served its purpose, it is forgotten. In God's eyes, human beings are not disposable. Through Jesus Christ God our Father calls each one to everlasting life. It is true that Jesus had to die first, as he foretold that "the son of Man is to be delivered into the hands of men" (Lk 9:44), but he rose again from the dead. The meditation on the span of life by the author of the first reading, does not sound optimistic as he ends it with the word, "the dust returns to the earth as it was" (Eccl 12:8). The reason is that despite his belief in God, he lived in an era when there was no clear understanding of after-life. But we have been promised immortality by the death and resurrection of Christ. It seems that a new clock has been so accurately constructed that it will lose or gain only one second in thirty-three million years. But no matter how accurately we measure time, we can not create time, nor extend time. Each of us will have only one lifetime on earth. That is why, belief in immortal life is the oldest wish of humankind.

MONDAY – WEEK 26 / YEAR 2

CONFLICT WITH STORMS

Readings: Job 1:6-22; Lk 9:46-50

Once I was going through a great furniture factory, when my guide pointed out to me a superbly grained and figured sideboard in the natural wood. "I want you to observe the beauty of this oak" he said. "It is the finest selected timber of its kind and the secret of the intricate and beautiful grain is just this: that the trees from which it was taken grew in a spot where they were exposed to almost constant conflict with storms." So with the human life beset by sorrows, tests and trials. If we stand the storms of sufferings, the wind of God strengthens and beautifies us. That is the promise given to us by the death and resurrection of Christ. Still, why good people like Job should suffer is a mystery. After suffering almost every form of devastating adversity, Job did not get a neat solution to the mystery of suffering. He simply placed a blind act of faith saying, "The Lord gave, and the Lord has taken away" (Job1:21). He was in effect confessing that we human mortals do not have the right to question the wisdom or the justice of an all wise and all good God. Hence, like Job, we simply believe that after the sorrow and strife, after the strain and stress, we will reap the peaceable fruit of unending blessedness.

TUESDAY – WEEK 26 / YEAR 2

CARRIED BY A STORM

Readings: Job 3:1-3, 11-17, 20-23; Lk 9:51-56

Wordsworth wrote a poem in which a bird is swept from Norway by a storm. It battles against the storm with desperate effort, eager to wing back to Norway. But all is in vain; so at last he yields, thinking that the gale will carry it to its death – but the gale carries it to sunny England with its green meadows and forest glades. Because Job did not really understand that the storm of his sufferings was carrying him to eternal bliss with God, he despaired and even cursed himself saying, "Let the day perish wherein I was born" (Job 3:3). On the contrary, Jesus not only allowed himself to be carried by the wind of suffering but relentlessly "set his face to go to Jerusalem" (Lk 9:51), for he knew well that it was there he would come back to life and achieve the salvation of the world. We too in our journey of faith are at times driven by heavy storms of trials. If we submit to God's plan for our life, even when it is painful, the storm will take us to God's blessed abode. We are not going to be perfectly happy here on earth. Jesus' resurrection gives us a wide-angle lens. Perfect happiness may start here but will only be completed in the next life. Hence we need to cling on to God even in sorrow, for we are safer in a storm with God, than anywhere without him.

WEDNESDAY – WEEK 26 / YEAR 2

GOD IS ENOUGH

Readings: Job 9:1-13, 14-16; Lk 9:57-62

Where there is smoke, there is fire. Hence, according to Job's friends who came to console him, Job must have committed some sin in the past because of which he was suffering. But Job protested against this conventional wisdom. He insisted that he was innocent and yet wondered why he should suffer (Job 9:15). In other words, he called God's dealing with him mysterious; but his friends were so sure of their perception that, in effect, they were unwilling to accept some aspect of mystery about God. The truth is that God has purposes other than merely exercising strict justice to each person, though our limited minds can not fully understand what those purposes are. Hence God asks that we trust him. In the Gospel Jesus asks his followers to abandon everything in complete trust. He insisted that a man should leave even the burial of his father to others, in order to follow him (Lk 9:60). Yes, it takes a lot of courage to put everything in God's hands; to give ourselves completely, our lives, our hopes and our plans; to follow where he leads us, and to make his will our own. Fearing that God's way would be painful, to go our own way alone, is a folly. The fact is that when we have nothing left but God, then we become aware that God is enough.

THURSDAY – WEEK 26 / YEAR 2

LONELINESS INTO SOLITUDE

Readings: Job 19:21-27; Lk 10:1-12

Loneliness has always been the inevitable experience of every human being. Among all forms of loneliness, what is most distressing is to be left alone with no one to understand us or care about us. Mother Teresa said, "Loneliness and the feeling of being unwanted is the most terrible poverty." Three friends came to see Job in his time of trials. Instead of offering him consolation, they condemned him as guilty of some terrible sin. Being abandoned even by his friends, Job was pushed to cry out to them. But he took consolation in his faith that God is good, and so he affirmed, "I know that my Redeemer lives" (Job19:25). Our feeling of loneliness does not mean that God has abandoned us. Jesus sent his disciples on a mission to preach in his name (Lk 10:1). Although they were physically separated from him, he was still with them in spirit. They were not alone. If we trust that God is still with us even when others abandon us, we will turn our loneliness into a fruitful solitude. In solitude, we become conscious of God's presence within us. In solitude, we find a new centre of strength and peace within ourselves, a centre that does not depend on any external circumstances, for God has come to occupy that centre.

REFINED LIKE SILVER

Readings: Job 38:1, 12-21, 40:3-5; Lk10:13-16

God tests our faith, not that he might know what is in us, but that we might know that "Daddy knows best." We say that we love God as our Father, but we might easily deceive ourselves unless that love of God is put to test. Job looked up to God in heaven and wanted to know why he had to suffer so much. He simply could not accept the fact that he too shared in the sinfulness of the human race, as did the evil cities of "Chorazin and Bethsaida" (Lk 10:13), condemned by Jesus. To Job's persistent question, "Why?" God's final answer was that he knows best. There was simply no way, a poor mortal like Job could comprehend the actions of God. In the end, Job accepted in faith the wisdom of God, saying "Behold, I am of small account; what shall I answer thee" (Job 40:4)? We say all the time, "I love you, God." And we do. But we become aware of the depth of our love only when we are tested. God's love for us drives him to test us in order to refine us like silver. When silver is refined, it involves pressure. So too, when we are pressured by trials, we must hold on and remain faithful to God and obey him in all things. Obedience to testing melts away our pride and crushes into dust our self-centredness, revealing a refined heart.

SUSPENSE IS NOT IN THE END

Readings: Job 42:1-3, 5-6, 12-17; Lk 10:17-24

My friend Alex and I love to spend time in bookstores. I head for the Theology section, then move to the Saints section. From there I might glance at Astronomy books. But no matter where I am in the store, I always know where I can find Alex. He loves mysteries. Strangely enough, he decides to buy a book by reading the last few pages. I wondered how he could enjoy a mystery when he knows how it will all come out. He replied that the suspense was not in the conclusion, but in how the writer handled the story, and knowing the ending enhanced the story. Alex is not alone. Jesus has made known our ending saying, "Rejoice that your names are written in heaven" (Lk 10:20). We have no clear idea of what heaven will be like. The truth is that the heavenly bliss will far surpass anything we can imagine; it will surpass even the restoration made to Job. Job, despite all his mysterious sufferings, yielded to God in the end. As a reward, God restored him goods even more than he had lost (Job 41:12). Jesus has already made known to us that God will restore to his faithful the heavenly bliss lost by our first parents. Is not the story of our lives enhanced because we have already the assurance that all will turn out well? It is.

MONDAY – WEEK 27 / YEAR 2

BEING A SAMARITAN

Readings: Gal 1:6-12; Lk 10:25-37

Recently I heard a condemnation of the poor starving people of India: "Why don't they get out and make more, like I did?" The speaker made his money out of oil. He did not put it there; it just splashed up his face. But the poor of India could dig until the end of time and not hit oil. The secret of helping the needy is to treat them as they are, not as they ought to be, nor as we want them to be, but as they actually are. The Good Samaritan did not ask, "Why did this man come this way so dangerous with thieves? Why could not the Jews who passed by help another Jew? Why should they leave it to a Samaritan to help?" He simply accepted the fact that there was a needy human being and went down to minister (Lk 10:34). Do we want to love others as the Samaritan did? Then, it is not enough to have merely an intellectual understanding of another's difficulty; we need to go little further to feel it as our own burden. Loving others calls for patience, tolerance and benevolence. It extends to those beyond our own sect, and is exercised not only to the good but even to the dull and the foolish that stumble. But to be patient and benevolent with them requires that kind of love, which sees in every human person God's own image.

ONE THING IS NEEDED

Readings: Gal 1:13-24; Lk 10:38-42

A man went to college to gain wisdom, but he came away with facts and figures. He turned to business and became cunning. He tried a craft and learned only skills with his hands. He then tried pleasures, but gained a feeling of emptiness. The man felt that he would never know wisdom. He grew weary of search. But one day he stopped at a church. He listened quietly to the Word of God being proclaimed. A small voice within him said, "Be still, and know that I am God." After a period of silent meditation on the words he heard, he felt some enlightenment in his mind, and believed that that was the beginning of wisdom. When Martha complained about being left to do all the work while Mary was only sitting and listening to the Lord, Jesus said to her, "Martha, one thing is needed; Mary has chosen the good portion" (Lk 10:42). By no means did Jesus disapprove of what Martha was doing. He was only emphasising the importance of listening to God in prayer. The Word nourishes our spirit as food nourishes our body. Before starting his active ministry, St Paul went away to Arabian deserts to spend days in communion with God (Gal 1:17). We all live such busy lives that we need to set aside time for daily prayer.

LIKE TREES IN THE FOREST

Readings: Gal 2:1-2, 7-14; Lk 11:1-4

The article "What good is a tree?" in *Reader's Digest* explained that when the roots of trees touch, there is a substance present that reduces competition. In fact, this unknown fungus helps link roots of different trees, even of dissimilar species. A whole forest may be linked together. If one tree has access to water, another to nutrient, and the third to sunlight, the trees have the means to share with one another. Like the trees in a forest, Christians are linked together by their faith in Jesus Christ. As we read in today's first reading (Gal 2:8), St Peter and St Paul taught that the true mark of a Christian is not the observance of the old Mosaic Law such as circumcision, but faith in Christ, and irrespective of our national origins or of our previous religion, we all become one in Christ. Being one in Christ makes us all children of God, for Christ himself is the Son of God. That is why, Jesus asked us to call God "Our Father" (Lk 11:2). If we are the children of the same heavenly father, we must love and support one another as the trees do in a forest. The spirit of a Christian community is achieved where there is the surrender of self for the other. Christian joy never comes to me by seeking it for myself; But it does come to me, when I bring joy to others.

THURSDAY – WEEK 27 / YEAR 2

WHAT COUNTS IN PRAYER?

Readings: Gal 3:1-5; Lk 11:5-13

A little boy was always asking God for this and that whenever he prayed. His mother once said to him, "My son, don't ask God for so many things; just report for duty." Such advice may make the child think that we ought to get away from prayers of petition. And yet, Jesus strongly encouraged prayers of petition: "Ask, and it will be given to you; seek, and you will find; knock, and it will be opened to you" (Lk 11:9). Devoted parents, even if they must struggle to keep their patience, are pleased when their children ask them for favours or help. Children ask because they have faith that their parents have power to help them and they have faith in their parents' love for them. When we pray, Jesus asks us to believe in God's almighty power and in his tremendous love for us his children. St Paul says that all the good works we do are the result of "hearing with faith" (Gal 3:5). So too, the effectiveness of our prayer rests on our faith in God's power and love. It is not the arithmetic of our prayer – how many they are; it is not the rhetoric of our prayer – how eloquent they are; it is not the geometry of prayer – how long they are; it is not the music of prayer – how sweet they sound, which God cares for. Faith is what counts in prayer.

"I BELIEVE IN GOD"

Readings: Gal 3:7-14; Lk 11:15-26

A cellar wall in Cologne Germany contained a beautiful testimony to faith in God, which workers found while clearing away debris from a bombed out-house. It reads as follows: "I believe in the sun, even when it is not shining; I believe in love, even when I do not feel it; I believe in God, even when he is silent." St Paul exhorts us to strive for faith, since "those who are men of faith are blessed with Abraham who had faith" (Gal 3:9). Faith rests on God, receives from God, responds to God, relies on God, rejoices in God and reproduces godliness in us. We all want to enjoy a meaningful and fulfilling life. But, just rituals will not do the trick. If there is no faith, rituals become meaningless fobs. As the saying goes, "When faith goes to market, it always takes a basket." Indeed, faith gathers the blessings of God in Christ. Jesus warns, "He who does not gather with me, scatters" (Lk 11:23). And we gather the blessings of the Lord through the sacraments. But sacraments operate upon us only to the extent of our faith. If our faith is as simple as that of children, our basket will overflow with God's blessings. One little girl expressed her utmost faith in God by saying, "Dear God! Please take care of yourself or we are all sunk!"

OUR RADIANT MODEL

Readings: Gal 3:22-29; Lk 11:27-28

Our society today is experiencing a major crisis of faith. In this computer age, we have made such vast strides in technology that we have become a self-sufficient and sophisticated people. God has become irrelevant in the lives of many, who put their faith in their own ingenuity. But Mary was a paragon of faith throughout her life. She believed in

God and in Jesus as his Son. St Paul said, "In Christ Jesus, you are all sons of God in faith" (Gal 3:26). So we are God's children by faith in Christ. Mary's exemplary faith made her the highly favoured daughter of God. But her faith was not empty of actions. She said "Yes" to every call that came from God. When a woman said to Jesus, in effect, "Your mother must be proud of you", Jesus replied, "Blessed rather are those who hear the word of God and keep it" (Lk 11:28). His reply was not a denial of what the woman had said. He only wanted to underline the importance of Mary's faith and obedience over her giving physical birth to him. No person has more fully heard the Word of God and no person has kept that Word completely than Mary. Mary gave full expression to the longing of the poor of Yahweh, and hence she is the radiant model for all believers.

MONDAY – WEEK 28 / YEAR 2

FREEDOM TO LOVE

Readings: Gal 4:22-24, 26-27, 31-5:1; Lk 11:29-32

Someone presents me a magnificent home and I am very grateful to that person, for this expensive gift is a sign of the goodness and love of that person for me. Scarcely, then, should I accept the gift and ignore the giver. God has given us through his Son Jesus eternal life and it is right that we lead a life pleasing to God in response to God's goodness. Such a response calls for our observance of God's laws. This does not mean that mere observance of law wins for us eternal life; what wins it is the love we express in that observance. That is why Jesus has blessed us with the freedom required to love God with all our heart. St Paul affirms it by saying, "For freedom Christ has set us free" (Gal 5:1). Therefore, freedom is self-determination to love God and neighbour. Freedom is not doing what we like. Our worst difficulties begin when we are able to do whatever we like. As Cicero said, "We are in bondage to law of God and of society in order that we may be free to love God and neighbour." Freedom is not the right to do as a person pleases, but the liberty to do, as he or she ought. Freedom standing by itself inevitably degenerates into license. Licence is unbridled freedom that quickly becomes the enemy of freedom.

WHAT IS INSIDE?

Readings: Gal 5:1-6; Lk 11:37-41

A young woman moved away from home and settled in an apartment in a large Metropolitan area. Her parents came out to visit her and they took pleasure in buying things for her new apartment. Before they left they saw her landlord and paid him three months' rent in advance. All appeared to be generous acts of love for the daughter. However, whenever a disagreement arose, they reminded their daughter of all that they had done for her. Finally, in desperation, the daughter sent them a check for the rent and the items her parents had purchased for her, with a note, "Please don't misunderstand, but I want you to take this check. A gift is no good with a string attached to it." We need to examine our motivation in all that we do. St Paul reminded the Galatians that the external regulations such as circumcision no longer mattered. What counted was "faith working through love" (Gal 5:6). Jesus condemned the Pharisees for insisting on the washing of hands before eating while inside they were "full of extortion and wickedness" (Lk 11:39). Some should often be ashamed of their best actions if the world could see their motives. They take great pleasure in doing a thing, often from some motive other than the ostensible one.

LIFE IN THE SPIRIT

Readings: Gal 5:18:25; Lk 11:42-46

A convicted murderer was interviewed recently. The interviewer asked the man whether he was sorry for what he had done. The murderer laughed and said, "Why should I be sorry? I wanted to kill the sucker and I did. I've often killed other people before, and I guess I will do it again if I feel like it." We know that evil is real. St Paul speaks about "the works of the flesh" (Gal 5:19), which is our human nature tainted by sin. The desires of the flesh blind and darken the soul and prevents us from seeing the will of God, as the mist prevents us from seeing the sun clearly. As water defiled with mud does not reflect any image, so our soul wounded by sin loses its capacity to follow either our natural reason or God's wisdom. Hence we need to surrender ourselves not to the flesh but to the Spirit, so that we can enjoy the fruits of the Spirit such as, love, peace, patience, goodness and self-control (v.22-23). To live by the Spirit is not easy but is possible, if we call upon the Spirit to make his grace effective within us, if we frequent the Sacraments, and make the Word of God as our rule of life. The Spirit-filled life is not a special deluxe edition of Christianity; it is part and parcel of the total plan of God for his people.

THURSDAY – WEEK 28 / YEAR 2

TO BE IN CHRIST

Readings: Eph 1:1-10; Lk 11:47-54

What the sun is to a flower, so is Jesus Christ to a Christian. The achievements of the Saviour through his Incarnation are astounding and numerous. Anyone wishing to describe them in detail would be like one who gazes at the expanse of the sea and attempts to count its waves. Because of our First Parents' original fall from grace, we are conceived in the state of sin, and having lost the title to heaven. But Jesus by his death has restored that title to us. Because of the original fall, we were deprived of bodily immortality and hence all die. But Jesus by his resurrection has made it possible for us to rise again to eternal life. Because of the original fall, we no longer have the in-built control over our base and evil desires. But Jesus through the indwelling of the Holy Spirit, has blessed us with an ability to control our desires. As St Paul affirms, God our Father "has blessed us in Christ with every spiritual blessing in the heavenly places" (Eph 1:3). The result is that Jesus is our way, the truth and the life. Therefore, as the root is in the soil, as the branch is in the tree, as the fish is in the sea, as the bird is on the air, we must be in Christ. Physically our life is in the world, but spiritually it needs to be lifted above the world, to be in Christ.

FRIDAY – WEEK 28 / YEAR 2

IT IS A GUARANTEE

Readings: Eph 1:11-14; Lk 12:1-7

In his later years, Martin Luther became gloomy. One day his wife came into his study dressed in black. Martin asked, "Who is dead?" She said, "God is!" Martin responded, "My soul! Why should you talk like that?" She said, "Because of your gloom." There can be no place for gloom but joy in a Christian's life. Joy is not a luxury or a mere accessory in Christian life. It is a sign that we are really in God's wonderful guarantee. As St Paul says, when we believed in God's Word and were baptised, we "were sealed with the promised Holy Spirit, who is the guarantee of our inheritance, until we acquire the possession of it" (Eph 1:13). What is a guarantee? When one wants to entrust a work such as printing a book, the one who undertakes the work will ask for a guarantee. One has to pay a certain amount of money as a guarantee. It is a pledge that the work will be done. The Holy Spirit is the guarantee that those who have him now will possess eternal life after death. A guarantee is small in comparison with the actual payment. So too, the fruits of the Spirit that we enjoy now, such as love, joy and peace are only a foretaste of what we shall enjoy in the next life. Therefore, Christianity is the most joyful religion. While it has its sorrows and stern disciplines, the end of it is a resurrection not a burial, a festival not a funeral.

SATURDAY – WEEK 28 / YEAR 2

A LONG MOUNTAIN CLIMB?

Readings: Eph 1:15-23; Lk 12:8-12

People love chopping wood. In this activity, one immediately sees results. But lots of things we do, take years of patient work before we can see any real results. A tutor or a therapist working with a handicapped child must often measure progress in inches of miles. Our personal goals may take very long to reach them. What keeps us from giving up? For believers, it is the hope that comes from knowing that our good deeds are all important to God, who guides our steps with his mighty power, no matter how slow our pace may seem. God will guide our steps until our death. Even after our death, with the power he exercised in raising his Son Jesus from the dead, he will raise our own dead bodies to new life. We may feel discouraged as we struggle through life as a car that struggles up a long mountain climb. But St Paul wants us to know, "What is the hope to which he has called you, what are the riches of his glorious inheritance in the saints and what is the immeasurable greatness of his power in us who believe" (Eph 1:18-19). May we always carry this hope in our hearts for it alone can sustain us in our difficulties. May we trust that God loves us and is always with us to help us to carry our burdens.

MONDAY – WEEK 29 / YEAR 2

GOD, A SPARE TYRE?

Readings: Eph 2:1-10; Lk 12:3-21

A big dog was watching a smaller dog chasing its tail! "What are you doing?" he asked. "I am looking for happiness", the smaller dog said. "Someone told me that happiness is in my tail." The big dog replied that he had heard that, too. But he discovered that every time he chased his tail it ran away from him. "So now," he said, "I just relax and do what dogs are supposed to do and I find that happiness comes to me." Those of us who are chasing after riches to find happiness, should just relax and do just what humans are supposed to do, namely, to rely on God who is the foundation of true happiness. The rich man in the Gospel lacked this foundation (Lk 12:19). There is no indication that he acquired his wealth dishonestly, but his mistake was that he had placed all his security on wealth, as if God was not needed. St Paul says that not even our good deeds merit our ultimate happiness in heaven, rather "it is the gift of God – not because of works" (Eph 2:9). Yes, everything, especially true happiness comes from God. God is not a kind of spare tyre. A spare tyre is forgotten for months until we suddenly have a flat on the road. It is a pity that many forget God in good times; then in an emergency they want him to be on hand.

CRITICAL TO THE BODY OF CHRIST

Readings: Eph 2:12-22; Lk 12:35-38

Have you ever watched an operation in a hospital with real blood and real sutures? I did. It was an operation for a kidney transplant. I saw what Mark, a good friend of mine, had to go through when he gave his kidney to his brother George. Mark made a big sacrifice, for people without kidneys can't survive. You can live without your eyes, your ears, the use of your hands or legs, but not without pancreas, kidney or liver. And yet, because we don't see these hidden parts of our body, we easily forget how critical they are to life. Likewise, many people who are well-to-do in the Church, which is the body of Christ, do not seem to take notice of those who are hurting in the same body. Referring to the fact that the Gentiles converted to Christianity became part of the body of Christ as the Jews were, St Paul wrote that Christ through the cross united them "in one body" (Eph 2:16). If so, how much greater unity should exist among the baptised Christians? How can the well to do in the Church close their eyes on those who are hurting, as if they are of no consequence? The truth is that the Church can't survive as the body of Christ without the needy, the weak and the vulnerable, for they give the rest of the body of Christ an opportunity to serve while offering their own sufferings for the welfare of that body.

THE MOTIVE IS LOVE

Readings: Eph 3:2-12; Lk 12:39-48

Fear is the most devastating emotion on earth. Very many seem to be either living or working in fear. The mother is afraid for her children, the father for his business, the clerk for his job and the worker for his or her competitor. There is hardly any person who is not afraid that some other person would do him or her, a bad turn. Therefore many of us transfer our fear complex on to our relationship with God. Only the superficial reading of today's Gospel, especially about the punishment of the unworthy servant, would indeed confirm that fear has to be the motive of Christian living. But the main point of the parable is not to arouse fear but love. It calls for generosity in our loving response to God's generous love, because "Every one to whom much is given, of him will much be required" (Lk 12:48). Underlining the generosity of God's love for us, St Paul points out how God has revealed to us even "the mystery of Christ which was not made known to the sons of men in other generations" (Eph 3:5). Has not God, then, the right to expect from us a loving relationship with him? Hence, our Christian life needs to be saturated with love, not fear. If we suffer long for God, may it be love's endurance; If we are kind to others, let it be love's service.

THURSDAY – WEEK 29 / YEAR 2

THE FIRE OF LOVE

Readings: Eph 3:14-21; Lk 12:49-53

Suppose you are a millionaire. You have everything life can offer: money, prestige, power and pleasure. Would you be willing to give up all your money, surrender your prestige, abandon your power and turn your back on pleasure? If you are willing to do all that, you have only begun in a remote fashion, to approach what Jesus the Son of God did, in becoming man and willing to die on a cross for our sake. He foretold of his death when he said, "I have a baptism to be baptised with" (Lk 12:50). As we stand at the foot of the cross, we begin to get a glimpse into the "breadth and length and height and depth" (Eph 3:18) of Christ's loving sacrifice. He did not die for nothing, because by his death he wanted to "cast fire on earth" (Lk 12:49). What fire? The fire of Love! A Hindu manufacturer who had come to one of my Christian prayer services told us this: "Years ago, when I was a boy, we heckled a missionary preaching in the bazaar and threw tomatoes at him. He wiped off the tomato juice from his face and then after the meeting, he took us to a sweet shop and bought us sweets. I saw the love of Christ on that day and that is why I'm here." Yes. Love is never wasted. It makes no difference where it is bestowed.

THE BOND OF PEACE

Readings: Eph 4:1-6; Lk 12:54-59

A small boy was excitedly opening a toy automobile, but found that it required a good deal of assembly. Try as he might, he could not get the carport together, and with a cry he threw some of the pieces across the room. The frustration of not being able to accomplish what seemed simple was devastating to the boy. Attempting to live a good Christian life can be just as frustrating sometimes. St Paul explains what a good Christian life is: It is "to maintain the unity of the Spirit in the bond of peace" (Eph 4:3). Some people seem to be disruptive by nature. Their conversation usually ends in arguments. If everyone wants to do one thing, they insist on doing the opposite. When they don't get their way, all they do is complain. The Sacrament of Baptism has united us with Christ and with one another. We are called to give expression to that unity in actual fact. Jesus asks us to watch for the signs of times. "When you see a cloud rising in the west, you say shower is coming" (Lk 12:54). So too, we should watch for the signs of cracks in our relationships. We need to mend them early before they split open. It is no good to defer until tomorrow to make peace, for tomorrow's sun may never rise to some. There is no point in always getting ready to unite, but never uniting.

TO SHARE A BURDEN

Readings: Eph 4:7-16; Lk 13:1-9

When others share our suffering, the harsh blows of life are softened. The changes and the chances of life can be better dealt with, when others join in and share the burdens. If such sharing grows to global level, there will certainly be less misery on earth. The followers of Christ are called to be examples of sharing the burdens of each other, at least within the Church. St Paul says (Eph 4:16) that the Church is like a body made up of many people with various talents and roles. As different parts of the body help each other for the welfare of the whole body, so we must help one another. When the hands want to thread a needle, the eyes come to collaborate. So too, believers have to support one another to carry out our respective duties. Let your stomach become upset, and your whole body feels the pangs of pain. So too, if one believer suffers, the rest have to feel it in some way, as if the whole community is suffering, and come forward to share the burden of the sufferer. To share a burden is to extend spiritual generosity. No burden is too heavy when shared by another. Sharing a burden tells the person that he or she is known, valued, and loved. Christ demands a high level of caring and sharing from his disciples.

MONDAY – WEEK 30 / YEAR 2

"WALK IN LOVE"

Readings: Eph 4:32–5:8; Lk13:10-17

We are made by love and for love. There are but two loves: love of ourselves, and love of God and others. Sin can be called, in a sense, the breaking of God's commandments. If so, sin is non-love, for all God's commandments can be summed up in two: love of God and others. Every time I love myself, it is less love for God and others. Self-love is draining away of love, for love is made to leave self and fly towards others. We become our own victims of misery, if we condemn ourselves to love no one but ourselves. Like the woman in the Gospel, physically bent for eighteen years (Lk 13:12), who could neither look up to God nor look around to see others, a selfish person feels like crawling to avoid being seen by God and others. And so, St Paul asks us to "walk in love as Christ loved us" (Eph 5:2). Why should I submit myself to self-love and suffer dreadfully, locked in myself, prisoner of myself, hearing nothing but my own voice and seeing nothing but myself? All sufferings in the world, all injustices, humiliations, and despairs are signs of non-love. Hence, may our love daily penetrate a little into all spheres of human life. The battle for a better world is a battle for love in the service of love.

LIKE THE RUSSIAN DOLL

Readings: Eph 5:21-33; Lk 13:18-21

Once I purchased a wooden, hand painted, peasant Russian doll that twists open at the middle to reveal another doll inside. You take the smaller doll out, open it, and another, even smaller one is inside. Open that one and you discover a tinier doll! The fun is in discovering all that is hidden inside each doll. To me, it is an excellent picture of all the models hidden in Christ. Jesus is our model for love. St Paul directs husbands to model themselves on Christ: "Husbands, love your wives as Christ loved the Church" (Eph 5:25). He could have held up Christ as model also for wives in their relationship to their husbands. If we open the love of Christ, we will find our model for sufferings for love's sake. Christ never died for our good works; they were not worth dying for, but died to restore us to heaven. If we open the love of Christ still further, we will find our model for gentleness. Even though at times he spoke with biting criticisms against all forms of hypocrisy, his heart is a gentle heart. If we open his love still deeper, we will find our model for forgiving others. While he hung up on the cross, he pleaded with his Father to forgive his executioners. Christ is God's everything for our total need, hence every virtue known to every human being is found in Christ.

THE NARROW DOOR

Readings: Eph 6:1-9; Lk 13:22-30

Gentle Jesus, meek and mild, never harming, always charming! Is he so? Perhaps it is the picture occasionally painted in a child's Sunday school lesson, but it is not the exact picture of the historic Christ. Jesus threw so many hard teachings at his disciples. It is little wonder they got miffed. He once said, "If you try to save your life, it will slip through your fingers, but give it away, and you will find it." In today's Gospel he says, "Strive to enter by the narrow door" (Lk 13:24). What is a narrow door like? St Paul says to children: "Obey your parents" and "Honour your father and mother" (Eph 6:1). This requires on the part of the children humility and acceptance of discipline. That is children's narrow door. He says to parents: "Do not provoke your children to anger but bring them up in the discipline and instruction of the Lord" (v.4). This requires on the part of the parents unselfish love and patience. That is their narrow door. Through such teachings, the Lord invades into our comfort zones. He tears aside the curtain of our easy-going consciences, and throws open the locked doors of our superficial lifestyle. He challenges us to enter by the narrow door, and if we do that, we can enter into new pastures of peace, and happiness.

THURSDAY – WEEK 30 / YEAR 2

FIGHTING EVIL

Readings: Eph 6:10-20; Lk 13:31-35

There are too many people, these days, who laugh at the thought of evil spirits and demons in the air. To them, faith means believing in things that are good such as heaven, Jesus, resurrection, and so on. Rarely do they consider believing in the reality of Satan, the embodiment of evil, and his hosts as having practical impact on us. St Paul did not even argue the point of the existence of evil spirits. He warns us "to take the whole armour of God" (Eph 6:13), not for a bloody political or economic conflict, but for conflict with sin, the ultimate cause of evil. Jesus himself faced evil in conflict, when he encountered men like Herod as we read in today's Gospel (Lk 13:31). The greatest evils of our time are usually those which violate justice and charity. We are called to fight against such evils and secure justice for workers, for example, dignity for the downtrodden and assistance to the poor. How are we to fight against evils? Not by hanging dried herbs on the door of our house; not by burning dried plants on fire on a particular day. But by putting on the shield of faith, the breastplate of righteousness, and the shoes of the Gospel of peace and by wielding the sword of God's Word. Our eyes can not see the evil, but it is real.

A LOVING FAMILY

Readings: Phil 1:1-11; Lk 14:1-6

I have had the pleasure of knowing one of the most loving families around. The entire family is an inspiration. The mother and the father are two of the most loving, caring and devoted people I know; and their two teenage daughters possess a powerful faith and are outward looking personalities. Their home is a haven of peace and harmony. They are always welcoming company. If any stranger is stranded in the town, it is this family that finally comes to help. The family is quick to acknowledge that their love comes from only one source, namely, Christ to whom they are bound together in love. It is this charity that St Paul praises in the Philippians, for they knew that their love for Christ must overflow into love for their neighbour; and of course St Paul recommends more love, saying, "I pray your love may abound more and more" (Phil 1:9). In direct contrast was the attitude of the Pharisees who objected to Christ's healing of the man with dropsy, just because he was healed on a Sabbath (Lk 14:2). True Christian love has power to change our world. It gives new hope to the discouraged, new strength to the weak, new joys to the sorrowing. It makes life more worthwhile to everyone into whose eyes it looks.

THE FINAL AWAKENING

Readings: Phil 1:18-26; Lk 14:1, 7-11

Many think that our greatest enemy is death. Is it? Others say that life is a dirty trick, a short journey from nothingness to nothingness. Is it? Is death the last sleep? No. It is the final awakening. For a Christian, death is the turning off the light because the dawn has come, which ushers the believer into eternal and blissful union with Jesus Christ.

Hence St Paul longed to die. "My desire," he said, "is to depart and be with Christ" (Phil 1:23). He saw death as the greatest gain possible. And yet, he knew that there was still work to be done for his people. The inscription "I expected this, but not just yet." could well be written on his gravestone. We need to have a similar balanced view of life and death. As Christians we need not fear death, but look forward to it as the fulfilment of life. And yet, we should accept the remaining time left on earth, to carry out whatever allotted to us in God's plan. Our place in God's plan may not be exalted. It could be the lowest place at the table of life. But we are sure, God would say in heaven, "Friend, go up higher" (Lk 14:10). Our humble submission to God now, will one day pay its dividends. Humility is not the depreciation of ourselves, but appreciation of God's plan for us.

MONDAY – WEEK 31 / YEAR 2

HAPPINESS IS PERFUME

Readings: Phil 2:1-4; Lk 14:12-14

All of us want to be happy, but many of us, all too often, do not seem to find it. In fact, there is a simple way. It comes by putting our focus on others. St Paul had this in mind when he wrote, "Count others better than yourselves; Let each of you look to the interests of others" (Phil 2:3-4). When Jesus said, "When you give a feast, invite the poor, the maimed, the lame, the blind" (Lk 14:13), he too wanted us to put the interest of others first. How? By inviting the influential people and our friends, our motive usually is to gain favour from them later; but invitation to the poor is for their own sake, since they can't repay the favour. Hence, the right way to find happiness is to put others first. Start by asking yourself, "What good can I do for someone today?" You can consider all the people around you, at home, at the job and in your neighbourhood. Then do something. It does not have to be a big favour; it can be as simple as a compliment on a job well done. Then do something harder: be nice to a person you dislike or who dislikes you. Finally, single out a person you usually ignore, and do something to make him or her feel special. Happiness is perfume you can not pour on others, without getting a few drops on yourself.

THE DESCENDING WAY

Readings: Phil 2:5-11; Lk 14:15-24

In Shakespeare's tragedies, the play usually opens with the hero rising to fame, wealth or power. Within him, however, there is a flaw of character at work. Just when he appears to have reached the top, fortunes begin to turn against him. His flaw is his undoing and he tumbles from the height of success to the depth of tragedy. His death is his end. Just the opposite was true of Jesus. From the moment he "empties himself, taking the form of a servant, being born in the likeness of men" (Phil 2:7), he went down the descending way until he died on the cross. But, death for him was not the end, but the beginning of his glory with his Father. God our Father invites us to follow Jesus in his descending way, as the man in the Gospel invited people for a large dinner (Lk 14:16). It is up to us to accept God's invitation. God assures that our descending way is the ascending way. It is the way of suffering, but also the way of healing; it is the way of humiliation, but also the way to the resurrection; it is the way of tears, which turns into tears of joy; it is the way of hiddenness, but also the way that leads to light that will shine on all people; it is the way of persecution and martyrdom, but also the way to the full disclosure of God's love.

JESUS IS SUFFICIENT

Readings: Phil 2:12-18; Lk 14:25-33

To those who believe in Jesus as the Way, the Truth and the Life, he is sufficient for their lives. His sufficiency was unmistakably demonstrated at his death. His death brought the dead to life, but at his passing, heaven and earth were plunged into mourning and hard rocks were split asunder. If I truly believe in the sufficiency of Jesus for my happiness, then it would be the most extreme folly and delusion on my part, to look elsewhere for true happiness. It is in order to make this point forcefully clear that Jesus said, by exaggeration, that his followers must be ready to sacrifice even one's father, mother, wife, children, brothers and sisters (Lk 14:26). Martyrs throughout the history of the Church bear witness to the fact that even life itself must be sacrificed in order to be faithful to Christ. St Paul was no exception. He wrote: "Even if I am to be poured as a libation upon the sacrificial offering, I am glad and rejoice" (Phil 2:17). "In a civilisation like ours," wrote C.S. Lewis, "I feel that everyone has to come to terms with the claims of Jesus Christ upon his or her life, or else be guilty of inattention or of evading the question!" The strange thing about Jesus is that we can never get away from him.

THURSDAY – WEEK 31 / YEAR 2

WE STAND AMAZED!

Readings: Phil 3:3-8; Lk 15:1-10

Suppose you have just finished typing a 100-page term paper. You discover one sheet missing. What would you do? You will forget about the other ninety-nine sheets and go looking for the one lost sheet. When you find it, you are so happy that you take the other ninety-nine sheets, throw them in the air and say, "Yip pee! I found my lost sheet!' That is how Jesus feels when a lost sinner returns to him. He asks: Does not a shepherd who had lost one of his hundred sheep "leave the ninety-nine in the wilderness and go after the one which is lost?" (Lk 15:4). Of course, the Lord loves the ninety-nine, too; but his heart is with the lost one. The love of Christ for each of us is amazing! St Paul who was once lost but found, experienced this tender love of the Lord and exclaimed, "Indeed, I count everything as loss because of the surpassing worth of knowing Christ" (Phil 3:8). Most people understand a God who forgives sinners who crawl to him begging for mercy. People can relate to a guff God, who makes sinners grovel in the dirt pleading for forgiveness. But do we understand a God who actually runs in search of sinners in order to forgive them? A God who seeks out rebels in order to save them? Little wonder, we stand amazed at the love of Jesus!

IF THERE IS NO GOD

Readings: Phil 3:17-4:1; Lk 16:1-8

Dostoevsky, the Russian author, wrote great novels about man's search for freedom. One of his best novels is *The Brothers Karamazov*. The theme of the novel, in the words of one of his characters, is: "If there is no God, all is permitted." The author's conviction was that without God there is no freedom, only chaos. People without God substitute anything for the Supreme Being. As St Paul says, "Their end is destruction, their God is the belly, and they glory in their shame" (Phil 3:19). In effect, they make themselves their own God and indulge only in license. But those who believe in God and believe that "their commonwealth is in heaven" (v.20), enjoy true freedom to be good and to do good. Christians who think a lot about the next world, are usually those who are doing most good in this world. They aim at heaven, and they get earth thrown in. But if they aim at the earth, they get neither. When we realise that our citizenship is in heaven, we begin acting as responsible citizens in this world; we begin to invest wisely in relationships; our conversations, goals and motives become purer and honest. And all of this serves us well not only in heaven but also on earth. Heavenly minded people are the ones who enjoy true freedom.

THE RIGHTEOUS MAMMON

Readings: Phil 4:10-19; Lk 16:9-15

Money is a wonderful thing, but it is possible to pay too high a price for it. Money, in some respect, is like fire. It is an excellent servant, but a terrible master. Life is so tragic for the person who has plenty to live on, but nothing to live for. If a person gets his or her attitude towards money straightened out, almost all other areas of his or her life will be straightened out. While saying, "make friends by means of righteous mammon so that when it fails they may receive you into the eternal habitation" (Lk 16:9), Jesus not only was warning us against undue attachment to money, but advised to give some of it to the poor and the needy. The Christians of Philippi did that to St Paul that made him very happy. "I rejoice in the Lord greatly", he wrote, "that now at length you have revived your concern for me" (Phil 4:10). Some who give freely seem to grow all the richer; but those who withhold tend to suffer want. We can not take our money to heaven with us, but we can send it there ahead of us. A farmer was known for giving extensively to the Lord's work. He explained it this way: "I keep shovelling into God's bin, and God keeps shovelling back into mine, and he has the bigger shovel."

MONDAY – WEEK 32 / YEAR 2

A GROUNDLESS DIVORCE?

Readings: Tit 1:1-9; Lk 17:1-6

The modern cry "Less doctrine and more liberty" is degeneration from the vertebrate to the jellyfish. Liberty without doctrine is like a sword in the hand of a lunatic. Every Christian needs to have an insatiable appetite for sound doctrine. A doctrine is sound if it leads us to Jesus Christ. When St Paul writes that a bishop should "hold firm to the sure word as taught" (Tit 1:9), he means that all presbyters must see to it that the authenticity of the teachings of Christ are preserved. Jesus, of course, warns that "temptations to sin are sure to come" (Lk 17:1). That is, scandals of false doctrine and erroneous practice would inevitably come upon the Church and we have to be on guard against them. As Catholics, we ought to recognise that the sources of sound doctrines are the Bible and the traditions of the Church. Why traditions? It is because the doctrines are only a kind of map. But that map is based on the experience of hundreds of people who were really in touch with God. Therefore, our faith is rooted in the Bible as it had been understood and lived for thousands of years. To separate doctrine from its lived tradition is to sue for a groundless divorce. God has joined them together, and what he has joined, we can not put asunder.

A TYPICAL PARISHIONER

Readings: Tit 2:1-8, 11-14; Lk 17:7-10

A pastor was talking to a poor lady who worked hard as a cleaning woman. He told her how glad he was to see her in her place in church every Sunday, so attentive to his sermons. "Yes; it is such a rest after working hard all week, to come to church, sit down on the soft cushions and not think about anything", she said. While her Sunday attendance is commendable, one wonders whether she can be a typical parishioner. The true parishioner is one who is in close fellowship with the rest of the parish community, enjoying the fellowship of a shared faith, shared parish work, shared joys and sorrows in the Lord. The early Christian community of which Titus had charge, was rather a small one. And yet, as St Paul's letter to Titus shows (Tit 2:2,6), the community was made up of all age groups. In spite of it, it is likely that the people of this community knew each other rather intimately. One unfortunate thing about our modern parishes is that the parishioners are not sufficiently acquainted with each other and hence lose the spiritual fruits of Christian fellowship. One wonders whether some of the professing parishes have gone in for theatrics, running a showboat instead of a lifeboat, staging a performance instead of experiencing fellowship.

A GRATEFUL HEART

Readings: Tit 3:1-7; Lk 17:11-19

Poet Rabindranath Tagore expressed it in this way: "I have thanked the trees that have made my life fruitful, but have failed to remember the grass that has ever kept it green." We take so much of God's blessings in creation for granted. What of his blessings to each of us personally given? There is an Irish proverb: "Get on your knees and thank God you are on your feet." It is incredible that the nine lepers who had been cured failed to return to give thanks to the Lord. May we imitate the Samaritan (Lk 17:16) who returned to thank the Lord. The Mass is a constant reminder of our need to thank God, for Eucharist is a worship of thanks and praise to God, for all of the good things he has given to entire humanity. How do we express our gratitude to God? It is not merely in words but by our life, a life that responds to God's goodness through our goodness to others. Still another specific form of response to God's goodness is, as St Paul writes to Titus (Tit 3:1), to be loyal citizens to our Government. In other words, our entire lives, not just prayers, must be a thanksgiving to God. Helen Keller said, "So much has been given to me that I have no time to ponder over that which has been denied!" My own often repeated prayer is: "Oh God who has given so much, mercifully grant me one more thing – a grateful heart!"

THURSDAY – WEEK 32 / YEAR 2

"FREELY, FREELY"

Readings: Philem 7-20; Lk 17:20-25

Some say that force is all-conquering, but in fact, its victories are short lived. Even to end an evil, force is not advisable, for forcible ways make not an end of evil, but leave hatred and malice behind them. A human being is a free person and hence, every act of submission to an exterior force, rots the person standing; That person is dead before being buried by the legitimate grave diggers. That is why God never forces any of us to do something. He does not force us to serve him; he does not force us even to love him; he wants us to love him and serve him freely. St Paul did the same with Philemon. St Paul would not force him to give up his right over his slave Onesimus who had fled from him seeking refuge in Paul. But Paul sent the slave back to Philemon for he wanted Philemon to release the slave freely out of a motive of Christian love. He wrote: "Though I am bold enough in Christ to command you to do what is required, yet for loves sake, I prefer to appeal to you" (Philem 8). Our loving service to God will please him if it is given freely. God knows that whatever needs to be maintained through force, is doomed. Have you seen pebbles in water? Not hammer-strokes, but dance of the water sings the pebbles into perfection.

FRIDAY – WEEK 32 / YEAR 2

LOVING IN ACTION

Readings: 2 Jn 4:4-9; Lk 17:26-37

On a full moon night, if I am romantic, I will sit outside in my backyard ogling up at the sky. Full moons make us think of love and there is nothing like being in love. Recall what it felt like when you were in love. Your heart grew faint and your breathing short, just picturing the soft eyes and tender smile of the one you adore. Being in a room with that person is a thrill. You ply him or her with questions just to hear the sound of the voice. When you are in love one thing is certain: you can't keep it to yourself; you just have to tell that person who grips your love. Likewise, we who love God would be happier if we express our love for him. But how? St John says that it is by keeping God's commandment and his commandment is that "we love one another" (2 Jn 5). But real love is in action. The greatest act of love that anyone can perform is to give oneself for others. Sometimes, it is easier to say "I'd die for you" than it is to say, "I'll live for you; Let me think of your interests before my own." This is living a sacrificial love for others. But such a love can only come to us as a gift from God. Because it takes superhuman strength to live really for others. And God will certainly offer this gift if we sincerely ask him for it.

CONCERNING MISSION

Readings: 3 Jn 5-8; Lk 18:1-8

If there be any one point in which the Church ought to keep its fervour at white heat, it is concerning mission. If there be anything about which we can not tolerate lukewarmness, it is the matter of sending the Good News to a dying world. It is so because Christ commanded his disciples to take the Gospel to every living individual and the Church exists by mission, as fire exists by burning. The first reading of today is taken from a letter written to a man named Gaius, who had welcomed some missionaries and given them hospitality, even though they were strangers to him. The letter encourages Gaius to give them the means necessary to continue their missionary journeys, "for they have set out for God's sake" (3 Jn 7). As part of the Church, each baptised Christian is expected to be a missionary at least in three ways: by contributing to the missions, by being witnesses of our faith to others, and by prayer for the spread of the Gospel. It is not enough to possess faith in our conscience. The faith is both communal and outgoing. Hence there is the obligation of involving oneself with it and of spreading it. Though our task is not to bring all the world to Christ, our task is unquestionably to bring Christ to all the world.

THE SPIRITUAL SIGHT

Readings: Rev 1:1-4, 2:1-5; Lk 18:35-43

We have physical sight. Do we have spiritual sight? There are those who see only what they want to see and disregard the rest. Then there are those who are colour blind that prevents them from seeing some dark areas in their life. Then there are those with spiritual cataract: they appear to see, but don't actually see. There are those like the alcoholic father who can not see the misery he is causing to his wife and children. In many, there is also an inability to see the invisible conflict that goes on in creation between the spirit of evil and that of Christ. This conflict took the form of physical persecution for early Christians, and for us now, in the form of flaunting temptations by worldly values such as money and pleasure. The book of Revelation was written both for early Christians and for us, to help us open our spiritual eyes to see that Christ had already won the decisive victory over evil and death, a victory in which all people of faith will share. It is to announce his victory over evil that Jesus said to the blind man, "receive your sight; your faith has made you well" (Lk 18:42). Temptations of this world may be small in comparison to persecutions; but still we must fight against them. Little things are little things, but faithfulness in little things, is a great thing.

TUESDAY – WEEK 33 / YEAR 2

ACTIVISM AND APATHY

Readings: Rev 3:1-6, 14-22; Lk 19:1-10

Two common failings of any Christian community are activism and apathy. We need action but not activism, which is hyper-action. Activism saps one's spiritual energy with the result that the activist becomes too physically energetic to explore the higher fields of the spirit. Some think that to be busy is a proof of happiness; but how can you be happy if your spirit is emptied? "I am ashamed of my emptiness", said Word to Work. "I know how poor I am when I see you", said the Work to the Word. Hence the Lord warned the early Church of Sardis of its guilt of activism: "You have the name of being alive and you are dead" (Rev 3:1). The opposite of activism is apathy. Science may have found cures for most evils, but has found no remedy for the worst of them all, which is apathy. The early Church Laodicea had become spiritually so apathetic that God told them, "I will spew you out of my mouth" (Rev 3:16). The lust for comfort, that stealthy thing, had entered into this community a guest, then became a host and then their master. If we are given to activism or apathy, we must change in the manner Zachaeus changed. Showing great spiritual energy, he actively sought to right the wrongs he had done to his neighbours (Lk 19:8). That was true change.

WEDNESDAY – WEEK 33 / YEAR 2

"MY HOME IS ON THE OTHER SIDE"

Readings: Rev 4:1-11; Lk 19:11-28

At dusk, a little girl entered a cemetery. An old man who sat at the gate said to her, "Aren't you afraid to go through the cemetery in the dark?" "Oh, no," she replied, "my home is just on the other side." That home is heaven where God dwells with his angels who never stop singing, "Holy, holy, holy, is the Lord God Almighty" (Rev 4:8). God's holiness is his perfection. When we recognise something of the goodness in our neighbours, when we appreciate beauty in creation, and when we experience human love, we are able to have a glimpse into the perfect goodness, perfect beauty and perfect love of God. What is more, we have been promised a share in the perfection of God in heaven. The parable of the talents in the Gospel, reminds us to use our God-given gifts, small or big, even if it is just one (Lk 19:13), to prepare ourselves to enter into our heavenly home. Are we using our talents only to improve our lives financially and socially? Or, have we used our gifts to come to a better knowledge of God with whom we will finally be united forever? We are not citizens of the world trying to get to heaven, but citizens of heaven making our way through this world. It is not the Christian doctrine of heaven a myth, but the humanist dream of utopia on earth.

THURSDAY – WEEK 33 / YEAR 2

MISSED OPPORTUNITIES

Readings: Rev 5:1-10; Lk 19:41-44

What will one think of a captain of a ship who does not know the destination of the journey and does not care about the storms and perils of the sea? What would one think of a pilot of an aeroplane who sleeps away or smokes cigars and is not bothered about stormy weather? We are captains of our souls. But we can not, on our own, guide ourselves to our destiny. That is why the Lord will be visiting us regularly with his grace, grace to keep our focus on our eternal home, grace to pass safe through the troubled waters of temptations, grace to avoid the rocks of the false values of the world. This means that we need to know the time of his visitation and use it, without getting completely distracted by temporal cares, a grave mistake that the Jews made. Jesus wept over the people of Jerusalem because they had again and again missed the opportunity of God's visitation and lost "the things that make for peace" (Lk 19:42). Shakespeare wrote: "There is a tide in the affairs of men which taken at the flood, leads on to fortune; Omitted, all the voyage of their life is bound in shallows and in miseries." This was the fate of the citizens of Jerusalem who missed opportunities for peace. How are we using the Lord's visitations in our own lives?

FRIDAY – WEEK 33 / YEAR 2

BROKEN BUT BLESSED

Readings: Rev 10:8-11; Lk 19:45-48

A woman gives birth; she is in pain, yet she feels joy. Some things are bitter and sweet at the same time. Christian life is bitter and sweet at the same time, a truth symbolically expressed in the book of Revelation. The angel asked St John to eat the scroll saying, "Take it and eat; it will be bitter to your stomach but sweet" (Rev 10:10). The scroll of the Gospel is sweet because it proclaims the great triumph of Jesus Christ through his resurrection, a triumph in which the whole Church shares. It is bitter because the triumph was achieved through sufferings and death, and the people of the Church must share in his sufferings too. No Christian escapes a taste of wilderness on the way to the Promised Land. How willing are we to struggle and suffer in the present to attain eternal life in the future? Do we feel at times broken by God? That is part of God's plan, especially if he wants to use us for the good of others. Out of our brokenness, blessings can be bestowed on more people than we ever dreamed possible. If the hand of God has broken you, you can be certain nothing will be wasted. God will gather up and use all the hurts both for you and for others; not a bit will be discarded or cast aside. Good Friday – is both bitter and sweet.

SATURDAY – WEEK 33 / YEAR 2

SOWING IN TEARS

Readings: Rev 11:4-12; Lk 20:27-40

One of the Bible sayings I love most is, "Those who sow in tears will reap with songs of joy." If you have ever reached through an invisible wall of pain to embrace God, you have sown in tears. If you have ever been rejected by a dear one and turned the other cheek in love, you have sown in tears. If you have patiently endured physical affliction or responded in love through a difficult marriage, you have sown in tears. God's promise is that those who sow in tears will reap abundant return of joy. This is because the Saviour of the world who died on the cross rose again and those who believe in him share in his resurrection. "The two olive trees and the two lamp stands" (Rev 11:4) seen by St John in his vision, can be taken to refer to Moses and Elijah. The presence of these prophets symbolise that everything that had happened in salvation history referred to Christ, found its fulfilment in him, especially in his resurrection. In today's Gospel, Jesus, in answer to a silly question posed by the Sadducees asserts that our own resurrection is a certainty

(Lk 20:37). Pain has a way of screaming for attention. But when we respond in faith to pain, we can taste the fruits of Christ's resurrection even here on earth.

MONDAY – WEEK 34 / YEAR 2

SUCCESS IS "BEING GOOD"

Readings: Rev 14:1-5; Lk 21:1-4

There is nothing new about people wanting and working to achieve success in life. Power, money, fame, prestige are the words that one associates with the idea of success. But, through the example of the poor widow in the Gospel, the Lord sets different standards to success. By any worldly standard, the woman would not be considered a success. She stands in stark contrast to the renowned religious leaders. Yet the woman made a success of her life, because by God's grace, she achieved victory over pride and selfishness. Her goodness manifested in her generous offering, won praise from Jesus (Lk 21:3). The Book of Revelation, too, is concerned about success, but it takes its standard for success from Jesus the Lamb of God, whose victory over evil and death was the true success all human beings should strive after. The one hundred and forty four thousand people mentioned in the reading (Rev 14:1) are not a mathematical count. The number is symbolic of all those who had succeeded in their struggle over evil in order to become good. If we were as industrious to become good as to make ourselves successful, we should become really successful by being good. It is a grand mistake to think of being successful without being good.

TO SUFFER INJUSTICE

Readings: Rev 14:14-19; Lk 21:5-11

"To do injustice is more disgraceful than to suffer it", said Plato. And yet, millions suffer in our world because of injustice done to them by others. One form of modern injustice is to keep the riches of this world to oneself and allow others to die of hunger. In any town in the third world, you can see persons queued up at the breadline, a woman in her attic eating what she had salvaged that morning from garbage bins, urchins in their orphanage dividing some scraps from old folks' home, and a thousand unfortunates, at this moment, throughout the world, twisting in pain and dying of hunger before their despairing families. Oppressed people of all times have yearned for righting of wrongs and for the achieving of justice. It is the Christian belief that the Lord would one day come to put an end to all injustice in the world. Today's first reading is the vision of the coming of Christ at the end of time. He wears a crown of gold to symbolise that he has conquered evil and he bears a sickle to show that he will judge against evil (Rev 14:14). But it is not enough for us just to wait for the Lord to come. It is God's plan that all conscientious people of faith should in the meantime strive to rid of injustice from the face of the earth.

TOWARDS FINAL VICTORY

Readings: Rev 15:1-4; Lk 21:12-19

How can an all good God allow evil and suffering? Implicit in this question is a fear that perhaps sin and evil are more powerful than God. But the book of Revelation proclaims that on the last day God

will show forth his goodness and power, by the total destruction of sin
and evil. On the day of Christ's Second Coming, the saints will cry
out, "Great and wonderful are thy deeds" (Rev 15:3). But victory over
sin and evil does not lie in the future alone. Since it has already been
achieved in the death of Jesus on Calvary, we can already experience
now the joy of that victory when, for example, we are truly converted
to Christ. But, by 'joy' we do not mean the transient pleasure that
comes from physical comfort, or false happiness of a simple mind that
is unaware of human degradation, or the 'virtuous' resignation of a
pseudo-mystic, or the blind optimism of the one who figures that it is
better to laugh than to cry. By 'joy' we mean profound peace which
emanates from a person who strongly believes in the victory of the
Saviour over sin and evil, despite all the chaos in the world. Through
the ages of the Christian era, this victory has been unfolding in
its joyful effect, and will reach completion in the Second Coming
of Christ.

THURSDAY – WEEK 34 / YEAR 2

A VICTORY TO CELEBRATE

Readings: Rev 18:1-2, 21-23, 19:1-3,9; Lk 21:20-28

I am only an amateur gardener. Hence when I notice fragrant and
beautiful crocuses in my backyard, I don't know how to account for
such a profusion of flowers, except to say we had a couple of weeks of
hard frost back in January. I am convinced that the freezing cold
forced a lot of beauty out of crocuses. Likewise, the nipping frost of
trials and afflictions in our lives are needed if we are to grow, to
revive, to bud and blossom. Suffering is evil, but Jesus has overcome
evil and we already have a share in that victory. That is why, if we
accept sufferings in faith, peace and joy blossom in our hearts. These
contrasting aspects of Christian life are portrayed in the book of
Revelation. In the first scene, we witness a mighty struggle against
evil, symbolised by Babylon, (Rev 18:2), a struggle in which we are
still engaged. In the second scene, we see a vision of joyful victory

celebration in heaven (19:1), a victory in which we already share on earth, but hope to share fully in heaven. Do you feel the nipping frost of loneliness, the biting cold of persecution, the icy sting of rejection or the numbing chill of heartache? For God's sake, persevere in your faith and dedication to the Lord. You have a victory to celebrate with the Lord.

FRIDAY – WEEK 34 / YEAR 2

ALL WILL BE NEW

Readings: Rev 20:1-4, 11-21:2; Lk 21:29-33

We like a new dress, a new pen, a new house, a new-born child, a newly blossomed flower, a new friend, a new book, a new song. In heaven, everything will be new, for everything will be consecrated to God. "Then I saw," St John writes, "a new heaven and a new earth" (Rev 21:1). What he means is the future heavenly renewal of the universe, in the final fullness of the Kingdom of God. This hope of our final destiny must keep us encouraged as we plod through life's pains in faithfulness to God's plan for us. The fig tree in the Gospel also gives us a word of hope (Lk 21:29). A fig tree, like most trees in winter, looks dead, but in fact, is bursting with new life ready to explode in the spring. The same is true of our life in faith. Although we may be enduring difficulties, within us, the Holy Spirit is acting as the nucleus of new life and rebirth, which will burst forth in our heavenly bliss. Life's hardships are God's way of helping us to get our minds on the hereafter. I don't mean 'hereafter' as a psychological crutch or an escape from reality. I mean "New heaven and New earth." To grip our hearts with heaven, God at times takes drastic measures. At first, you and I may not approve his methods, but later we will be grateful for it.

SATURDAY – WEEK 34 / YEAR 2

TOWARDS UNLIMITED JOY

Readings: Rev 22:1-7; Lk 21:34-36

Godly people joyfully delight in good things, and they nobly endure hard things, because they know their existence is meaningful, and they are destined for unlimited joy at the deepest level, which will be heaven. Because they keenly feel that nothing now quite meets the standard of their longing souls, throbbing ache within them drives them not to any complaint, but to anticipation of heaven. The book of Revelation presents the final scene of human history, our heavenly home. As St John saw in his vision, not just one but "twelve trees of life" (Rev 22:2) grow luxuriously, "the river of life" (v.1) flows there, not in trickles as in our baptism, but a river flowing down the middle of the streets. These symbols of abundance are the image of the fullness of life in heaven. "There shall no more anything be accursed" (v.3), as it was in the Garden of Eden, for heaven is the never-ending life with God. Saints who had a glimpse of heavenly existence got so homesick for heaven, that the yearning for it swelled in them like an ocean wave. Let us have a lively hope of heaven while living fully on this earth pleasing to God. If we learn to invest our days in eternity, our present existence will throb with sweet excitement.